ADAM'S HAUNTED SONS

Adam's Haunted Sons

Sister Laurentia Digges, C. S. J.

WITH A FOREWORD BY

BARNABAS AHERN, C.P.

NEW YORK: THE MACMILLAN COMPANY

LONDON: COLLIER-MACMILLAN LTD.

Library of Congress Catalog Card Number: 66–21162

SECOND PRINTING 1967

The Macmillan Company, New York

Collier-Macmillan Canada Ltd., Toronto, Ontario

Nihil obstat

Gall Higgins, O.F.M.Cap.
CENSOR LIBRORUM

Imprimatur

✠ Terence J. Cooke, D.D.V.G.

The nihil obstat and imprimatur are official declarations that a book or pamphlet is free of doctrinal or moral error. No implication is contained therein that those who have granted the nihil obstat and imprimatur agree with the contents, opinions or statements expressed.

The author wishes to thank the following for permission to reproduce the following copyrighted material.

Excerpts from *Collected Poems* by Conrad Aiken, 1955, *The Boy With a Cart* by Christopher Fry, 1951, and *Poems* by Gerard Manley Hopkins, edited by W. R. Gardner, 1948, reprinted by permission of Oxford University Press. Excerpt from "The Dry Salvages" in *Four Quarters*, copyright, 1943, by T. S. Eliot, reprinted by permission of Harcourt, Brace & World, Inc. Selection from "Little Gidding" in *Four Quarters*, copyright, 1943, by T. S. Eliot, reprinted by permission of Harcourt, Brace & World, Inc. Selection from "The Apple" © 1958 by John Moffitt, reprinted from his volume *The Living Seed* by permission of Harcourt, Brace & World, Inc. Selection from "The Dry Salvages" from *Complete Poems and Plays* by T. S. Eliot, 1943, "L'Annunciazione: From Bellini," © 1957 by Ned O'Gorman. Reprinted from his volume *The Night of the Hammer*, and "Still, Citizen Sparrow" from *Ceremony and Other Poems* by Richard Wilbur, 1950, are reprinted by permission of Harcourt, Brace & World, Inc. Excerpt from "Pentecost" reprinted with permission of The Macmillan Company

Printed in the United States of America

from *Time Without Number,* by Daniel Berrigan. Copyright © 1957, Daniel Berrigan. Excerpt from "Depression" reprinted with permission of The Macmillan Company from *The Crow and the Heart,* by Hayden Carruth. Copyright © 1959, Hayden Carruth. Excerpt from "The Prodigal," *Poems North and South* by Elizabeth Bishop, 1955, is reprinted by permission of Houghton Mifflin Company. Excerpt from "The Atoll in the Mind," *The Song of Lazarus* by Alex Comfort. Copyright 1945 by Alex Comfort. Reprinted by permission of The Viking Press, Inc. Excerpt from "For Nightly Ascent of the Hunter Orion over a Forest Clearing," copyright © 1961 by James Dickey and excerpt from "Armor" is copyright © 1962 by James Dickey. Both are reprinted from *Drowning With Others* by James Dickey, by permission of Wesleyan University Press. Excerpt from "The Triumph of Time," copyright © 1956 by Barbara Howes. Reprinted from *Light and Dark* by Barbara Howes, by permission of Wesleyan University Press. Excerpt from "Ladies by their Windows," copyright © 1954 by Donald Justice, and excerpt from "Sonnet," copyright © 1957 by Donald Justice. Both are reprinted from *The Summer Anniversaries* by Donald Justice by permission of Wesleyan University Press.

Excerpt from "Abraham's Knife," *Abraham's Knife and Other Poems* by George Garrett, published by The University of North Carolina Press in 1961. Excerpts from "Birds at the Feeding Station" and "Notes for a Marriage Vow," *The Holy Merriment* by Arnold Kenseth, published by The University of North Carolina Press, 1963. Reprinted by permission of The University of North Carolina Press. Excerpt from "The Carnival Act," *The Quiet Wars* by Samuel Hazo, © Sheed and Ward Inc., 1962, and reprinted here by permission. Excerpt from "Noah and His Ark," *The Double Root* by John Holmes, published in 1950 by Twayne Publishers, and reprinted here by permission. Excerpt from "Monologue of a Son of Saul," *Spring of the Thief* by John Logan, published in 1963 by Alfred A. Knopf, is reprinted here by permission. Excerpt from "After the Rain had Stopped, Eighth Elegy," *Poems from Limbo* by Rob Lyle, published by Dufour Editions, Inc., 1961. Excerpt from "Soliloquy on a Southern Strand," *Poisoned Lands* by John Montague, published by Dufour Editions, Inc., 1963. Excerpt from "Iago Prytherch," *Poetry for Supper* by R. S. Thomas, published by Dufour Editions, Inc., 1958. Both reprinted by permission. Selection from "The Second Elegy," *The Duino Elegies* of Rainer Maria Rilke translated by Harry Behn, published by Peter Pauper Press, 1957, is reprinted here by permission. Excerpt from "The Dreamer and the Sheaves" by I. R. Orton, *Images of Tomorrow* edited by John Heath-Stubbs, published by SCM Press, Ltd., 1953, is reprinted by permission. Excerpt from "Another Country," *Visiting the Caves* by William Plomer, published by Jonathan Cape, Ltd., 1965, is reprinted by permission. Excerpt from "'Chaka' V," *Poems* by F. T. Prince, published by Faber and Faber, Ltd., 1937, is reprinted by permission. Excerpt from "Orpah Returns to Her People," *A Crackling of Thorns* by John Hollander published by Yale University Press, 1958, is reprinted by permission. Excerpt from Homer's *Iliad, The Iliad,* translated by Richard Lattimore, revised edition published 1962. Copyright 1962 by The University of Chicago Press. Reprinted by permission.

Excerpt from "The Finding of the Ark," *Mirrors and Windows: Poems* by Howard Nemerov, published 1958 by The University of Chicago Press, is reprinted by permission of the author. Excerpt from "The Cry," *Col-*

lected Poems by Elder Olson, published 1958 by The University of Chicago Press, is reprinted by permission of the author. Excerpt from "Jacob" by Allen Kanfer, *The Yale Review*, Winter 1953, copyright by Yale University Press. Selection from "David" by James Wright, *The Yale Review*, Winter 1957, copyright by Yale University Press. Both reprinted by permission of *The Yale Review*. Excerpts from "The Days" and "Abraham," *Collected Poems* by Edwin Muir, second edition published in England in 1964 by Faber and Faber, Ltd., American edition published by Oxford University Press in 1965, are reprinted by permission of both publishers. Excerpts from "The Boyhood of David" by Adrienne Rich from *Poetry*, August 1957, is reprinted by permission of the author. Excerpt from "Winter Valley" by Raymond Souster from *Poetry*, September 1963, is reprinted by permission of the author. Excerpts from "Fern Hill" and "Author's Prologue," *The Collected Poems of Dylan Thomas*. Published in England in 1953 by J. M. Dent & Sons, Ltd. and in the United States in 1953 by New Directions. Copyright in 1953 by Dylan Thomas; © 1957 by New Directions. Reprinted here with permission from the publisher, New Directions Publishing Corporation. Also with the permission of J. M. Dent & Sons, Ltd., and the literary executors of the Dylan Thomas estate. The Bible text in this publication is from the *Revised Standard Version of the Bible*, copyrighted 1946 and 1952, and from the Apocrypha, copyrighted 1957 by the Division of Christian Education of the National Council of Churches, and used with permission.

For DEARIE *and* TIM
DEBBIE *and* LARRY
—*and* PETER

CONTENTS

Foreword

To write the first printed word about *Adam's Haunted Sons* means the privilege of introducing a book on the Bible that is distinctive in purpose and singular in value.

In our day "the waters of Shiloah, that flow gently" (Is. 8:6) have reached a new crest; books about Scripture rush from the press like a floodtide. Some are ponderously scientific in contents and style. Others, no less scholarly, are delightfully readable. Most are well illumined by the insights gained from the past few decades of research in excavated mounds and newly discovered libraries of ancient Near Eastern literature. Many bring to light, with profit to mind and heart, the rich, perennial truths that make the Bible a living book. Still, among all these works, *Adam's Haunted Sons* comes to the reading public with something special.

The author, while indebted to scholarship for the facts she marshalls and to biblical theology for the life-giving truths she presents, has centered attention on "the human and literary dimensions of the Bible." The texture of her book was woven on the framework of a very human loom; its composition was prompted by the vital challenge of teaching the Bible as literature to college English classes. A teacher's daily need to present what is solidly true and humanly interesting created the substance of this work. Sister Laurentia's personal insights have gained additional depth from the stimulating queries and suggestions of her students. The finished fabric, therefore, is something significant. Every gifted literary approach to human life reveals secrets that have transformed characters and situations; even more, when a master stylist writes of the men and women of the Bible, he brings his readers to see in the world of God's word a new heaven and a new earth.

Through a curious coincidence I read this book immediately after finishing (for the fourth time) Emily Brontë's *Wuthering Heights.* Looking back on the experience of reading both books in succession, I realize now that the same impressions and the same reactions endured throughout the consecutive reading. Miss Brontë studied the people around her and then wrote a story of lives transformed by inner loves and tensions. The countryside she painted—the Yorkshire moors around Haworth Parsonage, surrounded by hills with jutting crags, swept by tempestuous winds and warmed by soft breezes, enameled with heath and harebells—is the only part of the world she knew. But in *Wuthering Heights*, the Yorkshire country images kaleidoscopically the lives of men; all the familiar scenes take shape and color from the tangled destinies of Heathcliff and Cathy, Edgar and Isabella.

Many others have written of nineteenth-century life in England. Libraries are full of contemporary histories and biographies that students consult when they must append a learned footnote to some new scholarly thesis. But Emily Brontë's novel is still alive; its characters are immortal. Ellen Dean speaks to every age, and each man, like another Lockwood, listens to find something of himself in the Lintons and the Earnshaws—his good and evil, his joy and restlessness, the haunting of his heart by a dream, and the ceaseless search for his soul's desire.

Adam's Haunted Sons is reminiscent of *Wuthering Heights.* Emily Brontë, with the expertise of a literary craftsman, wrote of characters whom she had created in her own mind. Sister Laurentia, with her own masterful gifts of style, has written of "the tremendously vital human characters" who people the Bible. Their biographies are as fascinating as the story of the men and women who lived at Wuthering Heights and Thrushcross Grange. They were all authentic human sons of Adam, who, by his very name, is every man. Their story is our story. Though separated from us by millennia, these men who spoke a different language, followed strange customs, wore their own style of garb, and labored with primitive implements were still in heart and flesh men like ourselves. They laughed and sang, courted and cried, fought their battles and made capital of victory; and, like us too, they were haunted by the dream for which God made all men.

Today we need a book like *Adam's Haunted Sons*. Scientific and theological studies on sacred scripture have an indispensable role to play; they are necessary if we are truly to understand God's word and to develop correct patterns of religious thinking. But scholarship must be counterbalanced by comparable literary studies of the human characters whose personal lives were charged with the saving action of God and whose experiences color and enliven the world. If men of today come to think of Abraham, Moses, and David as mere puppets in an antiquarian's shop, the best part of the Bible's message has been overlooked. What does it benefit a reader of Exodus to know the exact route of the trek to Sinai if he is indifferent to the personal story of Moses, and remains untouched by the hopes that thrilled the soul of this great man and the agonies that tortured his heart?

All one needs to discover this best part of the biblical narrative is "the seeing eye and sympathetic heart" of the nineteenth-century romanticists. Long before the advent of biblical science, Robert Browning wrote his incomparable "Saul." Without the accoutrement of scriptural *wissenschaft*, Cardinal Newman and Basil Maturin, Janet Erskine Stuart and Bertrand Wilberforce studied the characters of the Bible and unfolded the story of their inner lives in fascinating studies in which each man can see, as in a limpid pool, the reflection of God's work in his own soul.

There is nothing adventitious or artificial in these reconstructions. The sacred writers themselves, though often following a stylized pattern of dialogue and historical narrative, have filled their pages with revealing insights into the inner life of their characters. Aaron's apology for not being able to eat the sin offering on the day his two sons were struck dead (Lev. 10:16–20), Moses' heartache over the waywardness of his people and his relentless wrestling with God in prayer, Samuel's mourning for the rejected Saul coupled with his intransigent refusal to see him again (1 Sam. 15:35), the fierce mother-love of Rizpah fighting off bird and beast from the bodies of her slain sons (2 Sam. 21:10), Ezekiel's heroic self-control when the Lord took away from him his wife, "the delight of his eyes" (Ezek. 24:16),

Judith's flaming satire against the cowardly priests (Judith 8:10–13), Nehemiah's deliciously homespun boast, "Remember me, O my God, for good according to all that I have done for this people" (Neh. 5:19)—insights like these into the hearts of men form the very substance of God's message to every man.

The Bible is truly God's book not only because He has inspired it but also because it shows Him at work in Adam's sons and, through them, in the world around them. The glory of God's saving activity cannot be seen apart from the lives of the men and women through whom He worked in a fully powerful yet totally human way. To know the God of the Scriptures one must study the people of Scripture—their joys and sorrows, their struggles and inner conflicts, their gropings, successes, and failures. Nature itself, because it is man's home, images his story and, therefore, as in a mirror, shows forth the power and the beneficence of God: "The voice of the Lord twists the oaks and strips the forest; and in His temple all say, 'Glory!' " (Ps. 28:9). Sister Laurentia has written *Adam's Haunted Sons* with a profound awareness of all this—of the compelling need to see God at work in the lives of men and in nature around them.

According to her own modest statement, she intended this book "for the general reader who would like to know more about the human and literary dimensions of the Bible, who wishes to explore the Bible with enjoyment, with zest." She has superbly achieved this purpose by delineating that element in Scripture which makes the message of God most meaningful for men. With seeing eye and sympathetic heart she tells of people like ourselves and of the world in which they lived. With gifted pen she presents every aspect of biography and every mood of nature as transformed by God's action in human hearts fashioned like our own and haunted, like ours, by God-given desires leading to the joys of a God-fulfilled dream.

BARNABAS M. AHERN, C.P.
Consultor of the Pontifical
Biblical Commission

Preface

THIS book is intended for the general reader who would like to know more about the human and literary dimensions of the Bible, who wishes to explore the Bible with enjoyment, with zest. It aims to banish fear and boredom, to share with others the fascination of the most famous book in the world with its tremendously vital human characters. Since these insights have been pursued in college classes treating the Bible as literature, they may prove useful to other classes and study groups as well as to the person who reads alone.

The chapters here follow the order of the Bible itself, and except for the first and fourth, they focus one by one on the dynamic human beings who live their changing lives in the scripture. The story of Babel, which is fourth, has no individualized characters, while Chapter I centers, not around any personality, but rather traces the wonderful unity given to the Bible by its frame—by the relationships between its first and last two chapters. For the same significant realities, the same rich symbols are found in Genesis 1–2 and in John's apocalyptic Revelation 21–22. In the beginning these appear as things of nature, shaped without man's concurrence; at the end they emerge transformed by artistry, by skill in craftsmanship—a peculiarly human trait. In the beginning the world has not yet been touched by man's power of choice; at the end he finds a world his choices have helped to make.

Adam's Haunted Sons goes only as far as David, for two reasons: because he brought Israel's hope to a climax by centering her life in Jerusalem, that city which even today holds so much meaning, and because with the Bible's riches to comment upon, the bulk of material was getting out of hand. The intention is to go on from David with a second volume.

The reader will have no trouble following this book with any translation he chooses. The Revised Standard Version is used here, and chapter and verse are cited in the text only for those passages not in the immediate context under discussion. In a few cases I have given proper names the spelling usually found in literature rather than that of the RSV.

This present book, an introduction to human and literary aspects of literature, does not pretend to profound scholarship, but is nevertheless indebted to many scholars and poets. Besides those mentioned, many other people and their books have helped to shape these thoughts. It is not always possible to retrace seven years of reading and discussion, however, and if I have at times failed to give proper credit, I shall do what I can in the future to rectify the omission.

Several persons should be named with special thanks: my mother who waited for her carbon of each chapter and so speeded my progress; Sister Rebecca, president of Mount St. Mary's College, Los Angeles, a severe, patient, invigorating, and creative critic; Sister Gerald who listened endlessly; Rev. Robert Stadler and Rev. Thomas Leahy, S.J., who believed a book like this could be written; Rev. Barnabas Ahern, C.P., Rev. John Reedy, C.S.C., Dan Herr and Joel Wells; Ralph Backlund for liking early chapters.

Permission to use chapters on Noah, Balaam, Gideon, Ruth, has graciously been given by the editors of journals where they appeared: *Worship*, *The Bible Today*, and *Ave Maria*. My classes in English 4B, The Bible as Literature, have also inspired and stimulated me. Far beyond the luck of most writers, I have been fortunate in my critics who are my friends, as well as in my two tribal loyalties—to the Diggeses and all who are theirs, and to the Josephs. May this book do them credit.

Introduction

THE men of the Bible are haunted—by a God they never asked for, by the dream of a country whose margin fades forever. Each single person, too, is haunted by an invitation to some work which relates to his people's God and to their far country. By their response to the twofold vision, of a God who is concerned about them and of a promised land, the people shape themselves and their unique destiny. By his answer, generous or reluctant, to his own call, each man creates his own personality, becomes what he does become for good or ill. Such urgency, such precarious choice makes for fascinating reading.

Yet though today's air is full of new excitement over the Bible stirred by fresh discoveries in archeology, study of the Dead Sea scrolls, the rediscovery of lost languages, the movement toward a more scriptural worship among people of many faiths, and though people want to read the Bible, still they are held back by feelings of boredom and fear.

Some begin bravely—nearly everyone has read Genesis—get as far as the middle of Exodus, and bog down, bored, in tables of ancient laws. Others, believing it to be God's book, fear that their faith may be injured, that they may think less well of their God, because the people he befriends are by no means ready-made saints.

Neither trouble is insoluble. To begin with, the Bible is not just one book, but a whole library of the best small books in the world, written by many hands over thousands of years. It holds all kinds of documents: enthralling stories, biographies, histories, great poetry, codes of law, census lists, formulas for worship, and less familiar varieties of writing such as wisdom speeches, prophecy, and apocalyptic visions. Each has its uses, but obviously all should not be read in the same way. The answer to boredom and fear is, therefore, first of all selection; and second, close reading—trying to see what is really there on the page in the Bible as we have it now.

Familiarity, in the beginning, with the immediately appealing parts, acquaintance with the Bible's living people, leads later on to interest even in their law codes and statistics, while alert attention to the words which tell how they act reveals their human qualities. These, in turn, evoke sympathy and a sense of understanding.

Such empathy banishes fear, especially when one discovers how the Lord accepts these people as they are—full of faults as is the way of humankind, yet touched by noble ideals and spurred on by a great purpose. To them he makes his revelation; to them he speaks a word which changes the course of history.

Before the Jews, mankind was bound to a cycle of perpetual return in nature with its repetition of seasons, its danger of stagnation and despair. With the irruption of the divine word into the cycle of becoming, history is born; time begins to move on a line towards a goal; recurrence changes to urgency and history gathers meaning because there is one who gives it purpose. The enduring vitality of these people comes from their sense of purpose which nothing can deflect, from their unquenchable hope. This explains their buoyancy. Even their laments cry out with energy, with a sense of abundant life. Always their eyes are forward. They are haunted by hope.

To urge the people on, the Lord makes three promises: of a land that shall be their home, of sons to inherit the land, of a unique relationship with himself: "You shall be my people, and I will be your God." By the themes of the promised country and the anticipated sons the Bible is held together as a book and invested with suspense. These themes look to the future. The relationship with God belongs to the present: he goes with them while they seek the land, he encourages their longing for sons to inherit the land. Following these threads the reader is led to watch some of the most vivid human beings in the world begin to search for this country of promise, fight to win it, settle it uneasily, lose it again, and begin all over to seek that home.

All the while, with the double vision of irony, the reader knows that the land they dream of—while it is a reality, an actual land along the eastern shore of the Mediterranean—is at the same time a symbol of a deeper reality; he knows that their first two promises of land and sons will be subsumed into the third, the call to be God's people. The call and promises are heard first by the patriarchs, Abraham, Isaac, and Jacob, and together, as the scholar G. Ernest Wright points out,[1] they become the first of five major events in the Old Testament.

After the call and promises, come Israel's rescue by Yahweh from the slavery of Egypt, the vision and covenant on Sinai, the winning of Canaan, and the triumphant unification of the tribes under David at Jerusalem. Around these five events the life and hope of the people center, and much of the Bible was written to keep them alive in history and in liturgical celebrations. Through them the people could discern Yahweh's commitment to them, and his calling for their loyalty in return.

To show this vital hope which shapes the Bible, and to demonstrate its memorable literary values—these are the aims of *Adam's Haunted Sons*. Here in the Bible are suspense and human reality, unity and order along with a wild variety. Literature is evocative, lingering in memory, employing symbol and event to stir feeling and thought; it works with human conflict and human motivation; it imposes pattern on the rich tangle of life's happenings. The aim, then, of this book is literary rather than theological: to accept the Bible as it stands today and to show how revelation in scripture comes shaped by human intent and human artistry; how it is concerned with human beings as they are influenced by the Lord's intervention. Accordingly, questions of sources, of historicity and the transmission of texts, are merely touched upon insofar as they are necessary to clarify literary aspects. Nor is there direct discussion of theology.

Since, however, God is acting here, one can no more treat the Bible without talking of him than one can discuss Shakespeare's most famous play and omit mention of Hamlet, prince of Denmark; nevertheless, in the present book the focus is on man. Through living personalities the divine mystery emerges. Through evocation, probing of personality, unraveling of relationships among events, literature does its work.

First in scripture comes Genesis, the book of beginnings. It falls into seven parts—four of prehistory: a creation idyll, the drama of the fall, and the short stories of Noah and Babel; these are followed by three historical sagas of Abraham, Jacob, and Joseph. Genesis, like many other books in the Bible, is a welding together of varied materials by one or more inspired editors. The materials come, as any good biblical introduction tells, from oral tradition, various written accounts, and documents shaped by and for purposes of worship.

Chapter 1 of Genesis, for example, was written fairly late in history by a priestly editor who felt strongly the majesty and transcendence of God. Chapter 2, earlier and more vividly primitive, shows a sense of God's immanence, his close relationship to man, his creature. These two attitudes are typical of the Bible's two views of the Lord. He is above and beyond all, yet he is always present and cares for his people with astonishing tenderness. The tracing of these layers of narrative is the work of many good scholars; it is, however, outside the province of this book, whose aim is literary exploration of the text as it appears in modern English Bibles.

Chapter I, then, of *Adam's Haunted Sons*, sets the scene by comparing the biblical picture of the land where mankind began with the bright symbolic city toward which he moves. The longing to find this last home is, as C. S. Lewis has said, each man's "inconsolable secret," which "we cannot hide and cannot tell, though we desire to do both. We cannot tell it because it is a desire for something that has never actually appeared in our experience. We cannot hide it because our experience is constantly suggesting it and we betray ourselves like lovers at the mention of a name."[2] This is the land of John's apocalyptic vision. When we, as Adam's sons, come to that city, then the homesickness which has haunted us will be quieted; then, as Augustine says:

> we shall be emptied and see
> we shall see and know
> we shall know and love
> and that in the end without end.

The First Country and Its Loss

CHAPTER ONE

In My Beginning Is My End

> I am the Alpha and the Omega,
> the first and the last,
> the beginning and the end.
> (REV. 22:13)

THE Bible opens and ends with hints and guesses about countries no man has seen. Genesis 1–2 tells of earth called up from chaos and unaltered as yet by man; Revelation 21–22 describes a new world which is the old one transformed by man's intervention. One is a world of nature; the other a world formed by deliberate artistry. Both accounts speak in symbols which evoke hidden meanings and signify a joy beyond experience. Neither is meant as literal description.

Rather, the words are like the stir of sound one listens to in a seashell. They evoke the rhythm of ocean, but no one supposes this is what the sea really sounds like. Neither do men suppose that the Bible gives exact information about Eden or heaven. Still, the hints and guesses have their own beauty, and lead the mind on to contemplate two modes of joy—those furnished by nature and those of art.

A close look at the beginning and end of any good book can reveal much about its themes, purpose, structure. To an astonishing degree this is true of the Bible. To follow Genesis 1–2 and then turn to Revelation (also called Apocalypse) 21–22 in order to see the beginning and end of man's wayfaring, gives a sense of the Bible's unity, the journey's continuity. To juxtapose these chapters sharpens suspense by showing the goal toward which the goal tends; their relationship exhibits the striking similarities and differences between man's first natural home and his last home built and ornamented by artistry.

In his book of Revelation, John seems deliberately to invite such comparison and contrast. Genesis opens with: "In the beginning, God created the heavens and the earth," while Revelation 21 begins: "Then I saw a new heaven and a new earth," and adds in the voice of the Lord: "Behold, I make all things new!" So poetry and theology both tell that man's final destiny will be a coming home, a return to find an open gate leading into a world familiar but strange. There all will be fresh creation, yet recognizable. Beings familiar since Eden will inhabit the heavenly city, yet the differences between garden and city go deep, and with reason.

Adam, who is everyman, begins in a garden with "trees pleasant to the sight and good for food," with rivers and birds and Eve his bride whose name means mother of the living. Adam comes at the end to a city where he finds all he thought he had lost, but transfigured now into glory. The difference between garden and city is that between nature and art, between a world of things which exist and grow in their own way, independently of man, and a world where things are transformed by artistry, by shaping hands and intellect—a world born of the choices man has made.

Through experiencing some of the meanings evoked by the symbols in Genesis, the reader is prepared for their recurrence and glorification at the end. With the opening chapters he is led by ancient literary artists to contemplate certain natural symbols that are significant of time and space, and to see them, in chapter 1, patterned in a sophisticated literary structure, emblematic of a fairly late artistry; chapter 2 is older and simpler. Both gather meanings around certain realities: the sea—strong, restless, a vast symbol for loneliness; rivers that flow to the four points of the compass; light, steady in its flow around earth, yet wavering, flickering, gleaming, always in motion; trees and all green plants in cool quietude; animals, akin to man, yet inscrutable in their self-sufficiency; man himself with his gift of dominion; woman and the beauty of her power to transmit life; the presence of God and his day of rest; death's dark shadow intensifying the sense of life, and a gate out of the garden. These will all reappear, in different fashion, at the end of the Bible, but first they must be seen in their natural significances.

> The waters stirred
> And from the doors were cast
> Wild lights and shadows on the formless face
> Of the flood of chaos.[3]

With the first words of the Bible, the sea is heard roaring in the darkness. Below are the waves of original chaos, the terror of destruction, of the restlessness and instability imaged in the sea's perpetual movement, of loneliness because of the sea's vast unpeopled expanse, of the dread which comes to man when he realizes how he is immersed in a sea of time—pressed upon by an irretrievable past and an unknown future, adrift upon a shoreless present.

The Israelites, a nonseafaring people whose land reached the coast of the Mediterranean only during a short period of their history with David and Solomon, felt strongly the mystery of the sea—a terror like that Melville pictures in *Moby Dick:* "to and fro in the deeps, far down in the bottomless blue, rush mighty leviathans, sword-fish, and sharks; and these [are] the strong, troubled, murderous thinking of the masculine sea." The sea's thoughts plot murder by a death made present in the fierce sea-dwellers, in whales, swordfish, and sharks.

Another writer, Matthew Arnold, in an entirely different context, depicts the loneliness of the sea, showing how the tide recedes from land with a

> . . . melancholy, long, withdrawing roar,
> Retreating, to the breath
> Of the night wind, down the vast edges drear
> And naked shingles of the world.
> ("Dover Beach")

He is talking of the desolation of a world without faith, but his words evoke a universal response. In the falling cadences of his lines one senses how man stands alone and diminished, looking over an empty expanse of night where the sea roars. But greater loneliness is in Genesis, for no man is there to hear the sea.

Yet creating power broods over the waters and calls order out of chaos. What emerges is a temporal world of natural happiness in a garden which belongs to the round earth. Here the symbols are natural beings in their natural state, and they often suggest the measuring of time, the dimensioning of space. Here in the garden man will live in a state of childhood happiness among green trees and in a friendly animal world.

The Creator's first deed is to poise the sky as a wall separating the waters above the earth from those below it. The Genesis poet pictures a solid sky, arched as a bowl over earth with the land floating upon subterranean waters. Darkness hangs heavy, but the Lord's first words sound: "Let there be light," and there is light—pure, simple, undifferentiated. Jung, the master of myth and psychology, says that this is the only creation story which has its beginning in light. Just as the waters were all one chaos, so this light is one flaming mass. Later it too will be brought to order.

Meanwhile, in its brightness the round earth emerges, and on it rivers, which in their way symbolize time and space, begin to flow. As for time, it is made of successive moments and multiple change, but there is also something that endures. Rivers are like this too: their waters flow on, ever changing, ever new, yet the river remains. In another sense, the river is memory which carries the past into the present, and time present flowing on to the future. As Eliot says in "The Dry Salvages," the "strong brown god" of the river is "time the destroyer . . . time the preserver," a reminder of things men choose to forget.[4]

Soon this river, flowing through Eden, divides into four branches—Pishon, Gihon, Tigris, Euphrates—seeking the four corners of the world. Dimensionless space is being dimensioned and order imposed, for the corners of earth signify the points of the compass by which thoughts of space are given direction. Under this image of plentiful water the Israelites will picture the land they hope for. Always the vision rises green in their minds. Moses will tell them of it: "The Lord your God is bringing you into a good land, a land of brooks of water, of fountains and springs flowing forth in valleys and hills, a land of wheat and barley, of vines and fig trees and pomegranates" (Deut. 8:8). Such is the dream of a desert people.

To shine is to be surrounded by the dark,
To glimmer in the very going out.
As stars wink, sinking in the bath of dawn,
Or as a prong of moon prolongs the night.[5]

In the meantime, the light shining over the emerging world has not yet been ordered. As with waters, so here, the first step is separation. "And God said, 'Let there be lights in the firmament of the heavens to separate the day from the night; and let them be for signs and for seasons and for days and years.'" So time is dimensioned. And the Lord makes "two great lights, the greater light to rule the day, the lesser light to rule the night; he made the stars also." It is a hierarchy of order, of obedience. And the prophet Baruch describes the way the stars rejoice in their docility:

The stars shone in their watches, and were glad;
he called them, and they said, "Here we are!"
They shone with gladness for him who made them
(APOCRYPHA, BARUCH 3:34)

With admiration for such regularity and control, the chorus keeps repeating: "and there was evening and there was morning, one day," and a second day, until it comes to the seventh, where the orderly shape of weeks is marked off by the day of rest. This day is one of the great legacies left to humankind by the Jews. God rested, and man too delights in leisure: quiet days in country places, evenings at home, times when the Lord says to his creatures, "Be still, and know that I am God."

Light, then, is ordered in itself; it imposes order on the flow of time, and it makes the order in the world perceptible to human eyes. What it reveals is a green world, clothed in plants which derive their sustenance from light.

Mounted on its triumphal chariot, Earth,
Shawled with the changing seasons, casts them off
In execution of a solemn dance. . . .
And hills start upward on a wave of green.[6]

A sense of the fragrant breathing plant world pervades the pastoral quietude of Genesis 2, which, in contrast to chapter 1 with its stylized stanzas, moves like a buoyant country dance.

Here again God phrases his commands in terms of orderly life: "Let the earth bring forth vegetation, plants yielding seed, and fruit trees bearing fruit in which is their seed." Each will propagate its own kind; each will perpetuate itself into future time.

But soon a tree, a member of the plant kingdom, will be used to stir up conflict and so present man with the possibility of disorder. Paradise has many trees, but two are singled out—the tree of life which will reappear in the heavenly city, and that mysterious tree which will soon tempt Adam to his fall. Alex Comfort, a British poet, sees the two reflected in the waters of every man's mind. Each man sees an "image of the mind's / Two trees, cast downward,"

> One tilting leaves to catch the sun's bright pennies,
> One dark as water, rooted among the bones.[7]

One tree bears the bright fruit of immortality; the other the dark choice of death.

> Animals run deep in dreams,
> and art keeps leading them forth
> to consciousness.[8]

Even closer to man than the plant world, and luring him with perpetual fascination, is the kingdom of animals. "Animals run deep in dreams," says the art critic Alexander Eliot. "To tame animals one learns courageously to see their shadows in oneself, making one's mind a vessel of creation, an invisible Noah's ark." Men watch them, feel kinship with them, and yet never understand them nor their archetypes within the self.

Out of primeval waters God calls birds "that fly above the earth," "the great sea monsters," "cattle and creeping things and beasts of the earth." They too, like plants, are to engender life, each according to its kind passing on its existence to new generations. If any human being had been there "after the birth of the simple light / In the first spinning place" of the tilted earth, he would have seen with awe, "The spellbound horses walking warm / Out of the whinnying green stable / On to the fields of praise." So Dylan Thomas, in "Fern Hill,"[9] thinks about the first of horses, walking dazed and spellbound because newly fashioned, warm from the hands of God; wandering through the green world and whinnying for praise.

> When I was young, it was much simpler;
> I saw God standing on a local hill,
> His eyes were gentle and bright birds
> Sang in chorus to his voice.[10]

Until now, God has created by his powerful word alone. In this the Bible account differs from other early creation myths which picture the gods struggling against chaos. Here God simply breathes his almighty word and all comes to be. But with man he takes pains, exercising craftsmanship, shaping with his hands the human form. Part of the naive charm results from the way the writer of chapter 2, called the Yahwist, gives human features and characteristics to God. These divine powers of artistry he will later share with mankind. Male and female, now, he creates them, each by a different process, and to man he gives power to rule, to hold dominion; to woman he gives the ability to bear life. In these ways they image forth the Lord who made them.

Man he forms "of dust from the ground," and breathes "into his nostrils the breath of life." Made of clay, he is forever rooted in earth; but his clay is infused with a breath of divinity which sets him aspiring after the infinite, makes him eternally restless, dissatisfied, reaching for the unreachable. Sharing the life of God, he shares knowledge, freedom, power to love, with the hazards that spring from such gifts in the keeping of a finite being.

Adam, whose name is given by God and means simply *man*, is soon given opportunity to exercise his dominion when the Lord brings, as in procession, "every beast of the field and every bird of the air," and waits "to see what he would call them." As the poet Richard Wilbur says, "To apply words to objects is to redeem them from namelessness." At times man feels that "the world is getting out of hand, that it is shaking itself free," reverting to chaos. And so he says to things: "You're a chair, you're a table, you're a tree." This is the primitive poetic act, and by it man "creates things and re-creates himself."[11]

Now Adam can call the animals and they will come. But his

power over them is not absolute. He has not made them. He calls each by its own name, not by his. Later on, one of them, the serpent, will shake off obedience and bring disaster. At the end of the Bible, too, there will be a different naming, a different kind of dominion; yet all this lies in the future.

> Like a beautiful olive tree in the field,
> and like a plane tree I grew tall. . . .
> Like a vine I caused loveliness to bud. . . .
> (SIRACH 24:14, 17)

Adam has named all the animals, but having found no helper like himself he is lonely. It is not enough that he can mirror the power of God. The Lord has a further gift to share, and so sets himself another task which calls for special care and craftsmanship. He casts the man into "a deep sleep" and takes "one of his ribs," and makes it "into a woman" and brings her to the man. By describing Eve as formed from the very bone of Adam, the writer conveys the essential closeness of man and woman, their need of each other if they are to reach maturity.

She is no alien being, and Adam welcomes her:

> This at last is bone of my bones
> and flesh of my flesh;
> She shall be called Woman,
> because she was taken out of man.

A bond of trust is thus forged by the bestowing and accepting of a name. Later Adam gives her yet another name, calling her Eve "because she was the mother of all living" (Gen. 3:20). With her too he is exercising dominion, for he precedes her, not in order of value, but in that of free obedience.

Woman, in the poetry of all centuries, has been symbolized in terms of a garden. Like the garden she is haven and refreshment to Adam; like it she is fruitful as her name signifies. With her coming man seems to have all he needs for happiness, yet a shadow broods over their idyll. Death lurks near, for the Lord God has "commanded the man, saying, 'You may eat freely of every tree of the garden; but of the tree of the knowledge of good and evil you shall not eat, for in the day that you eat of it you shall die.' "

The possibility of error is the price of freedom. Adam can, if he chooses, return the world to chaos. When, later on, he rebels, the reader finds with surprise that this garden has walls, is limited, for suddenly there is a gate, and Adam, outside through his own decision, sees the gate shut against him. His choice with its consequences is dramatized in the next part of Genesis. But in the meantime the world is at peace and governed by order. This order is forcefully portrayed by the unknown artist who shaped the first chapter of Genesis according to a strict pattern, so that the form supports the meaning in a vivid way.

> The shape of the poem says that:
> despite chaos, order exists;
> despite ugliness, beauty;
> despite evil, good;
> and they inhabit a world beyond change

Chaos, like some threatening beast, has been driven back to its lair, and order among creatures is precariously established. The first chapter of Genesis, by its artistic structure, emphasizes this theme of orderly creation. Possessing shape and symmetry like a poem, it moves through seven stanzas with recurring refrains; it poises its images in balanced halves, each half rising to a climax.

Each of the six days of work begins with the words "And God said," and closes with the refrain: "And there was evening and there was morning, one day," and the second day, and so on to the sixth. The phrase swings like a pendulum, sweeping away evening, bringing in daylight, and beginning again. Besides, the work days are characterized by God's pleasure in his handicraft, for six times the refrain rings out: "And God saw that it was good"; and at the last after the making of man, his joy is intensified, for he finds what he has made is "very good."

Beyond the patterns of days and refrains, chapter 1 shows symmetry in structure. Images in days one, two, three, balance with those of four, five, six, to form matching triads. The light, day, and night of the first day are matched on the fourth by the making of sun, moon, stars to govern day and dark. The second day's collecting of waters, consigning some to sky, some to sea, and thus clearing the land, balances on the fifth day with the making of fish in the sea, birds in the sky, and readiness of earth for animals and men. Grasses and trees, lowest of living beings, appear on the third day, while on the sixth God makes animals and men, highest in the scale of creatures. Here is the pattern:

1. Light, dividing of day and dark
2. Separation of waters, sky
3. Vegetation, having life, but low on the scale of living things
4. Luminaries governing day and night
5. Fish in waters, birds in sky
6. Animals and men, highest kinds of life

Noteworthy too is the climactic shape of the triads, rising toward days three and six where life appears. In some sense, the days twice ascend from energy to form to motion; from light which furnishes power, to form and order without which energy is aimless, to the self-movement, first of plants which live and grow, and then the higher movement of which men and animals are capable.

> Thou art still
> The son of morn in weary night's decline,
> The lost traveller's dream under the hill
> (William Blake)

So beautiful is Adam's first home and his idyllic life of childhood in a garden that he has bequeathed to his descendants a longing to return to the Eden of irresponsibility, to live in harmony with nature as the animals do, to find shelter again in his mother's womb where no decisions are demanded. Dante in his purgatory intimates that men must be freed of this longing before they can enjoy ultimate happiness. He therefore places Eden at the top of the purgatorial mountain so that every man who climbs must go through the garden and leave it behind before he is ready to step off into the translucent spheres of the heavens.

After all his labor of making the first world, God returns to simple rest, and a sabbath quiet descends on the seventh day. This peace of the ending looks toward another last day when creation will be complete in a different fashion—not in a natural garden of childhood joys, but in a city shaped and measured, a home which man's decisions have helped to build. Edwin Muir the poet says the sons of Adam long for

the passing of this fragmentary day
Into the day when all are gathered together,
Things and their names, in the storm's and the
lightning's nest,
The seventh great day and the clear eternal weather.[12]

When that "clear eternal weather" comes, and even storms have come home to their nest, then man will possess his true home, and in that city all will be one great sabbath, one everlasting day of peace and rejoicing.

My God, I heard this day
That none doth build a stately habitation
But he that means to dwell therein
(George Herbert)

To that city John turns his eyes when his apocalyptic visions are nearly finished. He has seen the forces of evil conquered and order achieved at the end of the world. And so his whole Revelation is a hymn to the triumph of order, gathering materials from Genesis and the prophets and the Old Testament apocalyptic writings, and building them into an intricate pattern of seven times seven visions. This design, however, will be discussed in another place; at present chapters 21–22 are most relevant.

Here is "a new heaven and a new earth," a world wrought by art and handicraft, a city where nature is deliberately shaped into architectural form, beautified by polished jewels and carvings upon stone and lintel, measured in ways that suggest symbolic completion rather than any literal width and height. Here, as in Genesis, the Bible talks of sea and river; light diffused and light from sun, moon, stars; the tree of life and the qualities of animals; man and woman and the presence of God; the joyful assurance of death conquered, and gates in the walls of the city.

This is a transtemporal, transcendent world, where space and time are irrelevant. Though John keeps the realities of the garden, he changes its landscape in four important ways: by transfiguring it into a city; by banishing chaos, fear, death; by placing in the city new artifacts produced by handiwork and intelligence; by transforming the Eden symbols, taking them beyond nature into art, and calling on them to signify freedom from time and space, the completion of a world no longer bound by transiency.

> [No more] the dark cold and the empty desolation.
> The wave cry, the wind cry, the vast waters
> Of the petrel and the porpoise.[13]

Genesis has shown the sea as a symbol of chaos, destruction, desolation, pressing in on man from all sides as present, past, future, press on him. Eliot, describing mankind's universal feelings about the sea, says:

> We cannot think of a time that is oceanless
> Or of an ocean not littered with wastage.[14]

Yet it is just such a "time that is oceanless" which the apocalypse envisions—the nontime of eternity. The litter of time's wastage, of chaos and desolation, are banished with a simple phrase freighted with meaning because of all that the sea has meant in earlier contexts: "The first heaven and the first earth [have] passed away," says John, "and the sea [is] no more." Just as the roaring of the deep introduces the creation story, so the vanishing of the sea prepares for a new life, a new home.

> The sun shall be no more your light by day,
> nor for brightness shall the moon
> give light to you by night;
> but the Lord will be your everlasting light.
> (ISA. 60:19)

The sea, a threat to man, is gone; now darkness where dangers lurk, must also go. The city has no place for fear. There "shall be no night there," and "they shall bring into it the glory . . . of the nations." This, as in the first world, is a diffused light, finding its source in neither sun nor moon:

> And the city has no need of sun or moon
> to shine upon it,
> for the glory of God is its light,
> and its lamp is the Lamb.

Sun, moon, stars no longer function to govern day and night, month and year, in a world of time. Yet their beauty is not lost, for in chapter 12 John has prepared for his vision of the city as the bride of God by showing a mysterious sign in the heavens, a woman adorned with sun, moon, and stars. Such is the new work of the heavenly bodies—to be glorious ornaments, but no longer to rule time.

Throughout the city, too, light is refracted from gold and glass, from sapphires, emeralds, amethysts, and all the jewels which make its walls and streets. These stones and minerals exist, not in their lackluster state of nature, but refined and polished by art. They recall all man-made lights; shining through colored windows, gleaming with iridescence from polished surfaces, moving with contrasting shadows over masses of sculpture or architecture. Still, these earth lights are, as Eliot again says, only "the light that fractures through unquiet water,"[15] not Light itself streaming from the mysterious center of the Godhead, and remaining a mystery to man's eyes.

> Behold, I will extend prosperity
> to her like a river,
> and the wealth of the nations
> like an overflowing stream. . . .
> (Isa. 66:12)

Not only light finds its source in the Lord, so also does the "river of the water of life, bright as crystal, flowing from the throne of God and of the Lamb." Again John has carried the symbol beyond nature by giving it a source in mystery; nor does he intend it to measure time or divide the quarters of space. It is simply there, flowing "through the middle of the street of the city"—a street of "pure gold, clear as glass." This river functions to bring beauty to the city, fruitfulness to the land, and refreshment to men who are invited to come and drink "water without price from the fountain of the water of life."

Since all is one heavenly city without division, there is no need for four rivers—for Tigris, Euphrates, Pishon, Gihon. Rather the unity recalls Dante's river of gold, banked with flowers, lighted by flying angels at the top of his heavens. Slowly as Dante watches, the river changes to a circle, the flowers emerge as living human beings, and the circle becomes a white rose encompassing all beatitude in another man's vision of John's city of glory.

Like a cedar on Lebanon I am raised aloft,
like a cypress on Mount Hermon,
Like a palm tree in En-gaddi,
like a rosebush in Jericho,
Like a fair olive tree in the field,
like a plane tree growing beside the water.
(SIRACH 24:13–14)

The waters give life, not to a profusion of plants as in the garden, but to one kind of tree—the tree of life which first grew in Eden. It springs up now as a figure of plenitude:

In the middle of the street of the city . . .
On either side of the river [grows]
the tree of life with its twelve kinds of fruit,
yielding its fruit each month.

Here is prosperity, a rich sufficiency of food for every month of the year, and the leaves of the tree, says John, bring healing to those who enter the city after the last conflict.

There is no mention now of the Genesis command to bear seed and propagate. That would be provision for the future, while in this world there is no future, but only, as Boethius the philosopher said long ago, "the perfect and simultaneous possession of interminable life." The key word is *simultaneous*—all is an eternal and intensely present now.

And he who talked to me had
a measuring rod of gold
to measure the city
and its gates and walls.
(REV. 21:15)

This twelvefold fruit of the tree by the river is one of the many instances of number symbolism important in the Bible. Seven, used in both Genesis and Revelation, being the number of days in the week, means completion. But twelve, which is not used in the story of the garden, means fulfillment on a larger scale, for it signifies all the months of the year; while, as an interesting footnote, six, which is half of twelve, means incompletion, essential frustration, and so John, earlier, has named the arch-enemy of the kingdom "six hundred and sixty-six" (13:18).

Twelve and one hundred forty-four, made of twelve times twelve, appear often in the book of Revelation whose theme is maturation, fruition, fulfillment. Here are twelve gates with twelve angels to guard them, and the names of the twelve tribes of Israel carved on the lintels. The city rests on twelve foundation stones, each made of a different jewel, and on them are written the names of the twelve apostles. These twelves symbolize a complete and vital present into which past and future are absorbed; and the inscriptions on lintel and cornerstone demonstrate once more the deliberate art which pervades the city, while all exactness in measurement marks a planned and finished artifact.

> Heraldic art without the lion .
> would not amount to very much. . . .
> The lamb, in coats of arms, is usually
> the paschal lamb.[16]

Of all the artistic transformations, one of the most pronounced is that of the kingdom of beasts. Lion and lamb not only lie down together, but their qualities of royal power and steadfast patience meet in the lamb who is the lion of Judah (Rev. 5), who shines with the glory of the Lord to give light to the city, and who shares a throne with the transcendent God. The lamb's appearance here at the end of the Bible is charged with drama. When all stand watching for the conquering figure of the lion, then it happens that the lamb appears instead, in company with the Lord God Almighty. This figure is "the root and the offspring of David, the bright morning star," the bridegroom of the city itself.

Many images in the Bible, and especially in the apocalyptic books, are not meant to be visualized. They are rather leaps of imagination into a world beyond the senses. Certainly, John's intention is not to paint realistically a lion who is also a lamb. The art of heraldry may give some insight here; a man who pictures a lion rampant on his coat of arms is abstracting from the natural world, choosing one possible quality of lions—their roaring attack which inspires fear. For his purpose, it makes no difference that lions do not stand upright and lunge forward as a man might.

So in the apocalypse, John is evoking the fierce strength of lions which so many Israelite shepherds, from Samson to David to Amos, had to face, and then tempering it with the patience of the lamb who goes unresisting to death, that lamb which earlier had become a symbol of the people's paschal liberation from Egypt.

> There is a river whose streams make glad
> the city of God,
> the holy habitation of the Most High,
> God is in the midst of her, she shall not
> be moved. . . .
> (Ps. 46:4–5)

All that Eve meant to Adam is gathered up and transfigured in the bride of Revelation. She is beauty, new birth, and welcome. In a poem that sings the beauty of Bellini's painting "Annunciation," Ned O'Gorman glorifies Mary with apocalyptic images:

> An angel stepping through her window said . . .
> I bring you flaring squares, circles,
> perpendiculars, and trapezoids. I bring you
> color from the sun.[17]

His geometric and shining figures echo John's vision, and can enrich in one's mind the picture of the woman made ready for final glory: "And a great portent appeared in heaven, a woman clothed with the sun, with the moon under her feet, and on her head a crown of twelve stars" (Rev. 12).

She is about to give birth, and being still partly an earth-woman, she cries out "in her pangs of birth, in anguish for delivery." When she brings forth her son, he is caught "up to God and to his throne," while she herself, threatened by a dragon, flees into a wilderness, where rivers and earth conspire to help her, and eagle's wings are lent her for flight. William G. Heidt remarks on the artistry of this passage: "There is magnificent contrast between the two figures so sharply etched against John's apocalyptic sky. The beauty of the woman is heightened by the dreadfully monstrous appearance of her assailants."[18]

This wonderful vision comes to mind when (chap. 21) an angel cries, "Come, I will show you the Bride, the wife of the Lamb," and the city appears, "the new Jerusalem, coming down out of heaven from God, prepared as a bride adorned for her husband." Woman and city merge in an identification closer than that of Eve with the garden. Whether or not John intended this bride to be the same as the woman of chapter 12, the temptation to see her adornment as sun, moon, and stars is irresistible. But these are not her only brightnesses.

Her light is "like a most rare jewel, like a jasper, clear as crystal," and around the city is "a great, high wall, with twelve gates":

> And the twelve gates [are] twelve pearls,
> each of the gates made of a single pearl . . .
> and its gates shall never be shut by day—
> and there shall be no night there.

The city is a figure of welcome, for her gateways, each one made of one great pearl, stand open to east, west, north, and south, and people of every tribe and tongue come streaming in, clothed in royal raiment and bearing gifts to the Lord. Such is the bride, the city, the home where God and man abide in communal sharing.

> He . . . had been given his life
> in fief, and authority had been his,
> the rich Christ had placed the standard
> in his hand . . .
> and set the ring upon his finger.[19]

Woman, as the city, stands alone, a single archetypal figure; man, in contrast, is identified with the whole of redeemed humankind, and man's special gift of dominion is typified in the activity of these rejoicing multitudes. They have, earlier in Revelation, indicated their glad surrender to God their overlord with the arts of music and song, and now in a solemn procession like a dance, they come before his throne to see his face and to have his name written on their foreheads.

When, in the garden, the animals came in procession to Adam, who gave names to each one, the action signified a certain overlordship on the part of the man. Still his dominion was limited; he called each animal by its own name. But here in the city, men now surrender their power, return to God the rule he has entrusted to them, and as a reward they are marked not by their own names but with the name of God. Because of their joyful obedience, the name of their Father becomes their own.

The gesture is one of childlike confidence. In his beautiful essay, *The Weight of Glory*, which was quoted earlier, C. S. Lewis marvels at the meanings of the word "glory." It signifies the pure and creaturely rejoicing in the divine accolade, the praise given to his creature by the Lord of all. Lewis remarks that "nothing is so obvious in a child—not in a conceited child, but in a good child—as its great and undisguised pleasure in being praised. . . . The promise of glory is the promise, almost incredible" of pleasing God, of being "a real ingredient in the divine happiness." To be delighted in by God—"it seems impossible, a weight or burden of glory which our thoughts can hardly sustain."[20] Yet this glory, as Revelation tells, is man's destiny.

> We shall not cease from exploration
> And the end of all our exploring
> Will be to arrive where we started
> And know the place for the first time[21]

Like some triumphant epic or great novel, the Bible draws its people, themes, symbols together at the end. The last chapters are foreshadowed in the first. Adam, though Eden will be closed against him, can look forward to a homecoming in a place more wonderful than Eden, a city which his hands and his will have helped to build. Here all will be new, yet nothing strange. Here in transfigured glory he will discover again the sky and waters and beasts, the bride and the presence of the Lord, for this is

> The dwelling of God . . . with men.
> He will dwell with them,
> and they shall be his people,
> and God himself will be with them.

The Lord who had walked when he pleased in the garden in the cool of the evening, abides in the city. It is his home as well as Adam's. And there his presence heals all sorrow:

> he will wipe away every tear from their eyes,
> and death shall be no more,
> neither shall there be mourning nor crying
> nor pain any more,
> for the former things have passed away.

Though they walk in the valley of the shadow of death, Adam's sons move in urgency. And the reader, having shared the visions of man's early and late homes, made vivid by evocative symbol and literary pattern, is urged forward—not for nothing does the word *come* appear five times in the last chapter of Revelation.

Next comes the first of dramas in which man loses his garden home and finds his feet set on a road of danger and sorrow, but lighted by hope. This road does indeed move forward. It progresses away from one symbolic place, a garden, and toward another symbolic home, the cool and glorious city. Through much of the Bible, however, the people are more concerned about a literal land than about the city with its plane trees by the waters in the streets. That city stands for their fulfilled relationship with the Lord, but they want an earthly city. And God promises even that, though it will not be theirs forever.

What happens is that the symbolic roles are reversed. The literal earthly land which seems so solid in its reality becomes itself a symbol for the greater, if less tangible, reality of the heavenly city, the transcendent happiness of an abiding place with God. On the conscious level, the people move in a series of ascents toward a promised land, a literal home, a certain spot on the surface of the earth. Abraham hears the promises; Moses sees the cities, valleys, mountains; Joshua and the Judges win their way in; David takes possession and unifies the country. Each man, from Abraham on, brings the people one step closer to the dreamed-of land.

From one point of view, the road looks more like a ladder than a highway—a ladder with uneven stairs—for under some leaders the people take greater steps. But always there is an ascent; the series moves upward to its climax with David. Only after his day is Israel forced by sorrow to learn that their country, stretching from Dan to Beersheba, and centered upon Jerusalem the holy city, is itself but a symbol of the greater, more costly land of promise. The first step of all is seen in the drama by which the garden is lost; this comes in the next chapter.

CHAPTER TWO

Adam's Fateful Choice

> The . . . constituents of the cosmos—the moon and waters, rock and tree, woman and serpent, are hierophanies, revelations of mystery
>
> (DANIELOU)

BY rich symbol and orderly pattern, the first and last chapters of scripture have offered visions of garden and city, the scene of man's origin and the place of his end. The next chapters, made of conversation and action, present a simple story with a profound theme—a story made vivid because the characters step out as on a stage and reveal themselves in their speech.

The theme is the old question of man's duality, of the contradictions in his nature: Why, with all his high ideals, does he fall so low, fail so miserably? What is the flaw deep in his being? The Genesis writer, gathering materials from already existing stories and shaping them to his important double theme of sin and hope for redemption, tells of Adam who misused his freedom to make a fateful choice. Gregory the Great once remarked that "the Bible has deeps and shallows where the lamb may wade and the elephant may swim." This story is an example. Theologians find it deep enough for their profound thought, and children are held by the spell it casts.

Its human power springs largely from its dramatic form. If conversation and conflict, human action and the results of free choice make drama, then the Bible is full of it—and this though the Israelites, with all their literary genius, wrote nothing for the stage. It is one important form they never developed, probably because dramatic art seemed too close to the idolatrous ceremonies of neighboring peoples. Yet, having an intense sense of human freedom, and a realization of the power of human decision, they wrote drama in spite of themselves.

Here are all its elements in a rudimentary form: setting, dialogue, significant action, psychological truth, conflict and irony, choice and the changes wrought by choice. Following the bare bones of dramatic structure, the tale moves through five steps: 1) an introduction which motivates all that follows; 2) a time of rising suspense; 3) a crisis when decision is inescapable; 4) a climax when choice is final; 5) the working out of the resultant changes.

And al was for an appil
An appil that he tok
As clerkes finden
Written in hir book
(MEDIEVAL SONG)

With the garden ready for man, the Lord is pictured as offering a last gift, the two-edged sword of freedom. "In the midst of the garden" grows "the tree of the knowledge of good and evil," a symbol of forbidden knowledge, a wisdom to which man is not entitled; a symbol, says Ignatius Hunt, in his preface to Genesis, of the right to decide for oneself, regardless of God, what is right and wrong. "Any seizure of this right is an attempt on God's sovereignty."[22] Adam knows clearly that he has power to attempt this: "You may freely eat of every tree of the garden," says the Lord, "but of the tree of the knowledge of good and evil you shall not eat, for in the day that you eat of it you shall die." Defiance is possible, and that possibility motivates the dramatic action.

The dialogue between the cunning serpent and the gullible Woman is a classic. It is not intended to be a word-for-word report.[23]

Now Eve, in a scene clear as on a lighted stage, stands before the tree. The adversary enters, disguised as a serpent. It is the writer's way of speaking out against the use of serpents in the degraded pagan rites of his time. Certainly this serpent is "more subtle than any other wild creature that the Lord God had made."

He begins with a cunning question: "Did God say, 'You shall not eat of any tree of the garden?' "

Naively the woman explains that they may pluck fruit from every tree except the one before them. She is like a child repeating a lesson only half understood: "God said, 'You shall not eat of the fruit of the tree which is in the midst of the garden . . . lest you die.' " Obviously she does not know the meaning of her own words; in particular she knows nothing of death.

The serpent suggests that this is all nonsense: "You will not die." And he begins to attribute some of his own subversive slyness to the Creator. "God knows that when you eat of it your eyes will be opened, and you will be like God, knowing good and evil." He is a master of half-truths; to possess knowledge is good, and to choose one's own destiny does make man godlike. But he fails to explain that the noble courtesy of free obedience leads to fulfillment beyond the creature's defiant self-willing.

Before his coming, Eve seems not to have looked carefully at the tree. Now she studies it, seeing that it appears "good for food, and that it was a delight to the eyes, and that the tree was to be desired to make one wise." The serpent's psychological skill has done its work. Now is the moment of crisis when irreversible choice must be made. Eve takes the fruit and eats it, and in her mouth she feels:

> The snake and the body of the snake
> the twist of choking in the grass
> the feet of scorpion on the tongue.[24]

She has made her dreadful choice, has reached out to an appearance of good and found it bitter, but the fate of mankind is not altered. That waits upon Adam's decision.

> This was the apple, ripe for his desire,
> This that he absently received of her
> As if bemused, and saw
> All things disfigured that were whole before.[25]

Until now, Adam has not been on the scene. At this moment he appears and the story rises to its climax. The telling is stark in its swift simplicity:

She took of its fruit and ate;
and she also gave some to her husband,
and he ate.

A modern poet captures a sense of allure and doom like that which must have hung over the scene while Adam made his choice: "The rich sound of leaves / Burns in his heart, sings in his veins," but desolation lurks there, waiting on his dangerous decision, and

> Now beyond the granite milestone,
> On the ancient human road. . . .
> The pilgrim listens, as the night air brings
> The murmured echo, perpetual, from the gorge
> Of barren rock far down the valley.[26]

Adam listens; he reaches his hand to the fruit of evil pride. The woods turn dark; the trees stand somber in the mist. Though he does not know it, he has just made himself an exile, one who will go on a long and lonely pilgrimage through gorges "of barren rock" and down far valleys. So the climax passes, and the turning point, the place of no return. Things can never be the same again.

> Man's loneliness . . . is haunted always with the certainty of death, dark death, which stops our tongues, our eyes, our living breath . . . with dust
>
> (THOMAS WOLFE, *The Hills Beyond*)

Offstage a new voice is heard, "the sound of the Lord God walking in the garden in the cool of the day." This tranquil phrase which comes like a last echo of the serene life now lost, is not heard again in the Bible. At God's call the human couple for the first time know fear; they hide, and he asks why. Adam answers that they are ashamed because they are naked, but this shame is as new as their fear.

He will not confess the real reason and so the Lord must say it for him: "Have you eaten of the tree of which I commanded you not to eat?" With this Adam begins to blame Eve, accusing her of giving him the fruit. It is a breach in love; the first human marriage has come to conflict, is no longer an idyll. Eve in turn blames the serpent. Having turned from God, the maker of unity, they find the harmony of the cosmos destroyed.

God's plan for living beings was a hierarchy of obedience. Man was directly subject to God, woman to her husband, the animals to man, and the plant world below the animals. With the fall, conflict is set in motion. The lowest of living beings, fruit from a plant, is used by an animal, the serpent, to tempt the woman, who in her turn lures man away from God. The great chain of being from the Lord to man to woman to animal to plant is wholly reversed; plant first, to animal, to woman, to man, and all against God.

Now in concrete images the Lord tells the consequences of their choice. Adam shall know hard work:

> In the sweat of your face
>   you shall eat bread. . . .
> cursed is the ground because of you . . .
> thorns and thistles it shall bring forth . . .
>   and you shall eat the plants of the field.

As Adam had taken fruit of earth in symbol of his rebellion, so earth will prove reluctant to yield its fruits to him. His wife, whose call was to bear life and cherish it, has chosen instead to transmit death. She therefore will know "pain in childbearing; in pain [she] shall bring forth children."

Adam and Eve, therefore, are injured, are flawed, in those two attributes wherein they most resemble God. By his gift of dominion, Adam images God's power, and now the man is weakened in his rule over creation; by her gift of fruitfulness, Eve shares in God's creative love, but now she finds the giving of life weighted with pain. Worst of all, both must meet inevitable death:

> You shall . . . return to the ground,
>   for out of it you were taken;
> you are dust,
>   and to dust you shall return.

It is the nadir, the lowest point, the return of chaos to the world.

Still there is hope. Through labor and sorrow, order can be won again, and through woman, who offered death, ultimate victory shall come because she gives birth to new life. The promise rings out in God's speech to the serpent:

> I will put enmity between you and the woman,
> and between your seed and her seed;
> he shall bruise your head,
> and you shall bruise his heel.

The phrases are mysterious, but they light a glimmer of hope at the moment of the fall. Somehow man, who is woman's seed, will win over evil, will be saved from his own misdeeds. For centuries since then, those who believe in the coming of a savior have seen the words as prophetic of him. Probably, too, it was this vision of a woman which inspired John's apocalyptic woman clothed with the sun and crowned by twelve stars.

And now, according to the story, the Lord provides "garments of skins" as protection from weather, garments made of natural materials little wrought upon by any handicraft. But when at last Adam and his sons come to the shining city of Revelation, they will stand before the throne of God clothed in white robes, in raiment fashioned by skill and artistry. And in their hands will be palm branches to signify victory, so that the tree, which has been a sign of death, comes to stand for triumphant life.

> The walls surrounding them they never saw;
> The angels often. . . .
> As long as the wings were furled, they felt
> no awe.[27]

The time has come for man to know exile from the garden. He is sent out, says the Lord, for fear "lest he put forth his hand and take also of the tree of life, and eat, and live forever." By sin he has forfeited his right to the fruit of immortality; it will not be his until he has passed those other gates and met with death. Only then shall he find in the city of joy the tree of life growing by the waters in the streets.

Looking back with Adam at the gate, the light of Eden focuses on an image of an angel's bright sword. Heretofore the garden had no visible walls, now it has a gate. The angel shuts it, and cleaves the long darkness ahead with a sword of light. It is as if he slashes an opening into a thick curtain and the two human beings make their way out into black shadows.

As they trudge into dark, their desolation evokes the primitive fear which rises in every man when he finds himself alone in mountains or forests with no glimmer of light, with darkness peering from between trees, around edges of hills. Looking backward they see that:

> Far inland shines the radiant hill,
> Inviolable the empty gate,
> Impassible the gaping wall;
> And the mountain over all.[28]

A wall of safety broken down, a door into a haven shut before one's face—these mean desolation. And the darkness cast over land by a mountain shadow gives a sense of brooding danger.

> The huge scream
> Echoed and re-echoed without end
> Since first the stronger pinned the
> weaker down,
> Ages back in the awakening slime.[29]

Soon the consequences of Adam's decision show themselves in murder, and in bloody revenge invoked by a murderer's son. These can be seen in the account of Cain and Abel, and the old boast song of Lamech, descended from Cain. The eldest son of Adam and Eve is Cain, and Abel is his brother. They act out the first real conflict between human beings, when brother sets his face against brother, and Cain kills Abel. It is the first of all murders.

"Now Abel was a keeper of sheep, and Cain a tiller of the ground." By making the wicked brother a farmer, living on settled land, the writer shows his preference for the wandering shepherd's life. This theme is later cried aloud by the prophets, who hold that Israel is faithful to the Lord in the hard nomadic life of the desert, but falls away when she settles down in comfort and prosperity.

Both Cain and Abel bring offerings to the Lord, and he is pleased with Abel's but has no regard for that of Cain, "so Cain was very angry, and his countenance fell." In accord with the sinewy spareness of Jewish writing, no reasons are given for Cain's rejection. Such narrative is like sculpture in which the hollows, the empty spaces, are as important as the solid parts. Presumably Cain has given his gift with some unworthy motive. Perhaps he aimed to force God to show favor; perhaps he made his sacrifice out of vainglory and a wish to surpass his brother. The writer does not tell.

Still, the next words imply some guilt, for God says:

> Why are you angry,
> and why has your countenance fallen?
> If you do well, will you not be accepted?
> and if you do not do well,
> sin is couching at the door . . .
> you must master it.

Cain must have made some choice for which he is held responsible; some sin is couching at his door.

Another biblical theme appears here, that of election, of God's freedom to call whom he wills. It is seen in the preferring of the younger son over his elder, of Abel over Cain. Human custom decrees the ascendancy of elder sons, but God can reverse men's habits, as he makes clear when he chooses Jacob, Joseph, David, and many other younger sons.

The wrathful Cain now says to Abel, "Let us go out to the field." He wishes to work his wicked revenge in a solitary place. It is one of those interesting inconsistencies in the narrative, showing that the stories are collages of varied sources, pieced and patched and even superimposed at times. Cain, according to the account so far, should have had no trouble finding solitude, for only himself, his brother, and their parents, Adam and Eve, have appeared. In the story, not enough time seems to have passed for other people to have been born. But the biblical writers live in a timeless world which takes its tone from the leisurely passing of days unmarked by change, days of people who work with moving flocks of sheep. In fact, a few sentences further on, Cain shall set out to found a city settled by many people. Where do they all come from? Such questions trouble the writer very little.

Cain has been rejected and is determined on vengeance. Whatever the reasons for God's displeasure, Cain quickly proves his capacity for evil when he and Abel arrive in the open field. There he rises up "against his brother Abel" and kills him. The murder is followed by another of those dramatic dialogues handled with so much skill in the Bible.

The Lords says to Cain, "Where is Abel your brother?"

"I do not know; am I my brother's keeper?"

"What have you done? The voice of your brother's blood is crying to me from the ground. And now you are cursed from the ground, which has opened its mouth to receive your brother's blood. . . . When you till the ground, it shall no longer yield to you . . . you shall be a fugitive and a wanderer on the earth."

Desperately Cain cries aloud that his punishment is greater than he can bear: "Behold, thou hast driven me this day away from the ground; and from thy face I shall be hidden; and I shall be a . . . wanderer on the earth, and whoever finds me will slay me." He has lost his relationship with earth, with God, with any peaceful life, and he may even meet the kind of violent death he has meted out to Abel. But even to him, mercy is given when the Lord assures him: "Not so! If any one slays Cain, vengeance shall be taken on him sevenfold." And the Lord puts a "mark on Cain, lest any who came upon him should kill him." Even though he is a murderer, his life is not forfeit to every chance comer. Still, like Adam, he is driven into exile, for he goes "away from the presence of the Lord, and [dwells] in the land . . . east of Eden."

> My words are like a turbid stream,
> wild waves that dash against a surging sea
> (AESCHYLUS)

It is left to one of Cain's descendants, the boastful Lamech, to echo the promise of the Lord's protection, twisting it to his own purpose. He struts before his two wives, Adah and Zillah, singing his ancient and bloodthirsty song of revenge:

> Adah and Zillah, hear my voice;
> you wives of Lamech, hearken to what I say:
> I have slain a man for wounding me,
> a young man for striking me.
> Cain is avenged sevenfold,
> truly Lamech seventy-seven-fold.

Because the verse just before this song tells of the forging "of all instruments of bronze and iron," some have thought it a triumph song occasioned by the making of the first metal weapons. This is possible, yet it remains true that the flood of death loosed by Adam's fall and actualized by Cain, is perpetuated by Lamech's vengeful spirit. In his boast he even quotes God's promise of sevenfold safety to Cain, distorting it until he makes it a pretext for killing. The discord set vibrating by Cain is echoed in the harsh tones of his grandson, and they resound to this day.

To such a sorrowful conclusion all the rich orderliness of the first creation, all the serene beauty of the garden, has come. The sense of tragic power in these early chapters is heightened by the dramatic form which presents man's attempt to disrupt creation. The happenings are made vivid especially through lifelike action and developed conversations, particularly those between Eve and the serpent, God and the human pair, and finally Cain and the Lord. Still, though disaster dogs man's steps, earth is a goodly place, and the race of men flourishes for a while, until wickedness grows so great that the Lord must invoke original chaos, the return of primeval waters, in the story of Noah. Adam's feet, meanwhile, are set on their long exile, their footsore journey, which is made more desolate because he has, as yet, no vision of a land which shall be his lasting home.

The next two stories, of Noah and of Babel, like this of Adam and Eve, tell of prehistory, of the days before God chose his people and gave them promises—those promises which set hope moving ahead of them like the pillar of fire which Moses will later follow. But first comes the tale of Noah and his flood.

CHAPTER THREE

Noah Makes a New Start

AMONG the haunting dream images which rise from man's subconscious mind and call up powerful responses is the vision—freighted with fear and longing—of being the last man left on earth. Then one dodges about the alleys of an empty city, or floats alone and helpless in a small boat far out at sea. Such ocean scenes form the stock-in-trade of Winslow Homer, the American painter, and modern poetry keeps returning to the ancient story of Noah afloat in a drowning world.

Though the tale of Noah is told in bare simplicity, it is charged with power to vivify imagination. This is characteristic of the kind of literature called myth. A myth, it has been said, is not a story that is false, but one that is true in several ways. So it is with the flood. It has some historical truth, and it prompts poets to discover other truths about human behavior.

That there was an extraordinary flood in Mesopotamia before 4000 B.C. is attested by other ancient stories, notably the Gilgamesh epic found in Nineveh, and especially by the discoveries of Sir Leonard Woolley, the British archeologist. In 1929 he startled the world with the message: "We have found the Flood." He had been digging at Ur of Mesopotamia, the city of Abraham's origin, when below the rubble left from about 3000 B.C. he came upon a layer of pure clay which could only have been left by flood waters. Below it were relics belonging to the Stone Age. A natural catastrophe had covered the older civilization with ten feet of clay, sealing it off, and survivors had built their city on top of the clay. Though this flood did not cover the whole round world, it was a great wash of waters.

Historical or not, the way of its telling still has the power of myth to evoke meanings. Even today it inspires poets to set the mind dreaming again, and feeling its way among the universal resonances of the rich and ancient story. As the Gilgamesh epic proves, the tale was already old when biblical writers adapted it to their purpose of showing man's rebellion and God's faithful providence, and these meanings are still valid. But today's poets explore other suggestions too, and one of the most rewarding is Noah's chance to start all over again in a fresh new world. It is a thing every man sometimes longs for.

Adam had a new world, but he fell, and the earth itself rebelled against man. Then he found, as T. S. Eliot says:

> The bitter apple and the bite in the apple
> And the ragged rock in the restless waters.[30]

Because of the "bite in the apple"—the disobedience of the free human being—therefore God said to Adam: "Thorns and thistles [shall earth] bring forth to you." Still, he left Eden with hope, knowing that one day the head of the evil serpent would be crushed. And upon his going out he began a family of his own, bore sons, and started building a new life, another new world.

But when his sons have lived some years on earth they forget Adam's new start and his high hopes. Then the earth is "filled with violence" and evildoing, and the Lord determines to "blot out man . . . from the face of the ground, man and beast and creeping things and birds of the air." This time it will not be earth, but waters that turn against man. God will call upon flood-waters above and below the earth to destroy all living things, all except one man, Noah, "a righteous man, blameless in his generation [who walks] with God." Noah with his family shall be saved to make the world new, to bring it into order again.

Every aspect of the story (Gen. 6–9) is fascinating, and calls on man to contemplate it: the preparation—when the Lord warns Noah, teaches him to build his floating houseboat, instructs him to take into it pairs of all the animals in the world; life during the flood—how people lived in the boat and what they thought about; the abating of waters and return to land for a new start; and finally the Lord's promise to safeguard this new chance and his sealing the promise in the beautiful sign of the rainbow.

Over . . . the blind house rain
Washes in thickening plumes. He turns
Again. What cost of pathos and ancient pain
Lies sea-like in his eyes! [31]

Before the floodgates open, God comes to warn his friend. Carefully he tells Noah how to build a safe boat. Its length will be "three hundred cubits, its breadth fifty cubits, and its height thirty cubits." Coated "inside and out with pitch," it will have a door and windows, and be three levels high. Some old legends say that Noah learned part of his carpentry in a book he inherited from Adam. This book told how to make everything men could need, and besides, it came in a box encrusted with jewels. These were dull in daytime, but shone so brightly at night that Noah could do without candles.

After the ark is ready, Noah, following God's instructions, brings in his wife, his sons with their wives, and pairs of every reptile, animal, and bird:

Two of everything was the rule Noah made.
Couple them into my only Ark, he said,
So to perpetuate the giraffe's true blood.
The dog, the boar, the donkey are not lost.
I'll wash generations upon the other coast,
Horse, heron, and housefly saved from the past.[32]

This procession of animals is made much of in the Bible story, being mentioned eight times in four chapters. In no other place in the Bible is man in such close relationship with the varied animal world. Interestingly, too, scholars trace here the splicing of different versions of the story done by some early editor, for in one place Genesis says Noah took pairs of all the animals, and in another that he took seven pairs of the animals that were legally clean. The writer treats his sources with such respect that he does not iron out the minor inconsistencies. This attitude will appear all through the Bible.

At any rate, the procession must have looked and sounded like nothing else on earth. A folktale says that the griffin balked, and that is why there are no griffins today—he stayed on earth and was drowned. Perhaps unicorns were there too. It is no wonder that children's toys and picture books dwell on the shapes and noises of all Noah's animals.

According to medieval plays, Noah had trouble with his wife as well as with the griffin. She protests loudly against leaving the companionship of her contemporaries, her friendly "gossips," behind, and says:

> I will not out of this towne . . .
> But I have my gossips everichone
> One foot further I will not gone;
> They shall not drowne, by St. John,
> [If] I may save their lyf. . . .
>
> Rowe forth, Noe, whether thou list,
> And get thee a new wife.

If he will not save her friends, he may sail away and find himself another wife. And then Noah must beat her to make her go aboard.

Once all are inside the Lord closes the door, and "waters and sorrows rise / and launch the floods again" (Rimbaud). "All the fountains of the great deep burst forth, and the windows of the heavens [are] opened. And rain [falls] upon the earth forty days and forty nights." Like other peoples, the Israelites thought of the world as existing in a kind of protective bubble, with waters above to make rain; waters around, in the ocean; and waters below, rising in springs and rivers. Ordinarily the power of Yahweh kept them from washing in to drown the earth. Now he sets them free for "forty days," a biblical expression meaning a very long time.

Legend again adds fanciful detail about the great rain. It says that the Lord removed two of the Pleiades and made holes in the vault of heaven to let the water through. Later on he lost these stars and stopped up the openings with two others taken from the Great Bear. That is why the Bear forever chases the Pleiades through the sky.

"The waters increased, and bore up the ark, and it rose high above the earth . . . and the ark floated on the face of the waters." This first house mentioned in the Bible, this houseboat, unsteady, tossed on the floods, begins to float. It is a good symbol of man's precarious hold on safety, his dependence on providence. As the Israelites find even with the Promised Land, no home can be held safe forever.

In my seashaken house
On a breakneck of rocks.[33]

Though the Bible tells us little about the feelings of people inside the ark, still human imagination persists in wondering about them. Three modern poets speculate about three different aspects of their life: first, the physical conditions inside; second, the view Noah's wife takes as she looks back, and third, what Noah sees when he looks forward.

Elizabeth Bishop in "The Prodigal"[34] thinks about all those living beings closed up together. Surrounded but not desperately threatened by danger, they must have felt secure and snug by contrast with the storm outside. Her poem is about the prodigal son in Christ's parable, who through his own fault is poor and in exile, but hesitates to go home. He feels that even his pigsty and "the brown enormous odor he lived by . . . with its breathing and thick hair" holds a familiar comfort, such as those in the ark knew. He sees, when he looks about his farmyard home,

. . . the cows and horses in the barn
beneath their overhanging clouds of hay.

With them nearby he feels "safe and companionable as in the ark."

Such safe companionship is the reason it takes the prodigal "a long time / finally to make his mind up to go home." Like Noah's wife in the medieval play, the prodigal is unwilling to move on into a better life. When the flood was over perhaps Noah may have felt some reluctance about leaving his haven and venturing out to start the world all over again. And most probably his wife was by now at home in the ark and just as hesitant to leave it as she had earlier been to leave the ground.

But maybe the ark was not so snug. A very old folktale says that the devil came disguised as a mouse and gnawed a hole in the floor. When water began to seep in, the dog stopped the hole with his nose, and that is why dogs' noses to this day are cold and wet.

Not so lighthearted are the meditations of poets who think about this woman and this man looking out at the flooding world. Samuel Hazo in "The Carnival Ark" is interested in Noah's wife. He places the scene in our day and intimates that the drowning world is worth no mourning because it is a tawdry world of tarnished pleasures, and the ark itself a ship of fun near the "spookhouse and the coca-cola lights." People climbing on it see their bodies "hourglassed and multiplied / by mirrors" that "reflect reflected faces to infinity." This ark:

> . . . rolls obedient to hidden engines
> Noah never knew when he survived
> the forty days and forty nights of rain.[35]

As the ark begins to float, the modern Noah's wife "stares dumbly" out on the pleasures left behind, not with honest regret, but with numb boredom. She is a woman of the wasteland, like the characters of the French novelist Camus, incapable of any real response of emotion, living in a grey cloudland of unreality.

An opposite thought comes to Richard Wilbur. He sees Noah as a figure of courage, a pioneer anticipating the future, anxious to begin building a better world, even while he is aware of his own isolation. Though the ark was full of stirring life, yet there must have been a great sense of loss, of waste, in Noah's thoughts. Wilbur's poem is called "Still, Citizen Sparrow." In it, ordinary men are sociable sparrows who "dart in the orchard aisles," busy about daily living, while Noah is the wide-winged vulture who sails "frightfully free" on the flood, and sees "the towns like coral under the keel / And the fields buried dismal deep."[36]

Both coral and vulture are good images. Coral is, of course, made of small houses submerged under the sea, like those Noah looks at, and the vulture is suggested by the Bible story because when the floods were over Noah sent a vulture flying out of the ark. That carrion bird did not return, presumably because it set about its business of clearing away the dead bodies left from the flood.

Like the vulture, Noah lies cruising "at the tall tip of the sky." Wilbur suggests that sparrows may be tempted to resent the detachment of the great lonely bird, but he proposes that they recognize the austere beauty of its flight, its heroic separation from company and security. There is need to "forgive the hero," to look kindly on the strong winged vulture; he cleans up the land, "devours death, mocks mutability, / Has heart to make an end, keeps nature new." Bird and Noah can bear to look on death from a high and weary place over the waters because they have a vision of a world cleansed and risen from death. If sparrows and ordinary men will look upward, they will see:

> That no more beautiful bird is in heaven's height,
> No wider more placid wings, no watchfuller flight.[37]

Beauty lies in such strength and detachment, an unearthly serenity, and so does hope, for the poem ends: "All men are Noah's sons." Had it not been for his courage there would have been no men to survive.

> Let us go to another country,
> Not yours or mine
> And start again.[38]

At last after Noah's weary watching, the rains slacken; there comes a wind over the earth and the waters subside. "The fountains of the deep and the windows of the heavens" close up, and the ark comes to rest upon a mountain which tradition has named Ararat. Steadily the waters recede until the tops of mountains appear; then Noah opens the "window of the ark which he had made." Framed there, he leans out toward freedom with a bird perched on his hand. Quickly it flies away. Dimension is added to the scene when we know that in early times mariners carried birds in order to loose them at sea, then their flight would guide the ships to the nearest land. This first bird is a raven or vulture, and legend says it was white, but because it deserted Noah, its feathers turned black.

Next he looses a dove which flies all night above those unsteady seas. Yet it returns beneath ark eaves, because it finds no resting place. Noah puts "forth his hand" to catch it, says Genesis, and takes it into the ark. He lifts into his dwelling the dove which signifies peace. After seven days he again sends out a dove, and it returns at nightfall, and "lo, in her mouth a freshly plucked olive leaf." Now he knows that the water is below treetops.

Noah's hope is justified, for when he sends his last dove flying it does not return. The vulture might have rested on floating corpses but the dove seeks trees or solid ground, so Noah knows he can leave the ark. He comes "forth, and his sons and his wife and his sons' wives with him. And every beast, every creeping thing, and every bird"—all come "by families out of the ark."

Now is Noah's chance to give the world a fresh start, to make all things new again.

In sign of this, the Lord gives him dominion over "every beast of the earth . . . every bird of the air . . . everything that creeps on the ground and all the fish of the sea." Into Noah's hands they are delivered. The fear of him and the dread of him shall be upon them all. His rule is like Adam's in Eden when he gave them names and they obeyed him. But Adam did not have to teach them to obey. Noah, beginning anew, will need to train them, for they no longer obey willingly; they will go "in dread" and fear because he will compel them, impose his will upon them.

> After the rain had stopped and
> their homes were gone,
> There was nothing in sight, but
> the stars were remarkably clear.[39]

Noah's first act in starting his new world is to build an altar and offer gifts to the Lord—gifts perhaps of foodstuffs remaining after the voyage, or of young animals born during captivity. It is a preparation for a sacred meal, and for the first time God openly pledges loyalty to man. He loved Adam and Eve; he looked with pleasure on Abel's sacrifice, but made no specific promises to them. Now he does. Noah, as he makes his sacrifice, must feel gratitude and anxiety. He and his family are safe, and have orders to begin a new life in a world cleansed from the past. Yet he has seen the Lord's anger in action, and so he feels fear, and accordingly his offering begs for continuing protection.

This he wins, for the Lord, smelling in the smoke of the burnt offerings a "pleasing odor," gives his solemn promise to hold back flood waves, and to keep order in the natural rhythms of the cosmos. Forever after this, the cyclic return of seasons shall keep appointed times:

> While the earth remains,
> seedtime and harvest, cold and heat,
> summer and winter, day and night,
> shall not cease.

Out of this second chaos of waters the Lord draws the cosmic order, and promises that order shall hold good while earth stands, that mankind shall know when to expect "seedtime and harvest . . . summer and winter."

Then the Lord, destroyer and savior, sets up a sign to remind himself of his promise. "When I bring clouds over the earth and the bow is seen in the clouds, I will remember my covenant." The rainbow will remind him of his promises to man. Paradoxically, the firm promise is sealed in the sign of the rainbow, trembling in air, evanescent and fragile. Still, ancient peoples thought of it as solid. American Indians, for instance, said the rainbow portended dry weather because its arch held up the waters stored behind the vault of the sky, and this is the very promise Yahweh is making to Noah. In another sense, too, the rainbow is solid, permanent because it is circular—it seems to extend on down around the round earth. The circle being endless, unbroken, undeviating, is a symbol of steadfastness.

Furthermore, this first and cosmic covenant promises order in the world, and the rainbow is a good symbol of order. It unites two diverse natural realities—water and light. As in the beginning God called light to illumine primeval waters, so now these contrary elements melt together, and from their fusion comes the exquisitely ordered spectrum, the varied and related colors of the prism. When God first said, "Let there be light," the brilliance was all of a piece, then he separated it and gave it order by assigning the heavenly bodies to carry each its own kind of light. Now he does something else, filling the sky with delicate gradations of color.

"Look upon the rainbow, and praise him who made it," says the book of Sirach, "exceedingly beautiful in its brightness. It encircles the heaven with its glorious arc; the hands of the Most High have stretched it out" (43:11–12). And Ezekiel sees the Lord himself surrounded by a rainbow:

> And there was brightness round about him.
> Like the appearance of the bow that is in the cloud
> on a day of rain,
> so was the appearance of the brightness
> round about.
> . . . The glory of the Lord.
>
> (Ezek. 1:27–29)

Again, the rainbow overarches the world in symbol of protection, of providing and guarding love. The rounded domes of Romanesque churches carry this same sense of providence, of the immanence of God, whereas the upward thrust of Gothic architecture stresses the transcendence and majesty of God and man's efforts to reach him by worship.

Noah's worship is like this. Arnold Kenseth, the poet, brings the scene vividly to mind. He first talks of "Birds at the Feeding Station," where many-colored wings are seen against snow, and watching them he asks, "What is more rainbow?"

> Such covenant
> Is here as Noah won. Green waters' weight
> Around his world, he saw the promises
> In colors drenching down from heaven's gate,
> And felt man's hope, awash and innocent.[40]

The birds circle and weave in flight, blending rainbow colors, and fashioning "tapestries of praise." So Noah's many birds, set free after the flood, must have flown, making rainbows of their wings, and singing praises of Noah's God, while the man walked out grateful into sun, into hope shining as the rainbow shines. Even this early man is imbued with the Bible's theme of unquenchable hope.

It is no wonder that the age-old legend haunts the imagination, and that its many meanings pursue man in his dreams. But though the rainbow is a celebration of peace and order, those days do not last long. Soon the descendants of Noah will build a tower of defiance and set the world at odds again. They will try to frame and own a city, a home to hold forever, and will find its possession precarious as the ark afloat on floods.

CHAPTER FOUR

Towers and Tongues at Babel

The proud man climbs and climbs
until all men call him great,
He seems to reach the summit
and the gods fling him down
(SOPHOCLES, *Oedipus the King*)

NOAH has set about his task of building a new world, and for a while all goes well. Yet as men increase upon the earth they become intoxicated with power. Like Adam and Eve, they wish to surpass their own creaturehood, to become like gods, to communicate with God on terms of equality. Among the Greeks such arrogance was called *hubris*, a pride hated by their divinities, an attitude that brought swift disaster. Those infected by it grew restless, always thrusting beyond themselves and scorning the help of the gods. The Bible has no single word for this attitude, but its writers also fear and condemn it. The evil does not lie in ambition as such, but in arrogating divine power to oneself.

This thrust of *hubris*, this bold presumption, is the theme of the Babel story (Gen. 11:1–9), in which men build a tower and attempt to scale heaven. In the telling, the writer offers answers to questions about two observable facts, and so gives his tale symbolic significance. One question concerns an unfinished tower, the other the diversity of human languages.

For the first, the writer might have seen on the plains of Mesopotamia those great towers called ziggurats whose ruins still exist. According to the records of Nebuchadnezzar of Babylon (605–561 B.C.), one tower, long before his time, had been built up to sixty feet and then left until he himself completed it. Possibly it could have been seen at the time when this story was told, and the teller may have wondered who first built it and why it was left unfinished. Today a ziggurat called Birs Nemrud at Borsippa, seven miles southwest of the ruins of Babylon, is claimed as the original tower of Babel, and a current superstition says that the man who passes near it will lose his memory, as the people of the tower lost the memory of their universal language.

It has long been connected with Nimrod or Nemrud (Gen. 10), a "mighty hunter before the Lord." The poet Dante places Nimrod, "a horrible giant," in lower hell among the traitors, because by building his tower of pride he betrayed his loyalty to God (*Inferno*, 31:49 ff.). About him Dante says: "Certainly when Nature gave up the art of producing these creatures she did well," and the description is a repellent one:

> His face seemed to me as long and wide
> as the pine cone at St. Peter's in Rome.

By comparing his face to a gigantic sculptured pine cone, Dante not only suggests immensity, but also a repulsive roughness of texture. This giant talks in nonsense syllables, and Dante's guide Vergil explains that "this is Nimrod, through whose evil thought" of building a tower to heaven, "a single tongue is not used in the world."

The second question also rises from observation. Men speak many languages. How did diversity begin? Did all tongues branch off from one common language? The Bible writer, shaping ancient folktales to his purpose, thinks they did. Philologists still argue the problem. But neither philology nor architecture is the main concern of the Genesis narrator. He is showing the effects of pride, and infusing his tale with his own religious sense of a transcendant God. As H. H. Rowley, the noted biblical scholar, says: The scripture "is permeated with a religious quality which is quite different [from other literatures], a religious quality which gives meaning to the whole, for which it has been treasured through the centuries and for which it is still treasured. For the Old Testament is a living book" whereas those others which sometimes furnish its raw materials "have only an antiquarian interest."

The Babel story fuses the two symbols of towers and tongues

to present its theme of man's proud rebellion. At the same time it explains in a popular way how different languages arose, and how Babel or Babylon, an enemy territory, got its name. In reality, *Babel* means *gate of the gods*, but it came to be equated with the Hebrew word *balal* which means *to confuse*, and the storyteller takes his chance to locate his story about the confusion of tongues at a Babylonian tower.

After the flood, says the tale, when all men were Noah's sons, "the whole earth had one language." Some of these people migrated eastward from the vicinity of Ararat to a valley in the land of Shinar or Babylon, and settled there. Sharing one language, they could work together, but their first cooperative venture was an act of pride:

> Let us build ourselves a city
>   and a tower with its top in the heavens;
> let us make a name for ourselves . . .
>   lest we be scattered abroad upon . . . the whole earth.

To preserve their solidarity they need a city. When it is built, they think, then they can raise a tower and force their will on the powers of heaven. Both city and tower here mean pride.

Many of earth's people have given their gods a home in the sky. To climb there without leave is an act of defiance, an invasion of privacy, an unlawful entry like robbery. Men have no right to force communication upon the mysterious and transcendent God. Rather, they are utterly dependent on his power, and it is for him to take the initiative—such is the Bible writer's thought.

Besides this, to "make a name" for oneself is to snatch at fame, to steal away a glory not belonging to man. It has been said that comedy is always about vanity, about small and strutting man, but tragedy is about pride, believing one's strength comes from oneself. The thrust of *hubris*, as in this story, does indeed invite tragedy.

Towering ziggurats are good symbols for pride, not only because of their height, but also because, being built like staircases, they are unresting, upward thrusting, shaped in ascending levels marked by platforms like giant steps. Moreover, they were built near temples and intended to make possible a communication with the gods. Their names, such as House of the Mountain, Mountain of the Storms, indicate that they were man-made mountains. Traditionally divinities have been at home on mountains, as were the gods of the Greeks on Olympus.

Now the Lord, from his home in the sky, begins to take notice: "Truly they are one people and they all have the same language. This is the beginning of what they will do." Therefore, says he to his heavenly court,

> Let us go down, and there confuse their language,
> that they may not understand one another's speech.

Man who had willed to force communication upon God, thus loses his power to communicate with his fellows. He is handicapped in his great human ability, and finds himself to this day struggling to reach others, discovering himself helpless to communicate the feelings that mean most to him. Philosophers, poets, novelists all grapple with the tragedy of man's need to communicate and his inability to do it. By confusing their speech the Lord scatters "them abroad from there over the face of all the earth, and they [leave] off building the city," and the tower is left unfinished.

Later on in Genesis there will be another stairway, a ladder seen by Jacob sleeping in the desert with a stone for pillow. In contrast to the Babylonian ziggurat which stretches up from earth and serves as ladder for man's defiance and for descending disaster, Jacob's ladder will stretch down from heaven and angels will climb it carrying worship up to God and blessing down to man.

This tower, concludes the writer, "was called Babel, because there the Lord confused the language of all the earth." Babel's name of confusion, mankind's diverse tongues, and the towers that loom on the plains have been explained by the story and the writer has driven home his point about the catastrophes which follow upon sinful pride.

The damage done to unity of speech, according to an opinion which reaches as far back as Gregory of Nyssa in the fourth century, was healed in symbol on the day of Pentecost when, as the Acts of the Apostles relates, the Holy Spirit came down in tongues of fire. Then, as the flames rested on the heads of

Christ's followers, they received the gift of tongues, of being understood by every man in his own language.

Daniel Berrigan, in "Pentecost,"[41] tells of the apostles' astonishment at their own powers. These men, "all their lives rounded in a backcountry brogue," begin to speak by the power of the Spirit, and find their listeners from all countries entranced. Especially do "the fine Athenian profiles" of the Greeks stand out with nostrils flared, "scenting their delicate language like odor of muscatel or honey." They are amazed at these fishermen, who cannot speak Greek, pronouncing it, nevertheless, with exquisite accent.

Then the poem addresses the apostles, telling them the meaning of the scene:

> Peter and John, it is Babel crashing about your ears.
> The Spirit . . . has riven the abominable tower
> with his descent.

Because the city of division, the tower of defiance, has been destroyed by the Spirit of God, therefore

> the undivided tongues
> are abroad, are a wildfire, front the twelve winds from these
> transfigured faces.

In their joy, these unlearned Galileans feel that they need "never again be constrained / by scarecrow gestures, by hem or haw," for eloquence is lent them by the Spirit's flaming tongues. It is a hint, a symbol of the apocalyptic day when men will again be united, and their problems of communication solved. But that day is not yet.

Meanwhile, the Bible, in the later book of Daniel, shows that the pride which built the ziggurats lingers in Babylon. Written during the Babylonian captivity, after 587 B.C., the book tells how Nebuchadnezzar, the king, walks "on the roof of the royal palace in Babylon" looking out over the city, and boasting:

> Is not this great Babylon,
> which I have built by my mighty power
> as a royal residence
> and for the glory of my majesty?
> (DAN. 4:30)

But while the words are "still in the king's mouth," there comes a voice saying that for his pride he shall lose the kingdom and shall dwell "with the beasts of the field," and "be made to eat grass like an ox." Then he is cast out, and his body is "wet with the dew of heaven till his hair [grows] long as eagles' feathers, and his nails . . . like birds' claws." A passage from one of the Greek plays reads like a comment upon Nebuchadnezzar:

The gods hate bitterly
the bray of bragging tongues.
The frown of their thunder blasts
their swagger from our walls.
(SOPHOCLES, *Antigone*)

Israelites and Greeks agree about the hatefulness of pride, and both speak its condemnation in strong terms.

The prophet Isaiah identifies the city of Babylon itself with pride, and chants a lamentation over the fall he foresees:

Fallen, fallen is Babylon;
and all the images of her gods
he has shattered to the ground.

. . . There ostriches will dwell. . . .
Hyenas will cry in its towers,
and jackals in the pleasant palaces. . . .
(ISA. 21:9, 13:21–22)

This is the fate which waits for the proud nation. The prophet makes it memorable by his images of ruin: idols shattered, and wildcats, owls, jackals, prowling and howling through the fallen walls and pillars.

John, too, talking of Babylon as the prototype of all proud cities, echoes Isaiah:

So shall Babylon the great city . . .
be found no more;
and the sound of harpers and minstrels, of flute players
and trumpeters, shall be heard in thee no more;
and a craftsman of any craft
shall be found in thee no more;
and the sound of the millstone
shall be heard in thee no more;

and the light of a lamp
 shall shine in thee no more;
and the voice of bridegroom and bride
 shall be heard in thee no more. . . .
(Rev. 18:21–23)

Such is the lament for Babylon the great. The passage is a poem in itself with its sevenfold *no more* tolling like a bell, and its progressive pattern of images symbolizing loss—no more music, no more crafts making useful and beautiful objects, no more bread made by work at the mill, no more light shining from homes of peace, no more hope of new families heard in voices of bridegroom and bride.

This story of Babel is the last of the tales of prehistory in Genesis. Their theme has been man's invoking of chaos from the order planned by God. The pattern is clear in three tales: rebellion followed by catastrophe and this succeeded by mercy and new hope. After primeval chaos stirs and rises into order at God's command, the creation begins. Adam, however, sins by trying to snatch the secrets of God, to win unfairly a knowledge not intended for him, a wisdom beyond his capacity. Thus he invokes a new chaos, for earth itself rejects him. He becomes a wanderer upon its face and finds it reluctant to yield its fruits. When Adam and Eve, repentant, set their faces to the future, they have a chance for a new life which is in some sense more satisfying because more difficult and challenging than Eden. Still, after their sin, Cain their son disrupts human relationships in this new world. He murders his brother Abel, and men after him grow more wicked, defying God in his capacity as lawgiver, seeking to be a law unto themselves.

Then a chaos of waters returns; Noah is forced to wander on the face of the flood, and all other men go down to death under its weight. After the flood Noah is given responsibility to put a cleansed world into order again.

But once more this hope fails when men sin by abusing the gift of speech. Helped by their unity of language, they build a tower, determined that it shall reach the skies. But the sky itself rejects them, human relationships fall into chaos, and communication becomes intolerably difficult. Still hope will rise again when God chooses a single man, Abraham, and trusts a new kind of future to him.

These stories of Adam, Noah, and Babel form a prologue to the Bible. They tell of man's ingratitude and the Lord's saving intervention which brings new hope. All three end with men exiled, set homeless on the face of earth to seek a new abode, but with no definite place in mind, no promise as yet guiding them to any new home. This pattern will shape much of what follows, but with a difference. Until now the design of action has been an alternating up and down, or rather, a circling like a ferris wheel on which men ride high then are brought down again. The people move as nature circles in the return of seasons. With Abraham, the next man in the story, the circle of recurrence becomes a line, a road towards a promised country.

Though men will continue to fall, there will always be some who keep the goal in view. Henceforward Abraham's people will be set apart by the urgency of their forward march, their vision of a land promised by the Lord—a vision which undergoes successive transfigurations as they gain insight through revelation. From their longing to perpetuate possession of this land comes their thirst for the fulfillment of the Lord's second promise—the pledge of sons to inherit the land. Finally, this promised land is to be more than just a temporal home. It will be the abiding place of God. David, when long years later he wins Jerusalem, will try to guarantee the divine presence by bringing the ark of the covenant to his city, and the Lord will bless him for the effort. But this deed too will be only a symbol of the reality, and David's city only a sign promising that lasting city which John tries to describe in the last pages of the Bible.

Still, in the promised land of Canaan, the earthly home that Israel seeks, the Lord will meet them. Though all along he journeys with them, yet in a special sense he waits for them at the end of the long road. Abraham, a man uniquely fitted for fatherhood, is the first to hear the three promises, the first to begin the people's march toward the land of promise.

Promises of Another Country

CHAPTER FIVE

Abraham: The Birth of a Father

THE first man to hear the Lord's three promises and to set his feet toward the promised land as a goal is Abraham, whose vocation is to be a father. So well does he fulfill his vocation, that even today three great faiths look to him as father: the Jewish people because of Isaac, his son, progenitor to Jacob whose other name is Israel; Islam because of Ishmael, eldest son to Abraham, with whom they claim kinship; Christianity because of Christ, who is named as descendant of Abraham. He is indeed a father; this is the keynote of his life. Although his story in Genesis comes shaped by many tongues and hands, by the vicissitudes of oral and written transmission, still a unified portrait emerges—an account of one called to fatherhood. Abraham's whole life tends toward this.

With him, the Lord sets moving the forward line of history, what Mircea Eliade has called the "terror of history," where things are "forever irreversible," and man is faced with irrevocable choice.[42] Abraham must choose between hope and despair —hope for the future symbolized in the son, despair because it seems impossible that he should enjoy peaceful fatherhood.

"Abraham I cannot understand," says Kierkegaard in *Fear and Trembling*, "In a certain sense there is nothing I can learn from him but astonishment. He stands in absolute relation to the Absolute."[43] Watching this man, astonishment sweeps over the viewer; he stands awed at the absolute faith, the unquenchable hope Abraham shows before the mysterious ways of a transcendent God. Why must this man face such anguished decisions?

The reasons lie in Kierkegaard's word *relation*. Abraham is called to be a father, to symbolize that strange and fundamental relationship called fatherhood. To this end he must first learn to be a son, to exist in a filial relationship, and then to practice the lessons of fatherhood for himself. The father to whom he relates is not so much Terah who begot him but rather Yahweh himself, the Lord whom Paul names that Father "from whom every family in heaven and on earth is named" (Eph. 3:15). He must follow God's orders with filial dependence and at the same time shoulder the responsibilities of a father.

After each important decision or act he hears God's voice promising him a homeland, sons to inherit the land, and further relationships with God himself. His call, along with these promises, will shape the history of his people, for great as Abraham is, he is not the hero—the people are. But bewilderment must often have plagued him because to human vision the Lord seems to contradict himself. He initiates Abraham's hope for a son by his promises, partially fulfills and renews the promise, gives a son and then demands that son's death.

Each time of joy is clouded by doubt and trouble, yet through all changes Abraham moves toward new heights of sonship and paternity, new dependence on an all-powerful Father as condition for a fulfilled fatherhood of his own. Only when he is an old man can he rest from conflict. Then he can look with quiet eyes on the son, the land, the future of his people—who are the chosen of God, and like himself stand "in absolute relation to the Absolute." Of this man, Genesis (12–25) gives an admirably unified picture structured upon five steps whereby he learns to exercise fatherhood toward his household of dependents, his nephew Lot who travels with him, Ishmael and Isaac after him who are sons of his body, and at last the whole people of Israel.

> Abraham. . . . In hope he believed against hope, that he should become the father of many nations.
>
> (Rom. 4:18)

Abraham's family appears in the Bible when Terah, his father, dwelling in the fertile crescent of land between the Tigris and Euphrates rivers, moves from the rich city of Ur in Chaldea to Haran in northern Syria. These people were idolaters, for Joshua remarks that the fathers of Israel, including Abraham, "lived of old beyond the Euphrates . . . and they served other gods." Modern archeology has discovered that Ur was wealthy and cultured, and that it practiced child sacrifice. This practice will cast its shadow on Abraham's life.

When Terah dies in Haran, then Abraham's story begins. He hears God's voice.

> Go from your country and your kindred and
> your father's house
> to the land that I will show you.
> And I will make of you a great nation,
> and I will bless you,
> and make your name great,
> so that you will be a blessing.

The scene is full of mystery, a sense of transcendence that Abraham lives with all his years. As Auerbach remarks in *Mimesis*, a book that compares the literature of the Bible with that of the Greeks, we do not know where the speakers are, where the Lord has come from, nor in what shape he appears.[44] His promises, too, are mysterious. He will lead Abraham to a land that is not named —a land he will show to him; he will make "a great nation" of this man who has no sons. And most mysterious of all, through him will come a blessing to the whole world: "You will be a blessing," says the Lord.

By the word *blessing* a relationship with divinity is already implied; Abraham and his people will live in close friendship with that God who calls to light and it obeys, who looses floods and walks on winds. This God will concern himself with the fortunes of this family and never again absent himself from their minds. From their worship of him will spring the profound awareness of transcendence and the sense of purpose in fulfilling God's will which have so deeply affected the world's history. Moreover, Abraham's blessing is to reach all nations—a prophecy particularly interesting in the light of his fathering the three great groups of Islam, Israel, and Christianity. To his three promises, now, the Lord commits himself and calls on Abraham for a reciprocal commitment.

While the promises are dark with mystery, the call is clear. Abraham must leave his home, become a nomad, separate himself from a city of many gods to worship one transcendent God, and shoulder responsibility for a household. Now begins a journey to a land unknown, which calls to Abraham in obscure ways:

> The cries of sheep rise upward from the fields
> Forlorn and strange; and wake an ancient echo
> In fields [his] blood has known but has not seen.[45]

The pastures of the promised land draw him with a longing the poet's lines evoke. In one sense he experiences mankind's deep-seated desire to return to Eden, but in another and truer sense he turns toward a land of the future.

Edwin Muir has an image for his journeying, one that unites the seeming uncertainty of his roads with the steadfastness of his purpose:

> The rivulet-loving wanderer Abraham
> Through waterless wastes tracing his fields of pasture
> Led his Chaldean herds and fattening flocks
> With the meandering art of wavering water
> That seeks and finds yet does not know its way.[46]

Like a stream that lets itself go with the contour of the land, flowing, deflected, turning, apparently without goal, yet undeviatingly seeking the sea, so Abraham moves. He leaves Haran and turns westward to Canaan; arrived there he goes across country to "the place of Shechem, to the oak of Moreh." At that time "the Canaanites were in the land." Here God appears and promises the whole land to his posterity, but since aliens dwell here he moves on "to the mountain on the east of Bethel, and pitched his tent." When famine strikes he goes down to Egypt. Along his roads he builds altars to Yahweh. It is not so much that his wanderings come to no haven, as that his journeys are only one stage—not he, but his whole family are the chosen; he is father rather than lone individual.

> So Abram went, as the Lord had told him;
> and Lot [his brother's son] went with him.
> (GEN. 12:4)

Soon Abraham returns to the southern part of Canaan and begins to show his fatherhood towards his nephew, Lot, a member of his household. He provides for Lot, rescues him from captivity, intercedes for him with the Lord. His providing happens when he discovers his herdsmen quarreling with Lot's because the flocks have grown too great for the same pasturelands. Abraham, therefore, leads Lot to a high place and points to the sweep of countryside:

> Let there be no strife between you and me . . .
> for we are kinsmen.
> Is not the whole land before you?
> If you take the left hand, then I will go to the right;
> or if you take the right hand, then I will go to the left.

His wide gesture tells his generosity; but Lot tends to calculation. He looks about him and sees that:

> the Jordan valley was well watered everywhere
> like the garden of the Lord,
> like the land of Egypt . . .
> this was before the Lord destroyed Sodom and Gomorrah.

Lot chooses the Jordan valley, but the writer suggests that he will regret his choice. This is the place doomed to destruction.

This garden country is like Eden, the garden of the Lord, but Eden was lost; like Egypt, but in that fertile land Israel will be enslaved. The hints of doom are clearer when the narrator casually remarks: "Lot dwelt among the cities . . . and moved his tent as far as Sodom. Now the men of Sodom were wicked, great sinners against the Lord." Here the two men part after their bargain, and immediately the Lord appears and renews his promises to Abraham:

> Lift up your eyes, and look . . .
> northward and southward and eastward and westward;
> for the land which you see I will give to you
> and to your descendants for ever.

It is as if God follows Abraham's expansive gesture with his own wider one. All this land will belong to Abraham's posterity, but still he has no sons. So Abraham moved "his tent, and came and dwelt by the oaks of Mamre, which are at Hebron, and there he built an altar to the Lord."

Lot, in his new home, has begun to prosper when suddenly he is carried into captivity in a raid by neighboring kings. Abraham, in the only warlike action we see him take, goes to the rescue, calling together "three hundred and eighteen . . . men, born in his house," and pursuing the enemy "as far as Dan" in the north country. Returning home after victory he encounters Melchisedek, a mysterious king of Salem, a priest who offers bread and wine. To him Abraham does homage and offers tithes, a strange thing for a victorious chieftain to do. Hundreds of years later the epistle to the Hebrews mentions this scene nine times, dwelling on its mystery.

When Abraham comes home the promises are repeated, and God insists that his "reward shall be very great." But the man wants only one reward—a son, and there seems no hope for that: "O Lord God," he answers, "what wilt thou give me, for I continue childless. . . . Behold, thou hast given me no offspring; and a slave born in my house will be my heir." God, however, reassures him, saying, "This man shall not be your heir; your own son shall be your heir." Then leading him outside, God continues: "Look toward heaven, and number the stars. . . . So shall your descendants be." And Abraham puts his faith in the Lord. The childless man believes that God can give him descendants countless as the stars.

To win further ratification of the promises, he now offers sacrifice in a strange and solemn ritual. Bringing two birds and three animals for offering, he cuts his heifer, goat, and ram in halves and lays the pieces down opposite sides of a path, with one bird on each side. There he stands the whole day long, driving away the birds of prey that swoop down. But when the sun sets, deep sleep falls on him, "and lo, a dread and great darkness fell upon him." The voice of God speaks out of mystery, adding a somber note to the promises:

> Know of a surety that your descendants
> will be sojourners in a land that is not theirs,
> and will be slaves there,
> and they will be oppressed for four hundred years.
> But afterward . . . they shall come out
> with great possessions.

Then for confirmation "a flaming torch" moves down the path between the pieces of flesh. It is a nightmare vision, and a nightmare insight: only after centuries of sorrow will the promises reach fulfillment.

Abraham has provided lands for Lot, rescued him from captivity, and now a third occasion for compassion arises. Though this nephew is a good man, yet he has chosen to live among the wicked of Sodom. Now the Lord can no longer endure that city's evil ways, nor those of its twin city Gomorrah. The story is masterly in its balancing of contrasts: noon and evening, Abraham and Lot, a tree near a tent's open door and a busy gate in a city wall, friendship and reserve, mercy and brutality, concern for others and preoccupation with self, the crash of ruin and quiet desolation.

The account begins in peace. Abraham sits at the door of his tent "in the heat of the day." He sees three visitors approach, and in eager hospitality runs from his tent "to meet them, and [bows] himself to the earth." The open door symbolizes welcome and freedom; through it friends come in and home-dwellers can go out. With Eastern courtesy he deprecates his own services: "My lord, if I have found favor in your sight, do not pass by. . . . Let a little water be brought, and wash your feet, and rest yourselves under the tree, while I fetch a morsel of bread, that you may refresh yourselves." And he hurries away to find Sarah, his wife.

"Make ready quickly three measures of fine meal," he says, "knead it and make cakes." And he runs "to the herd," takes "a calf, tender and good," and gives it to the servant who hastens to prepare it. All is hospitable bustle; Abraham, that leisurely and dignified man, hastens; he runs; he tells his servant to be quick.

He brings curds and milk to the shade of the trees and the visitors eat. Afterward they ask about Sarah and are told she is in the tent. They reiterate the promise, saying that by next year she shall have a son. Sarah, listening behind the door, laughs at the impossible hope, for she has grown old in her childlessness. The messengers ask why she is amused, but Sarah denies, saying, "I did not laugh"; for she is afraid. The visitors, though, remark quietly, "No, but you did laugh." The scene brings a smile—Sarah's eavesdropping, her laugh, her attempt to deny it, and then the simple contradiction.

Only gradually, as the story moves, does it become clear that these are supernatural visitors, and that one of them is possibly the Lord himself. Now the guests rise and begin to walk towards Sodom, Abraham going along "to set them on their way." One shows his affection by dropping back to talk to Abraham, musing meanwhile: "Shall I hide from Abraham what I am about to do? . . . No, I have chosen him . . . to keep the way of the Lord." Suspense rises as the reader wonders what the message can be.

At last the words come: "Because the outcry against Sodom and Gomorrah is great, and their sin is very grave, I will go down to see whether they have done altogether according to the outcry which has come to me." Abraham evidently knows the cities are as wicked as report would have them; he foresees some grave punishment, and Sodom is the city of his nephew Lot. With a friend's liberty and a father's concern he remonstrates: "Wilt thou indeed destroy the righteous with the wicked? Suppose there are fifty righteous within the city; wilt thou then destroy the place and not spare it for the fifty righteous who are in it? Far be it from thee to do such a thing." His pleading is for others, his concern not only for Lot but also for the Lord's own honor. Being a good bargainer he gradually lowers the number of just men needed to save the city from fifty to forty-five to forty to thirty to twenty to ten. And each time the promise is given: mercy will come if there are but ten good men.

Skillfully the narrator ends the contest, leaving the reader to infer that not even ten just men live here. He remarks without comment: "So the Lord went his way . . . and Abraham returned to his place."

Then the scene shifts dramatically. Two of the visitors come to Lot in Sodom; the Lord is not with them. Whereas they had met Abraham at bright noon, now it is evening and earth grows dark. Lot sits, not at his own tent door, but at the town gate, a place of business among these people. His actions show none of Abraham's haste. He is a city man, courteous but not given to enthusiasm. The Bible says "he rose to meet them," not "he ran."

"Turn aside, I pray you," he says, "and spend the night, and wash your feet; then you may rise up early and go on your way." The visitors are as courteous and reserved as he. They do not accept at once, but demur: "No; we will spend the night in the street." Still, when he urges them, they turn to his house, where he bakes unleavened bread, and prepares a meal for them. The menu is not described as lavishly as Abraham's.

Scarcely have his doors closed when the men of Sodom prove that their bad name is well deserved. They besiege the house, demanding that Lot surrender his guests to their abuse. He refuses, offering his daughters instead. It seems strange today to see the duties of hospitality held more sacred than the fatherly protection Lot owes his children. The visitors, however, save the day by striking the men outside with blindness. Then they announce doom to come:

> Have you any one else here?
> Sons-in-law, sons, daughters, or any one . . .
> bring them out of the place. . . .
> The Lord has sent us to destroy it.

When he lingers, the visitors take him, "his wife and his two daughters by the hand," and lead them out saying: "Flee for your life; do not look back or stop anywhere in the valley; flee to the hills, lest you be consumed."

But Lot, the city man, fears the wilderness. He pleads, not for others as Abraham had done, but for himself:

> I cannot flee to the hills,
> lest disaster overtake me, and I die.
> Behold, yonder city is near enough to flee to,
> and it is a little one.
> Let me escape there—is it not a little one?

He, too, is a bargainer, repeating the word *little* to persuade the messengers it is a trifling favor he asks. It is as though he feels guilty for having chosen to live in the big city, but perhaps a smaller one might be permissible. He is offering to leave the prosperous city of his first choice, but placing his faith in another city—in human companionship, human means, just as he did when he chose the fertile lands of Sodom. The absolute trust of Abraham is not his.

The angels yield, and the family sets off for Segor, the "little city," entering it at sunrise. Thereupon "the Lord rained on Sodom and Gomorrah brimstone and fire . . . out of heaven; and he overthrew those cities, and all the valley." While the terrible rain falls, Lot's wife, in spite of an earlier warning not to look back or linger, does turn to look. Probably she is regretting the loss of her home, and feeling fascination for the danger left behind. No sooner has she looked than she is frozen in her path, transformed into a "pillar of salt." And to this day figures looking strangely human stand about the Dead Sea where Sodom used to be.

After the fire, the world falls silent, and Abraham goes out "to the place where he had stood before the Lord." Looking toward Sodom, he sees nothing but smoke rising up from the plain. So it was, says the story, that God "remembered Abraham," and for his sake led Lot away from the catastrophe.

All now is desolation; the silence is like that which fell after the failure of Abraham's plea, when he turned and went home alone, knowing the cities were doomed. The vast loneliness he looks on reminds one of paintings like those of Tanguy, pictures presenting a long flat horizon, an endless plain, with empty distances made more desolate because some small human figure stands looking out toward the horizon.

As appendix to this story comes one more scene in which the writer names Lot as ancestor of two ancient enemies of Israel. Lot grows afraid in his little city of Segor, and climbs with his daughters into the hills. They believe that all human beings have perished and they alone are left. In order to insure the continuance of their family, the daughters make their father drunk and commit incest with him. "Thus both the daughters of Lot were with child by their father." The first-born bore a son, and called his name Moab; he is the father of the Moabites to this day. The younger also bore a son, and called his name Ben-ammi; he is the father of the Ammonites to this day. So the narrator displays his scorn for two national enemies.

> You shall call his name Ishmael. . . .
> He shall be a wild ass of a man,
> his hand against every man
> and every man's hand against him.

All along, there has seemed little hope of a son; Abraham has been able to act as father to no one closer than his nephew. Now at last his desire will be partially fulfilled when he has a son of his own named Ishmael. Still, this son is not to be the true heir.

Abraham's wife, Sarah, finding herself childless, follows the custom of the times and offers her maid servant Hagar to him, in the hope that she may have children through her means. Abraham complies, but when Hagar finds herself with child, she looks "with contempt on her mistress." Sarah retaliates by forcing her to flee to the desert, where an angel finds her "by a spring of water in the wilderness . . . on the way to Shur." He makes a strange prophecy about her child. He shall be called Ishmael and shall father a great race, but everyone's hand will be against him, and "he shall dwell over against all his kinsmen." No wonder Melville in *Moby Dick* names his tough and lonely hero after this solitary desert dweller: "Call me Ishmael." It is the most famous opening sentence in American literature—a whole character sketch in three words.

After the birth of Ishmael, God makes his promise yet more solemn by revealing his name to Abraham. He calls himself I AM —God the Almighty, the One who is dependent upon no one. He also changes Abraham's name which until now was Abram; henceforward it will be Abraham, father of a multitude. Furthermore, Ishmael is not the heir, for God says again that a son will be born to Abraham by Sarah, his true wife. He laughs in his heart at the thought that they, in old age, shall have a child, and asks only that God will grant life to Ishmael, for his eldest son is dear to him. Ishmael, says the Lord, shall indeed be "the father of twelve princes," but the son of promise will be Isaac, born of Sarah. "I will establish my covenant with Isaac, whom Sarah shall bear to you at this season next year." The promise is growing more definite.

In return for the Lord's pledge, God calls on Abraham to enter into a solemn covenant with him, and to seal this covenant with the sign of circumcision. All the men of his family are to bear in their flesh the mark of their covenant with Yahweh. This ceremony, which had been an ancient pagan custom, is thereby given fresh and sacred significance.

At the promised time, Isaac is born, but before his destiny unfolds, one more scene is given to Ishmael. It happens during the feast which celebrates the weaning of the infant Isaac. During the festivities, Sarah sees Ishmael playing with her son Isaac, teasing him probably, for the mother grows angry. She insists that her husband send Hagar and her boy away. At this Abraham is saddened "on account of his son." He rises early to help Hagar prepare for her journey, fetches bread and water, and watches as they make their way toward the desert of Beersheba. When her water is gone, she leaves "the child under one of the bushes," and sits down at "about the distance of a bowshot," for she says, "Let me not look upon the death of the child." But the Lord has a care for the child, and sends an angel saying: "Fear not; for God has heard the voice of the lad. . . . Arise, lift up the lad, and hold him fast with your hand; for I will make him a great nation." Surely the ancestor claimed by Islam has his own majesty. With the words of rescue, Hagar takes heart, moves on until she finds a well, and comes to safety. To part from Ishmael was bitter for Abraham, yet a more bitter trial is coming.

> Behold, the fire and the wood;
> but where is the lamb
> for a burnt offering?
> (GEN. 22:7)

At Isaac's birth, Sarah laughed with gladness and gave him a name which means "laughter." Remembering her own early laugh of unbelief she cries out, punning on his name, "God has made laughter for me." But her joy is short-lived. It happens that God puts Abraham to a test, and he hears the divine voice:

> Take your son, your only son Isaac, whom you love,
> and go to the land of Moriah,
> and offer him there as a burnt offering
> upon one of the mountains of which I shall tell you.

It is a three-way trial. On the ethical level it must have appeared that he was being led back to the worship he knew in Ur, where children were offered to the gods in sacrifice. On the human level, to act so constitutes a sin against the love he owes his son. On the level of revelation, he must have wondered if he has truly understood the divine command—if this can really be the voice of God. Yet he sets out in silence on his anguished journey.

The story is bare in the telling, yet the sparse details carry the reader along in unbearable suspense. The only open expression of emotion lies in Yahweh's words: "your only son . . . whom you love." So he shows his awareness of the father's love. And Abraham's weight of grief presses heavier with each step of preparation and journey. He rises at dawn, saddles his mount, calls two servants and Isaac. He cuts wood for sacrifice, and even this detail tells of the desolate land to which his journey tends, for in any but the most barren desert he should have been able to find wood.

Abraham sets out, and two days later he looks up to see the mountain. It is as if he has traveled all this time with his eyes on the ground, oblivious of everything but the one terrible deed which faces him. When at last he speaks, the sound is shocking in the vast silence. He leaves the servants and even the donkeys behind now, for Isaac carries a container with fire ready kindled, and the knife. To start fire in the wilderness is difficult, and the knife chills with its ironic implications: Isaac and the servants have no idea of the victim it will slay; only the reader and Abraham share the burden of terrible foresight.

A present-day poet, George Garrett, in "Abraham's Knife" tells how the scene must have been:

> Where hills are hard and bare,
> rocks like thrown dice, heat
> and glare that's clean and pitiless,
> a shadow dogs my heels. . . .
>
> True sacrifice is secret, none
> to applaud the ceremony, nor
> witness to be moved to tears.
> No one to see. God alone
> knows, Whose great eye winks not,
> from Whom no secrets are hid.[47]

The harsh rocks loom ahead; desert sand slows the man's dragging movement, and all around is the stillness of waste places. Only God is there to watch Abraham's deed and heart.

One companionable phrase in the Bible, "they walked both of them together," sharpens the poignancy of the scene, and so does the affectionate use of names in the snatch of dialogue:

"My father!"

"Here am I, my son."

Then the boy remarks that they have fire and wood, but "where is the lamb" for the sacrifice?

Sharply the double meaning of Abraham's reply rings out: "God will provide himself the lamb for a burnt offering, my son." In Abraham's eyes, God has already seen to it, for he believes the victim will be Isaac. The boy, however, seems to think they will find an animal, for he asks no more questions. And so they will. The reader, looking toward the ending, knows with relief that Isaac is right, that the words of Abraham, meant as evasion, are true. The Lord will provide the victim—and not the one Abraham expects. But for the father there is as yet no cessation of pain.

Upon the mountain Abraham prepares methodically to carry out his sacrifice. Dreadful tasks, like ordinary ones, are approached by doing one small thing after another. He builds an altar, sets wood in order upon it, binds his son, and lays him upon the wood. The factual understatements add to the horror. Christians often call the scene the *sacrifice* of Isaac, but the Jews of today name it rather the *binding* of Isaac, as a way of emphasizing its meaning, for it signifies an end of child sacrifice among these people. No longer, after this, can such an offering be considered a good deed by any man who thinks the thoughts of the Lord.

The climax comes with the sentence: "Then Abraham put forth his hand, and took the knife to slay his son." It is one of the barest and most powerfully charged sentences in literature.

Suddenly the tension breaks. Another call comes from heaven:

> Do not lay your hand on the lad
>   or do anything to him;
> for now I know that you fear God,
> seeing you have not withheld your son,
>   your only son, from me.

So the boy is saved, and the promises are renewed: "I will indeed bless you, and I will multiply your descendants . . . as the sand which is on the seashore . . . and by your descendants shall all the nations of the earth bless themselves, because you have obeyed my voice." On the level of ethics, this rescue condemns the practice of child sacrifice; on the human level, Abraham is set free to love his son with an increasing love; on the level of revelation, Abraham has proved himself totally committed to Yahweh, and has heard God's commitment to him made yet more firm.

> Go to my country and to my kindred,
> and take a wife for my son Isaac.

When Isaac has grown up, Sarah dies, and Abraham takes the last step of fatherhood by helping his son establish a household of his own, thus insuring a future for the family. But first comes the burial of Sarah which is marked by ancient folk customs showing Abraham's affection for her, his oriental leisure in bargaining, and his taking perpetual possession of one small corner of Canaan, that land which the Lord will give to his posterity.

After a time of lamentation for his wife, Abraham goes to the folk of that land and negotiates for the purchase of burial ground: "I am a stranger and a sojourner among you; give me property among you for a burying place, that I may bury my dead."

With Eastern ceremony they make their offer: "You are a mighty prince among us. Bury your dead in the choicest of our sepulchres; none . . . will hinder you." But Abraham, bowing low, insists on full legal payment, to guarantee possession of the plot, and probably also to show honor to his wife. Paying "four hundred shekels of silver," he obtains "the field of Ephron . . . to the east of Mamre, the field with the cave which was in it and all the trees that were in the field." This much of the promised land will be his forever, and here Ishmael and Isaac will bury him beside Sarah.

He has yet one more fatherly provision to make before he dies. He therefore calls in a loyal and talkative old manservant and tells him to go to Haran in Mesopotamia, to "take a wife for my son Isaac." His plans show that he knows his family is a people set apart, not destined to intermarry with Canaanites and lose their identity.

The servant makes the long journey northward to Haran where Abraham's brother Nahor dwells. Arriving at evening, he rests his camels near a well and prays that the maiden destined for Isaac may be inspired to offer water for himself and his camels. Soon Rebekah, a beautiful young maiden, granddaughter to

Nahor, comes out with a pitcher on her shoulder. Like Abraham in hospitality, she hurries to minister refreshment. " 'Drink, my lord'; and she quickly let down her jar," and again, "quickly she emptied her jar into the trough" for the camels, "and ran again to the well." Meanwhile the man marvels at the way the Lord has sped his errand.

Offering gifts of jewelry to her, he asks for lodging. Her reply is simple and practical: "We have both straw and provender enough, and room to lodge in." Her family proves as hospitable as she, and listens in patience while the old man tells each detail of his commission, repeating Abraham's every word. His talkativeness shows that the account has come down through oral tradition, that it was long told by word of mouth before being written down. Homer has many similar passages where a character retells an earlier event without a change of words. Such repetition is aimed, not at readers with a page before them, but at listeners who cannot go back over a story to catch details they have missed. It serves also to emphasize important events.

When Rebekah's family have heard the message they call her in, and she consents to return with the old man, and to marry Isaac. Their farewells are full of good wishes and prayers that she may be the mother of "thousands of ten thousands," and that her descendants may "possess the gate of those who hate them." The words are prophetic—from her will rise that posterity numberless as the stars, promised to Abraham through Isaac.

Meanwhile at home Isaac walks in the evening near the well where Hagar has experienced desolation. Rebekah sees him far off, dismounts from her camel, covers herself with her veil, and goes to meet him. All her actions are marked by decisiveness—a quality which will affect the fates of her sons. Isaac now brings "her into the tent . . . and she [becomes] his wife; and he [loves] her." So he is "comforted after his mother's death."

After this, Isaac, who exists in the Bible primarily as a relationship, as son to Abraham and father to Jacob, fades into the background of the narrative. And soon attention is focused on the sons of Isaac and Rebekah, especially on the younger son, Jacob. He will be the heir even though in many ways he stands in sharp contrast to his grandfather Abraham. Abraham has first appeared as a full-grown man; Jacob's story begins even before his birth; Abraham's call has come directly through the voice of the transcendent God; Jacob's will emerge gradually from human circumstances and human plans, ratified later by the Lord. Abraham has walked solitary—a figure looming against the desert sky, bearing a revelation of mystery; Jacob is social and his visions come in terms of immediate sensory reality.

Abraham has been concerned most of all with the promise of a son; Jacob will think continually of the land promised by Yahweh. Yet different as Jacob may be from his mysterious and lonely grandfather, it is through him, with his twelve sons, that Abraham's hope for a posterity without number begins to be possible, through his line that Abraham will at last father that One in whom all nations shall find a blessing, through Jacob that Abraham's call to fatherhood will fructify beyond his wildest dreams.

After Abraham's call and promises are confirmed in the lives of Isaac and Jacob, the people will move on toward those four other decisive happenings already named in the introduction to this book: the march into freedom under Moses; the vision and covenant given to Moses and Israel at Sinai; the conquest of Canaan; and the glorious kingdom under David. These are the turning points of their history, leading them toward God who is their beginning and their destiny. These five events shape their living liturgy of thankfulness for the past, and especially hope for the future.

CHAPTER SIX

Jacob's Useless Walls

> If only we might find somewhere a pure, contained,
> yet mortal strip of orchard of our own
> between the stream and stone! [48]

To move from Abraham to Jacob is like waking from a dream of pastoral simplicity to find oneself staring at kaleidoscopic activity in a market place. Abraham lives in a world which seems peopled only by himself and the majesty of the Lord; he stands open and defenseless before God. He is the man of courage, the epic hero. Jacob is the hero of the folk tale, resourceful, wily, hurrying after human concerns, and his tale is full of popular elements: domestic detail, frank humor with admiration for successful trickery, triumph of the younger son over his elder, and even love at first sight.

In an entirely human fashion, he works to build walls of security, to protect himself from the unexpected. And always, when he moves from shelter, God the unexpected swoops down on him. Abraham, from his first theophany, his first vision of the Lord, is enamored of divine transcendence and gives himself in one free and irrevocable commitment. Jacob, too, hears God's promises and walks in awareness of mystery, yet he becomes a man of God slowly and with errors. He demonstrates freedom in process, freedom limited by circumstances, his own doings, and God's intervention. He has none of Abraham's calm acceptance, but wants to work his own will even with Yahweh.

Because he desires safety and prosperity, he looks on the Lord mainly as giver of good to man, and bargains with him for home and well-being, trying to win blessings by guile. He might be called the crafty Ulysses of the Hebrew story. Like Ulysses, too, he is resourceful, and he would give anything for a sight of smoke rising from his own chimney, yet must spend much of his life on roads far from home. He is the planner, the trickster, yet out of his craft and in spite of his guile the Lord leads him to his true destiny, even while he chastises Jacob's faults. As Wright and Fuller say in *The Book of the Acts of God*, a commentary on scripture, "God does not choose sinless people for his work; he takes men as they are and makes even their sin praise him."[49] Or as Tolstoy has said: "God sees the truth, but waits."

Jacob's call, like Abraham's, is to fatherhood; he will receive and transmit God's promises to his posterity, will lead the people further on their journey. But in the call and its fulfillment God respects his individual personality, his unique circumstances, and allows him to work things out gradually. Though Jacob is vastly different from Abraham, yet he too is chosen, and the Lord is always with him, shaping his destiny even when the man is unaware of the divine purposes.

His life calls up many questions; for example, if he had been less passionately attached to home and possessions, would he have been driven from that home? Had he loved the land with a calmer love might he have died there instead of in Egypt? Had he trusted God to give him his heritage instead of manipulating human relationships to gain it, would the sorrows of his old age have come, as they do, through his family relationships?

He clings to his home with fierce possessiveness, yet his very attempts to hold it force him to fly from home. In consequence, his days fall into a pattern of three periods of home life alternating with three in exile: at home with Isaac and Rebekah, on the road to Mesopotamia; at home with his uncle Laban, on the road back to Canaan; at home there once more, and forced into the exile of Egypt. Twice his own trickery forces him to flee; and the last time he is impelled by the craft and vengeful spirit of his sons.

Whenever he is at home he acts to work out his plans by human means, to throw a wall of security around himself—an understandable human effort. When he travels into the desert, into places without protecting walls, he encounters the mystery and terror of God who takes the initiative into his own hands, and leads him toward the day when he will be no longer Jacob, the supplanter, but Israel, the one who triumphs, the winner of a lifetime bout with God. Meanwhile, the reader is drawn to him as a human being because of his walls and his defenselessness.

> God writes straight
> with crooked lines
> (PORTUGUESE PROVERB)

The beginning of Jacob's story shows him three times grappling with his brother to gain possession of the family inheritance, and then being driven away by the trouble he himself has stirred up. Even before his birth the writer shows him struggling with Esau. His mother feels the twin children wrestling in her womb; disturbed, she goes "to inquire of the Lord," and is told:

> Two nations are in your womb,
> and two peoples, born of you, shall be divided;
> the one shall be stronger than the other,
> the elder shall serve the younger.

When her time comes, she bears twins, who from the beginning are rivals. "The first came forth red, all his body like a hairy mantle; so they called his name Esau." Afterward "his brother came forth, and he had taken hold of Esau's heel; so his name was called Jacob," which means the one who supplants, the heel-clutcher, the man of cunning and acquisitiveness. Later on, the Lord will change this name to one significant of his destiny.

As they grow up their rivalry is intensified by the favoritism of the parents. Esau becomes "a skilful hunter, a man of the field," while Jacob is "a quiet man, dwelling in tents." Isaac favors Esau because "he ate of his game," but Rebekah prefers Jacob. Though Esau is the elder, and therefore the legal heir, their mother must have told Jacob about the prophecy which destined the heritage for him, and he soon begins to lay plans for becoming the head of the family.

One day when Esau comes "in from the field . . . famished," he finds Jacob preparing food, and says to him: "Let me eat some of that red pottage, for I am famished!" From the red vegetables, as well as from his ruddy complexion, he derives his other name of Edom, "the red." At the time the story was written Israel's unfriendly southern neighbors were the Edomites, and so the teller accounts for their descent, designating them as sons of Esau who lost his heritage, rather than of the victorious Jacob.

To Esau's request, Jacob answers: "First sell me your birthright."

And the brother foolishly agrees: "I am about to die; of what use is a birthright to me?" His impatience and exaggeration are amusing and pathetic. The cautious Jacob calls for him to bind himself by oath, and only then does he give Esau some "bread and pottage of lentils" and Esau eats and drinks and comes away, as if the loss of his birthright were of little moment. Obviously his simplicity is no match for Jacob's cleverness. With vivid economy the writer sketches their personalities: Jacob, cool and calculating, the planner, the one who provides; Esau, impetuous, unable to see beyond present discomfort to the important future, not of quick intelligence, but openhearted and guileless.

Jacob's bargain, however, is not safe until ratified by his father. One day Rebekah overhears the old blind Isaac say to Esau: "Behold, I am old; I do not know the day of my death. Now then, take your weapons . . . and hunt game for me, and prepare for me savory food . . . that I may bless you before I die." As E. A. Speiser, translator of Genesis in the Anchor Bible says, the formula, "I am old; I do not know the day of my death," was used in these times to signify a man's intent to make his last will and testament.[50]

Naturally, then, Rebekah grows anxious. She calls Jacob and tells him: "Go to the flock, and fetch me two good kids, that I may prepare . . . savory food for your father . . . and you shall bring it to your father to eat, so that he may bless you before he dies."

Jacob is perfectly willing, but puts one objection: "My brother is a hairy man, and I am a smooth man. Perhaps my father will feel me, and I shall seem to be mocking him, and bring a curse upon myself and not a blessing."

Rebekah reassures him, "Upon me be your curse, my son." She does not know how much irony lies hidden in her words—an irony that appears after the deed is done. Now, practical and decisive as always, she dresses Jacob in his brother's clothes and covers his neck and hands with hairy kidskins so that Isaac will not discover the fraud. When Jacob enters Isaac's presence, the old man calls him close, and catches the smell of Esau's garments on Jacob. The father falls to praising the freshness of outdoor life which clings to him, while he blesses Jacob in poetic phrases:

> See, the smell of my son
> is as the smell of a field
> which the Lord has blessed!
>
> May God give you of the dew of heaven,
> and of the fatness of the earth,
> and plenty of grain and wine.
> Let peoples serve you . . .
> and may your mother's sons bow down to you.

The plan has succeeded; Jacob will possess the inheritance, but only uneasily, and after trouble and exile.

Scarcely has Isaac pronounced the blessing and Jacob gone out, when Esau returns, learns what has happened, and the reader's sympathies are drawn to his distress. He breaks out into a "great and bitter cry," when he hears his father say: "Your brother came with guile, and he has taken away your blessing." Unable to control his voice, Esau weeps aloud, saying: "Is he not rightly named Jacob? For he has supplanted me these two times. He took away my birthright; and behold, now he has taken away my blessing." And pathetically he pleads, "Have you not reserved a blessing for me?"

The lost blessing, however, is irrevocable. All Isaac can offer is an oracle of Esau's future:

> Behold, away from the fatness of the earth
> shall your dwelling be,
> and away from the dew of heaven on high.
> By your sword shall you live,
> and you shall serve your brother;
> but when you break loose
> you shall break his yoke from your neck.

Someday Esau shall be free of this brother. For now, Rebekah and Jacob have had their way; nevertheless, their measures are unjust, and punishment will come. Upon Rebekah the curse she has unthinkingly invoked will fall. Esau, brooding over his misfortune, grows so angry that Rebekah fears for the life of her favorite son. She send him for refuge to Haran where her brother Laban lives. "Stay with him a while, until your brother's fury turns away . . . then I will send, and fetch you from there."

Rebekah, though, is mistaken; she will not bring Jacob home again. He will return, but when he comes she will be dead. All her love and planning result for her in the loss of her favorite son. As for Jacob, so far he has insured his earthly inheritance, but he has heard no heavenly call, received as yet no promise direct from the Lord, though the Genesis writer makes it clear that God is at work behind these human doings. Jacob's call and promises wait upon the days of his journeying, when he is away from protecting walls, from the home he loves with such anxiety.

> Thou knowest the walls, altar and hour and night:
> The swoon of a heart that the sweep and the hurl
> of thee trod
> Hard down with a horror of height.[51]

Jacob sets out for Haran in Mesopotamia, and at nightfall searches out a stone for a pillow and goes to sleep. This stone takes on significance in collections of anonymous folklore. One story says that next morning the stone sank down and became the keystone of the world, and later was used as the central support for the temple of Jerusalem. Another legend has Jacob gather not one stone, but four, from four famous altars of sacrifice: those of Adam, Abel, Noah, and that on which Abraham placed his son Isaac.

A nameless medieval artist, illustrating Aelfric's Anglo-Saxon translation of Genesis, pictures Jacob lying on these four stones, leaning on one elbow, and looking uncomfortably into swirling clouds where the Lord stands on a ladder gazing down at him. This ladder, bridging the distance between finite and infinite, is related, as has been seen, to the tower of Babel, but with an opposite meaning—signifying not defiance but shared communication and the Lord's protection. It also recalls an image that appears in folklore everywhere—that of a tree springing from the center of earth, serving as passageway to the heavens, and holding up the sky. Scandinavians call it Yggsdrasil, and say the earth is safe as long as it stands steady.

At any rate, the Bible says that Jacob dreams of a "ladder set up on the earth, and the top of it reached to heaven, and behold, the angels of God . . . ascending and descending on it!" And contrary to the illustration in Aelfric's book where the Lord stands above earth, the dream tells that Jacob had a sense of the Lord's nearness to him, and he heard God's voice: "I am the Lord, the God of Abraham your father, and the God of Isaac; the land on which you lie I will give to you and to your descendants . . . you shall spread abroad . . . and by you . . . shall all the families of the earth bless themselves. Behold, I am with you and will keep you wherever you go, and will bring you back to this land." Here, as S. H. Hooke says, "Jacob discovers that a God whom he does not know is interested in him, and has actually descended the ladder which leads from heaven to earth in order to stand beside him, for so the Hebrew should be rendered. He finds himself caught up into the vast purposes of God and is afraid."[52]

For the first time he is possessed of that sense of a transcendent God so characteristic of his grandfather Abraham. Filled with fear and reverence at the thought that God has been here, he exclaims:

> How awesome is this place!
> This is none other than the house of God,
> and this is the gate of heaven.

And he sets up his stone pillow as a monument, naming the place Bethel, the house of God.

But he follows the deed with a typically bargaining prayer. For all his great vision, he is the old Jacob. Preoccupied with thoughts of home and safety he makes a conditional promise: "If God will be with me, and will keep me . . . and will give me bread to eat and clothing to wear, so that I come again to my father's house in peace, then the Lord shall be my God." He wants bread, clothing, a safe journey, and a welcome home. For these favors he will reciprocate with his allegiance, and will give presents to God: "and of all that thou givest me I will give the tenth to thee." How different he is from his grandfather Abrahim, and yet the Lord has chosen both, given his promises to both.

Arise, my love, my fair one, and come away;
for lo, the winter is past,
　　the rain is over and gone. . . .
The fig tree puts forth its figs,
　　and the vines are in blossom. . . .
Arise, my love, my fair one, and come away
(SONG OF SOLOMON)

Jacob goes on from Bethel and comes "to the land of the people of the east." Here in the open plain he finds a well, with three flocks of sheep beside it. He falls to talking with some shepherds, when a beautiful young girl appears in the distance. He learns that her name is Rachel, and she is daughter to Rebekah's brother. When he falls in love with her we have one of the earliest examples of literature of love at first sight. For love of her he grows so strong that he can shift the stone covering the well—a stone so heavy that the other shepherds cannot lift it. But when "all the flocks were gathered there," then the shepherds, together, would "roll the stone from the mouth of the well, and water the sheep."

Since Jacob is too impatient to wait, he lifts the stone himself and waters Rachel's sheep for her. Then she hurries home with the news that their kinsman has come, and Laban runs out to meet him, embraces him, covers him with kisses, and brings him to their dwelling. Evidently Jacob goes to work for Laban soon after his arrival, for a month later they are negotiating about wages. "Should you serve me for nothing? Tell me," says Laban, "what shall your wages be?"

Without hesitation the younger man answers: "I will serve you seven years for your younger daughter Rachel." Then the Bible makes its own comment on his human love, "So Jacob served seven years for Rachel, and they seemed to him but a few days because of the love he had for her." Not many love lyrics say so much in short compass.

Now, however, Jacob who has tricked his brother, finds himself tricked in turn, for Laban has another daughter, Leah, whose eyes are "weak, but Rachel [is] beautiful and lovely." On the wedding night Laban substitutes this older daughter for the lovely Rachel, and the bridegroom wakes to find himself married to a wife he has not chosen.

When Jacob, in anger, takes Laban to task, the father merely answers that "It is not so done in our country, to give the younger before the first-born. Complete the week of this one, and we will give you the other also in return for serving me another seven years." To this Jacob agrees—he is willing to work fourteen years for Rachel—and when the week is ended he makes her his wife. So at last he has his bride, and loves her all his life.

As their families grow, however, conflict arises because Leah has many sons while Rachel has but two—Joseph, and much later Benjamin. These become their father's favorites, and their destinies will be affected by his partiality.

During these fourteen years Jacob works hard, and Laban's flocks increase under his care. At the end of the time he begins to think of his own household and to plan for its prosperity. He proposes that Laban shall give him "every speckled and spotted sheep and every black lamb" born that year. Carefully Laban first removes all such colored animals from his flocks, taking them far away before he gives consent.

Jacob, thereupon, works a kind of primitive magic on the flocks of white animals that are left in his keeping. He strips patches of bark from tree branches and places these wands before the ewes at the time of conception—a device for profit admired long afterward by Shakespeare's Shylock. The ewes, having looked at the patches of white and dark on the branches, bring to birth varicolored lambs, and Jacob claims them all. Laban, of course, is angry at being outwitted; the trickster who deceived Jacob at his wedding now endures trickery in his turn.

> We'll begin again, we'll remake the city of mercy, I want to go back home
>
> (Camus, "*Le Renégat*")

Laban's sons grow wrathful at Jacob's chicanery; they insist that their father has been robbed, and the whole family looks coldly on him. Jacob, therefore, calls his household and tells them that the Lord has commanded a return to the land of his birth. During the preparations for departure, Rachel steals Laban's household gods without telling Jacob. These images, as Speiser tells us in his introduction to the Anchor Genesis, are more than harbingers of good fortune. They are tokens which indicate the rightful heir to property. Rachel, aware of the long years of Jacob's work, is undoubtedly anxious that he shall have a share of her family's inheritance.

When all are ready, Jacob sets his children and wives on camels, and departs, taking his cattle and all he has gained during his sojourn. Soon Laban misses the stolen gods and comes after the caravan, accusing Jacob of cheating him, and carrying away his "daughters like captives of the sword. . . . Why did you flee secretly . . . I might have sent you away with mirth and songs. . . . And why did not you not permit me to kiss my sons and my daughters farewell? . . . You longed greatly for your father's house, but why did you steal my gods?"

Jacob, of course, knowing nothing of Rachel's theft, is loud in his protestations: "Any one with whom you find your gods shall not live. In the presence of our kinsmen point out what I have that is yours, and take it."

Suspense grows as all watch Laban enter one tent after another, until he comes to Rachel's. "Now Rachel [has] taken the household gods and put them in the camel's saddle, and sat upon them." When she makes excuses and refuses to rise, Laban's search fails. She has shown herself like her husband in her concern over hearth and home, and in her guileful ways.

When Jacob reproaches Laban for his suspicions, the latter offers peace, and they make a covenant, setting up a heap of stones to mark the place. That enmity is healed, but an older one remains because Jacob is troubled at the prospect of meeting Esau.

Accordingly, he sends some of his company ahead on the road with gifts for his brother, who has heard of his approach and comes his way with a large company. Jacob begins to pray by reminding the Lord of his promises:

> Deliver me, I pray thee, from the hand of my brother . . .
> for I fear him, lest he come and slay us all.
> But thou didst say, "I will do you good,
> and make your descendants as the sands of the sea."

Although during the twenty years with Laban there has been no mention of any conversation between God and Jacob, still

Jacob is mindful of the promises, and the writer makes it clear that God has had hold of all the tangled threads of Jacob's doings, and was working out his purpose of making Jacob into Israel—a man successful with God.

> Thou mastering me
> God! giver of breath and bread. . . .
> Over again I feel thy finger and find thee.[53]

That night when all his company have gone ahead across the ford of Jabbok, he finds himself alone, and has his second great vision, for a mysterious "man wrestled with him until the breaking of the day." A sense of awe surrounds the scene: it is night, and the antagonist seems at times to be an angel, a messenger of God, then again to be Yahweh himself.

In similar circumstances, the poet Gerard Manley Hopkins cries out in anguish while he wrestles with an invisible opponent:

> But ah, but O thou terrible, why wouldst thou rude on me
> Thy wring-world right foot rock? lay a lionlimb against me? scan
> With darksome devouring eyes my bruised bones, and fan
> O in turns of tempest, me heaped there; me frantic to avoid thee
>   and flee?

In desperation the speaker tries to wrench himself away from lionlimbs powerful enough to wring and twist the world, from eyes that peer through the dark at the man heaped on the floor in helplessness. Jacob in his wrestling must have felt such desperation. He has opposed his brother and won a heritage, contended with Laban and come off enriched, now he matches his strength against the Lord himself.

The vision is not an image seen with eyes, but a kinesthetic perception, a meeting felt in the sense of pull and thrust and strain. It has a fearful surrealism like a nightmare. Finally, this supernatural opponent, finding he cannot get free, touches "the hollow of his thigh; and Jacob's thigh was put out of joint," and says, "Let me go, for the day is breaking." But Jacob strikes a bargain: "I will not let you go, unless you bless me."

It is the familiar Jacob, but with a difference. His attitude is still reciprocal; he is still a bargainer. But while earlier he sought food and shelter, now he wants a spiritual gift, a blessing. He is transformed, but still recognizably the strategist. The blessing is given, and a new name—"Your name shall no more be called Jacob, but Israel, for you have striven with God and with men, and have prevailed."

God has let himself be beaten in what the poet Allen Kanfer calls "This one night bout with loser taking all." God loses, but at the same time he laughs:

> Laugh and spread it in Gath: Elohim takes
> All takers: all the wounded limp with joy. . . .
>
> Of such, such is the kingdom blown between
> Ascending ladders and the earthy maxims.[54]

Jacob, between his high visions on his journeys and his earthly concern for gain, is working out his call, learning to become a man of God. His call and the promises are given to him between ascending heavenly ladders and maxims of the world which say that security is all, that possessions are the safe walls that shut out loneliness and fear.

After the night, Jacob looks up and sees Esau coming, and "four hundred men with him." Though he is terrified, Esau's simple generosity soon puts him at ease. Jacob runs to meet his brother, embraces him, and weeps, then ceremoniously introduces his company, leaving Joseph and Rachel, the best loved, to the last. After an exchange of gifts, Esau returns home, and Jacob comes "safely to the city of Shechem, which is in the land of Canaan." Here he ratifies his loyalty by building an altar to the Lord, and then using his own new name, he dedicates it under God's other name of Elohim, calling this the place of El-Elohe-Israel.

> Fortunate is the man who has not known
> the gods' vengeance!
> Where the anger of heaven strikes,
> that house is shaken. . . .
> I have seen for long this gathering
> sorrow
> (Sophocles, *Antigone*)

Once home again, Jacob is not left to enjoy life in peace. He has won property by deceiving Esau and Laban; now his troubles come from those of his own household: he is driven from his newly settled home, loses Rachel in whom his love abides, is forced to cut off his eldest son from inheritance, and is at last brought by hunger into the exile of Egypt, where this home-lover dies in a strange land. As S. H. Hooke says, "The story runs on, and we do not see a triumphant Israel living up to his new name, but a figure round whom the consequences of other people's sins and failures gather."[55] Much time and trial must still pass before he is fully transformed into that Israel who wrests victory from God and brings his people to the place where God will work his second wonder, following the promises. Only in Egypt, where he has not planned to go, will opportunity come out of the people's travail, so that the Lord will lead them forth to freedom and towards nationhood.

Soon after the settling in Canaan, one of the neighboring chieftains, falling in love with Jacob's daughter Dinah, seizes her by force. Her brothers are "very angry because he had wrought folly in Israel by lying with Jacob's daughter, for such a thing ought not to be done." The young man offers gifts and honorable marriage, and suggests that the two peoples make peaceful alliance. Treacherously the sons of Jacob consent, stipulating only that all the men of the place shall be circumcised.

"Then we will give our daughters to you . . . and we will dwell with you and become one people." The Canaanites agree, and undergo circumcision, but on the third day when their wounds are very painful, "two of the sons of Jacob, Simeon and Levi, Dinah's brothers, [take] their swords and [come] upon the city unawares," and kill "all the males." Jacob reproaches them bitterly: "You have brought trouble upon me by making me odious to the inhabitants of the land." If they gather to attack, "I shall be destroyed, both I and my household." In fear of such reprisals, they then leave their home and find another place, still within Canaan's borders, to live.

They go first to Bethel where God had appeared in the vision of the ladder, and Jacob prepares to offer new worship with his family, whom he has ordered to purify themselves, that they may offer sacrifice to the God who has been with them in their journeying.

In response to his offering, God renews his promise of "the land which I gave to Abraham and Isaac," and of a great posterity. And he adds a new note by foretelling that "kings shall spring" from Jacob. Probably the writer is looking back from his later age and remembering the glory of David and Solomon who traced their lineage to Jacob. At Bethel, too, Deborah, Rebekah's old nurse dies, and is buried "under an oak" in that place. It throws a different light on Jacob to find him cherishing his mother's nurse during all these travels, and showing sincere grief when she dies.

Jacob finds cause for deeper mourning when they move towards Ephrath. Here Benjamin, youngest of the sons is born, but Rachel dies "in hard labor, after naming the child Ben-o-ni, the son of my sorrow. After her death, Jacob renames him Benjamin, which means child of my right hand. Long years after, when he is an old man in Egypt, Jacob remembers this time, and tells Joseph, the other son of Rachel:

> When I came from Paddan,
> Rachel to my sorrow died in the land of Canaan
> on the way,
> when there was still some distance
> to go to Ephrath;
> and I buried her there on the way to Ephrath
> (that is, Bethlehem).
>
> (GEN. 48:7)

The careful enumerations of details, the exact locations and his explanations of the two names, all intensify the pathos. This is the more true because he himself is destined to die in a foreign land, and his body will be brought back, not to be buried near his beloved Rachel, but in the family tomb at Mamre with Leah and his grandparents Abraham and Sarah. Two of the sorrows of his declining years have settled upon him—the exile and disgrace caused by the cruel treachery of Simeon and Levi, and the death of Rachel.

The third family sorrow comes because Jacob's eldest son Reuben proves unworthy to become the heir. He "went and lay with Bilhah his father's concubine; and Israel heard of it." Because of this, Reuben loses his place as head of the family, and when Jacob gives his last blessing to his sons, he can promise nothing but misfortune for his eldest:

Reuben, you are my first born . . .
the first fruits of my strength,
Unstable as water, you shall not have pre-eminence
because you went up to your father's bed.

Jacob's final sorrow and his exile to Egypt belong properly to the story of Joseph. Through his love for this favorite son, this child of Rachel the beloved, Jacob will one day be brought into a land of strangers, and in his old age will set up his household for the last time in a place far away—far from that land he has worked and prayed and conspired to hold. He will lose this son and cling the more stubbornly to Benjamin, the other child of Rachel; he will seem for a time to lose Benjamin, too.

But in the end he will find both again in the land of exile. For "the pattern of redemption [has] to be wrought out in Egypt, and the things that seemed to be against him were all part of the divine purpose to bring him against his will, to the place where that purpose should find fulfillment" (S. H. Hooke). He is being made worthy to give his name Israel to the people of God. They are destined to be saved, through him and Joseph, from famine, brought to a land where they will grow in numbers, gain a sense of unity under suffering, and be led into a new life of freedom after slavery.

How Jacob and the people came to Egypt is told in the adventure story of Joseph, which stands apart from the accounts of Abraham, Isaac, and Jacob. Joseph, like these, is a man of God, but his communication with divinity is less direct, is mediated through dreams. Abraham has talked face to face with God, as Moses will later do; Jacob has met the Lord in visions whose import is unmistakable; Joseph's revelations are given through dreams whose meanings are hidden until the Lord helps with their interpretation.

Joseph's story differs, too, because of its greater unity of structure, its twists of dramatic irony, its obvious literary craftsmanship. Jacob's has been a saga and a folktale, a narration of family relations and domestic intrigue; Joseph's is a literary romance, a tale of marvelous adventures in a strange country.

God's promises and his call, given to Abraham, Isaac, and Jacob, are now an unforgettable theme in Israel's history. Bestowed before men have done anything to earn them, they convince the people that their God is a faithful Lord, that he, the all-powerful, has taken notice of a lowly people, that he cherishes them and lends them his strength. This relationship is a new thing in the world, and their songs never tire of expressing wonderment because he that is mighty has done great things for them.

In return, God has exacted no payment beyond the simple acceptance of himself as their Lord. His call and promises are but the first of the pivotal events in the Old Testament. Joseph's story will strengthen the people's conviction about God's providing love, and after Joseph two more salvation events will occur during the days of Moses: the rescue from slavery in Egypt culminating in the triumphant march to freedom, and the vision and lawgiving on Sinai, when the people will pledge themselves as a nation to Yahweh. Joseph, whose story is next, is not one of the greatest fathers of Israel, but he too has his call and his place in God's plan, and his story is one of the finest in the Bible.

CHAPTER SEVEN

Joseph Dreams of Sheaves

> The Joseph story is the most sophisticated and polished of the stories of Genesis. . . . Every device is used to stimulate the imagination.[56]

AFTER the visions of Jacob come the dreams of Joseph. After the home-loving Jacob comes his son, an exile. As Jacob had gone unwillingly on a journey because he roused his brother Esau's ire, so Joseph must go because he has called up his brothers' rage. For Joseph it seems that God's promises will not come true since he lives as an alien, far from the promised land, and his sons, born of foreign wives, are seemingly destined to be heirs in Egypt, not Israel. Nor does Joseph himself ever hear the voice of the Lord speaking the promises. Yet because he is true to his people's commitment to Yahweh, therefore for him too the promises hold. He also will be an instrument shaped to the hands of God.

Joseph's story begins with the warm pungency of sheaves in the sun, the clean sharp smell of night under desert stars, a tingle in the nose caused by sheep milling in the dust. From this dry land he comes to the odor of the fruitful Nile and the green, cool gloom of its waterside grasses. The narrative begins with Genesis 37, is interrupted by 38 which concerns Judah, and takes up once more in 39, from which it flows without pause to the end of Genesis.

In the story are many familiar literary motifs: dreams with their interpretation and fulfillment, the lucky younger son triumphing over jealous brothers, the hero's temptation by the master's wife, the rise of a poor boy to riches and power, the long lost child restored to his father. Here, too, are glimpses of lives strange to our land and time: harvesters tying up sheaves of grain, herdsmen scattered in the hills, camel caravans against the horizon, prison life and palace life in Egypt where great faces of cattle loom up from the succulent reeds by the river. The account, like an epic, is built around the fortunes of a single hero; like a saga it weaves family relationships into an intricate plot, giving pleasure through recognition, reversal of fortune, and dramatic irony; and like a romance it tells of unusual adventures —a kidnapping, prophetic dreams, and amazing turns of destiny.

It is an almost perfect example of the storyteller's art, especially in its handling of movement in space. In earlier stories, the reader is always placed in the scene of the moment and sees the actors enter and play their parts and withdraw. "But in the Joseph cycle the reader continues to follow the characters after they have left the stage. While Joseph hunts for his brothers, their discussion of his fate is quoted; while Joseph is on his way to Egypt, Jacob's grief over his loss is described. . . . Technically the cycle is [a] most expert example of sheer narrative."[57] But the tale is dramatic too.

As in drama, much of its meaning unfolds through conversations. And true to dramatic form it falls into five acts. In the first the successful hero meets his brothers' rivalry and falls into misfortune imaged by a bloody coat; in the second he rises to power but falls again when his cloak is used as false evidence against him; in the third he ascends from slavery to a throne because he can interpret dreams. Here, too, the clothes image appears when in prison he is given new raiment to wear before Pharaoh who summons him.

The fourth act is full of conflicting emotions. Twice Joseph's brothers come to Egypt and stand before Joseph the ruler, recognized but not recognizing, while he takes a revenge in which clothes play a part. The last act draws all threads together when the old Jacob is brought by the brothers to be reunited with his lost son, and all find a new home in Egypt. These five acts repay close scrutiny for they are full of vivid action, stirring emotion, and depths of meaning under their bright surface.

The sheaves bow down
Yet he is not king but steward.[58]

At first meeting the reader watches the boy Joseph stir the wrath of his elder brothers. He begins by tale bearing—carrying ill reports of them to Jacob. Then he flaunts the fine clothes his father has given him out of favoritism, for "Israel loved Joseph more than any other of his children, because he was the son of his old age," and was moreover, the son of Rachel whom Jacob worked fourteen years to win. This son is beautiful in form and face as his mother was, but his elder brothers were born of the ill-favored Leah or of slave mothers. But worst of all, Joseph is naive enough to tell his brothers about his dreams in which they are demeaned and he is exalted:

> Hear this dream which I have dreamed:
> behold, we were binding sheaves in the field,
> and lo, my sheaf arose and stood upright;
> and behold, your sheaves gathered round it,
> and bowed down to my sheaf.

It is easy to imagine the brothers' feelings: "Are you indeed to reign over us?" Then in a second dream he sees sun, moon, and eleven stars doing reverence to him. This time his father reproves him by asking, "What is this dream? . . . Shall I and your mother and your brothers indeed come and bow ourselves to the ground before you?" So his brothers "were jealous of him, but his father kept the saying in mind."

Joseph has dreamed of gathering grain. This imagery is to be expected in the light of his family's country occupations. Yet it means more: through the grain he garners in Egypt long after, his brothers will, all unknowing, seek him out, bow down before him, and so make his dreams come true in a way they do not expect.

The second dream, in which sun, moon, and stars do him honor, also points, though more obscurely, to the future when he will be sold into Egypt. Egyptians from early times studied and worshiped the stars. At Karnak and elsewhere they built temples with lines of columns pointing to where the sun rose on midsummer's day. Only once in 365 days did the rising sun shine straight along that line, and so they learned to measure the year. Besides this, they held Sirius, the brilliant Dog Star, so much in reverence that they built temples constructed to guide its light in and down a long hallway to illumine a spot on the central altar. In this manner the light of the star became an actual part of the building's plan. Finally, their important god, Ra, ruled the noonday sun. He crossed the sky in a boat by day, and at night, in another ship, he rested while he was carried from west to east below the world, to be ready for sunrise next morning. To this land of sun, moon, and stars, Joseph will come.

The memory of this first pair of dreams will now remain quiescent until the climax, in act four, when seeing their fulfillment Joseph will recall them. In the meantime, the brothers burn with fires of envy because of his tale bearing, his father's partiality, and most of all because of his pride in his dreams. As in the stories of Cain and Abel, Jacob and Esau, the conflicts hinge on the rivalry of brothers, and as in tales the world over, the younger brother suffers but wins out in the end.

One day Joseph is sent by his father to search for his brothers, who are keeping sheep in the lonely country around Dothan. They see him afar off and resolve to murder him, but after some disagreement, they compromise by selling him to a passing caravan on its way to Egypt. Then dipping Joseph's embroidered coat in the blood of a goat they bring it to Jacob as proof that the boy is dead. Joseph had carried tales about them, now they carry news of his death; Joseph had triumphed over them because of this cloak, now they disfigure it with blood and use it as sign of his downfall. The coat is the first of four clothing images which add meaning to events in the story. As the caravan vanishes across the desert, the brothers settle down. Their rival is removed and act one is at an end. Yet even through their malice the Lord is bringing Joseph to the place where he can serve God's people, and is preparing their way into the land which will bring them sorrow, an increase in numbers, and at last a great deliverance.

My master has . . . put everything
that he has in my hand . . .
How then can I do this great wickedness,
and sin against God?
(GEN. 39:8)

Though Joseph comes to Egypt as a slave, he soon again becomes a favorite. All that he does prospers, because "the Lord [is] with him"; and his master, Potiphar, captain of Pharaoh's guard, trusts him with all his affairs. This ability to win trust is seen again later with a jailer, and even with Pharaoh himself. But troubles are in store because Joseph has inherited Rachel's beauty. The wife of Potiphar is captivated and tempts Joseph, but without success. He will not betray his master nor sin against God. Like the famous knight Sir Gawain, in medieval romance, Joseph remains true to the man whose trust and hospitality he enjoys; like Gawain, too, he is betrayed by a garment.

Because Sir Gawain conceals a magic girdle given him by a beautiful temptress, his opponent is able to wound him. Because Joseph, fleeing from Potiphar's wife, leaves his cloak in her hands, she uses it as evidence that he has dishonored her. Her ruse succeeds and Joseph goes to prison. His coat, earlier, had served as false proof of his death, now another garment is falsely displayed as sign of his sin. Act one had ended with Joseph exiled and enslaved; act two shows a deeper fall—the slave is now in prison. Yet the depths to which he descends serve later to make his rescue more dramatic, as the depths of slavery to which the people will come here in Egypt will make their march to freedom all the more glorious.

While dreams possess us,
the balance of our character
shifts in our sleep.

Again, as could be expected, Joseph is not long in prison when he becomes a favorite of the jailer who assigns to him the care of other prisoners. "And the keeper of the prison committed to Joseph's care all the prisoners . . . because the Lord was with him; and whatever he did, the Lord made it prosper." Like his forefathers, he is a friend of God, but his relationship is not so intimate as theirs. "Throughout the Joseph story, although the hand and purpose of God are everywhere evident and explicitly acknowledged, the only way in which God is represented as communicating with anyone is by means of dreams. Personal communication is only resumed when we come to the saga of Moses."[59]

Two of Joseph's fellow prisoners, Pharaoh's butler and his baker, are now disturbed by prophetic dreams. The butler dreams of a vine with three shoots from which he plucks the grapes to press for Pharaoh's wine. The baker dreams that he carries three baskets of pastry on his head for birds to peck at.

Then Joseph asks them, "Why are your faces downcast today?" They answer that there is no one to interpret their dreams. He says, "Do not interpretations belong to God? Tell them to me." He has a serene assurance that God will help him. Then he willingly interprets the first dream.

It means that the butler, in three days signified by the three vine shoots, will be freed and return to his place, serving wine at Pharaoh's table. Then the baker calls for his turn, and Joseph complies reluctantly, saying that after three days, indicated by the three baskets, the baker will be executed. The baskets high on his head mean that his body will hang high on a gallows, and the birds will come and prey on his flesh, just as they have eaten the pastries. After this the baker is mentioned no more.

Joseph, however, asks the butler to plead with Pharaoh: "Remember me, when it is well with you, and do me the kindness . . . to make mention of me to Pharaoh, and so get me out of this house. For I was indeed stolen out of the land of the Hebrews; and . . . I have done nothing that they should put me into the dungeon." Once free, though, the butler forgets, until two years later when Pharaoh has dreams which disquiet him. When no one can interpret them, the man finally remembers Joseph, recommends his wisdom, and the king sends for him. The message sets off excitement in the prison. Joseph is dressed in clean clothes, his beard is shaved off, and he appears at court. Clothes, which had earlier appeared as false signs of his death and evildoing, now become true signs for a rise in fortune—new hope, a new life.

Pharaoh tells Joseph he has dreamed of seven fat cattle grazing by the Nile, then devoured by seven famished beasts; of seven prosperous ears of corn eaten up by seven thin ears. The young man explains that both mean the same thing: Egypt will have seven years of prosperity, signified by the fat cows and full ears, and then seven years of famine when the fruits will be devoured. Pharaoh, like Potiphar and the prison keeper, is impressed, and appoints this wise man risen from slavery to rule Egypt next to himself. He is to prepare Egypt for the coming famine.

Such a sudden rise from prison to a throne next the king's is a feature in stories the world over. Literally Joseph goes from rags to riches, from prison garb to royal raiment. Act three has ended with a folktale wish fulfillment—a poor boy's sudden rise to fortune. He now proves a good administrator, gathering grain and filling the barns of Egypt, so that when famine comes he holds provisions for all. The stage is set for act four and the accomplishment of his first dream, though he has as yet no idea that he will rescue his own brothers and change the course of his people's history.

> Stone over stone, in the thin morning, they plod
> Again, until they come to a field where mowers
> Sweep their scythes under the dry sun.[60]

Famine comes as foretold, to Egypt, and to far-off Canaan. The scene shifts there, and the old Jacob is heard reproaching his sons: "Why do you look at one another? . . . Behold, I have heard that there is grain in Egypt; go down and buy grain for us there, that we may live, and not die." The sons make ready. "But Jacob did not send Benjamin, Joseph's brother, with his brothers, for he feared that harm might befall him." Though Jacob is acting just as he did with Rachel's other son, Joseph, still the ten brothers show no resentment. They will now let their father have his favorite.

Arrived in Egypt, they are brought before the potentate, Joseph. In a scene full of dramatic irony he recognizes them at once, but they do not know him. As they bow before him, Joseph remembers "the dreams he had dreamed of them." Here in this field of Egypt, his sheaf of grain stands erect and full, and his brothers bend in his presence. He shines as so brilliant a star, that the sun, moon, and stars of his family must do him reverence.

Immediately he begins a campaign to unsettle these brothers of his. He will have his revenge, but will not injure them, and so he alternates harshness and kindness in a series of quick changes until their old arrogance has dwindled. Speaking through an interpreter to conceal the fact that he knows their language, Joseph roughly accuses them of being spies. They protest their innocence in a flood of words, telling him all about themselves, and how their father is at home with Benjamin the youngest brother. They even mention Joseph himself, saying that they had another brother, but he is now dead. The words are ironic—perhaps they have convinced themselves that Joseph is dead, but all the while he stands prosperous before them.

He seizes on this information they have blurted out and orders them to return home and bring this youngest brother to Egypt. His motives are more than revenge this time. He wants to see Benjamin, the only other son of the long-dead Rachel. "By the life of Pharaoh, you shall not go from this place unless your youngest brother comes here . . . that your words may be tested . . . or else . . . surely you are spies." And he puts them in prison for three days. In this way he threatens grief to his father like that the brothers had inflicted long ago. It is a test to see whether they have changed.

Putting them in prison is another stage of revenge. Because of them he had suffered slavery and imprisonment; they shall taste the same bitterness. Three days later, however, he frees them, and sends them home, keping only one as hostage. This is Simeon, eldest of those who had consented to murder him at Dothan. The brothers, unaware that Joseph can understand, say to one another:

> In truth we were guilty concerning our brother,
> in that we saw the distress of his soul,
> when he besought us and we would not listen;
> therefore is this distress come upon us.

And Reuben answers them: "Did I not tell you not to sin against the lad? . . . So now there comes a reckoning for his blood." Joseph, listening, is deeply moved, but does not betray his identity. For sheer suspense and dramatic control of events, the scene is unsurpassed.

They set out for home and on the way one man opens a sack of grain to give fodder to his beasts. He is uneasy when he finds in the sack the money which he thought he had paid for the supplies. Joseph has put it there, planning to upset their self-satisfaction. "At this their hearts failed them, and they turned trembling to one another, saying 'What is this that God has done to us?' "

At home they tell Jacob the whole story: "The man, the lord of the land, spoke roughly to us, and took us to be spies. . . . But we said to him, 'We are honest men, we are not spies, we are twelve brothers . . . one is no more, and the youngest is this day with our father in the land of Canaan.' Then the man . . . said to us, 'By this I shall know that you are honest men: leave one of your brothers . . . and go. Bring your youngest brother to me.' " Then opening the sacks of grain, each one finds his own purse with his money in it, and they are "dismayed." This is no oversight.

Jacob, moreover, adds to their discomfort by reproaching them: "Why did you treat me so ill as to tell the man that you had another brother?"

They reply, reasonably enough, that they told him no more than he asked, "Could we in any way know that he would say, 'Bring your brother down'?" Then Reuben offers his two sons to Jacob as surety that he will bring Benjamin safely home, while Judah says he will make himself answerable for the boy. The brothers are indeed changed from the time when they could coldbloodedly tell their father his son was dead.

After much delay, Jacob is forced by continuing famine to let them go and take Benjamin along. In epic style they go bearing gifts: "some of the choice fruits of the land . . . a little balm and a little honey, gum, myrrh, pistachio nuts, and almonds." And their father adds: "Take double the money with you; carry back . . . the money that was returned in the mouth of your sacks."

> Take also your brother, and may God Almighty
> grant you mercy before the man,
> that he may send back your other brother and Benjamin.
> If I am bereaved of my children, I am bereaved.

As soon as Joseph sees them coming with Benjamin he orders a feast prepared, and sends his steward to invite them to his house.

But they are dismayed: "It is because of the money . . . so that he may . . . fall upon us, to make slaves of us." And volubly, as is their way, they go on to the steward: "Oh, my lord, we came down the first time to buy food; and when we came to the lodging place . . . there was every man's money in the mouth of his sack; so we have brought it again with us, and . . . other money . . . to buy food. We do not know who put our money in our sacks."

Quietly the steward answers: " 'Rest assured, do not be afraid; your God and the God of your father must have put treasure in your sacks for you; I received your money.' Then he brought Simeon out to them."

When Joseph comes home, they hasten to placate him with gifts, and introduce Benjamin. "Then Joseph made haste, for his heart yearned for his brother, and he sought a place to weep." On his return, the meal is served, and the brothers are twice puzzled: although they have not told their ages, they are seated in order, "the first-born according to his birthright and the youngest according to his youth"; and "Benjamin's portion was five times as much as any of theirs." Carefully the storyteller prepares for his denouement. Soon they will discover how it is that Joseph knows their ages, and how close is his tie with Benjamin. Meanwhile they drink and make merry at table while Joseph plans another shock.

Unknown to them, he has ordered their money returned to their sacks, and worse still, has had his own silver cup placed in Benjamin's. No sooner are they gone than the steward comes after them, "Why have you returned evil for good? Why have you stolen my [master's] silver cup?" Just as they have before blurted out too much about their home, so now they protest too loudly: "The money which we found in the mouth of our sacks, we brought back to you . . . how then should we steal silver and gold? . . . With whomever of our servants it be found, let him die, and we also will be my lord's slaves."

"Then every man quickly [lowers] his sack" and opens it. "And the cup was found in Benjamin's sack." At this moment of crisis their fate balances between life and death, but the Bible says nothing of their feelings, conveying them all the more powerfully because of this restraint.

Brought once again into the presence of Joseph, Judah puts up an eloquent plea:

When I come to . . . my father, and the lad is not with us,
then, as his life is bound up in the lad's life,
he will die;
and your servants will bring down the gray hairs of . . . our father
with sorrow to Sheol.
Let [me] remain instead . . . as a slave . . .
for [I] became surety . . . to my father. . . .
and let the lad go back with his brothers.

His words are full of compassion; plainly he remembers the promise made before he left home, to give his own life, if necessary, to bring his brother home.

Now Joseph can control himself no longer: "Make every one go out from me," he cries out. No stranger is to witness this reconciliation. Then weeping aloud he tells them:

I am your brother, Joseph,
whom you sold into Egypt.
and now do not be distressed, or angry with yourselves,
because you sold me here;
for God sent me before you to preserve life . . .
and to keep alive for you many survivors.

The scene is marked by dramatic recognition, generous forgiveness, and foreshadowing of a great deliverance to come, for the famine itself has been sent by Yahweh to prepare for the next act in the sacred drama, the saving of the whole people.

Their rejoicing, however, is not complete until Jacob can share it, and Joseph sends an urgent message:

Make haste and go up to my father
and say to him,
"Thus says your son Joseph,
God has made me lord of all Egypt;
come down to me, do not tarry."

The brothers turn towards home with Joseph's parting words in their ears: "Do not quarrel on the way." He seems to be recalling the days of their youthful violence toward him and urging them to hold to the change of heart they have shown.

With Egyptian wagons to carry his gifts of food, and "festal garments" for every brother, besides "five festal garments" for Benjamin, they hasten home. In this fourth appearance of the clothing symbol, its meanings are again transformed. Gifts of raiment now signify not enmity and death, as with the bloody cloak, but reconciliation and new life; not deception as with the use of Joseph's coat by Potiphar's designing wife, but a truthful pledge of Joseph's help; not Joseph set free from prison and dressed in fresh garments to come before Pharaoh, but the brothers set free from famine and sent with glad tidings to their father. Yet ironically enough, though these gifts signify good news for the immediate future, still their acceptance marks one step in the people's journey toward slavery in Egypt.

Their homecoming, with the Egyptian wagons, is invested with excitement and stress for the bewildered old father. He stands dazed and unbelieving at first. "And they told him, 'Joseph is still alive, and he is ruler over all the land of Egypt.' And his heart fainted, for he did not believe them." But when they have told him all, and he has seen the wagons with their goods, he revives: "It is enough; Joseph my son is still alive; I will go and see him before I die." Once more he will leave the walls of home, and once more Yahweh will confront him on the road.

> There is a joy that has no home.
> It meets me in lonely places. It is like
> Nothing on earth. It has no name.[61]

He starts from Sichem, southward to Beersheba, where he is encouraged by a new theophany, a vision in the dark with a renewal of the promises. At night on the desert the voice of the Lord comes saying:

> "Jacob, Jacob."
> And he said, "Here am I."
> Then he said, "I am God, the God of your father;
> do not be afraid to go down to Egypt;
> for I will there make of you a great nation."

This migration to Egypt is an event of first magnitude in the history of salvation, a crucial stage in the people's journey toward their destiny. In the vision, the Lord shows his recognition of Jacob's love for this land; though he must go to Egypt, yet, says the Lord, "I will bring you up again"; Jacob will at last be buried at home in Canaan.

This third of Jacob's visions is most like those of Abraham, who heard the voice of God in a kind of spaceless, timeless moment, for now Jacob's is not mediated through images of sight like the ladder, nor though kinesthetic sensations as in the wrestling bout at Peniel. All of Jacob's visions, however, come at night, while Abraham sometimes conversed with God in the brightness of day on the desert.

When Joseph in Egypt hears of Jacob's coming, he makes ready his chariot and rides "to meet Israel his father in Goshen," the northern part of Egypt. This is one of the places in the story where the handling of space is done with literary skill. Again and again the writer shifts interest from north to south, from Canaan to Egypt and back, to show simultaneous events, and yet the thread of narrative remains untangled. At the meeting, Joseph falls into his father's arms, weeping, and Israel cries out, "Now let me die, since I have seen your face and know that you are still alive."

But business waits, and Joseph, the man of affairs, must set about it. He goes to tell his good news to Pharaoh and to win the pastureland of Goshen for the family. Later on he brings Jacob to court, where Pharaoh admires his venerable age, "and Jacob blessed Pharaoh." During such rejoicing, Jacob's only words to Pharaoh are, "The days of the years of my sojourning are a hundred and thirty years; few and evil have been the days of the years of my life, and they have not attained to the days . . . of my fathers." The words sound strange on the lips of one whose ways have prospered, and whose life has been honored by the friendship of the Lord. As he has grown old he has lost some of his youthful assurance, and has bowed under the weight of suffering. After this one interview he returns to Goshen while Joseph remains near the court, working to end the famine and build up the power of Pharaoh.

At the end of seventeen years in Egypt, Jacob falls ill and Joseph, with his sons, come to visit. As old men will, he rambles in his speech, remembering his communications with God, the death of Rachel, and some of the troubles that are past, after which he blesses Joseph's sons and speaks oracles about the future.

> God Almighty appeared to me at Luz
> in the land of Cannan and blessed me,
> and said to me,
> "Behold, I will make you fruitful . . .
> and I will make of you a company of peoples,
> and will give this land to your descendants after you
> for an everlasting possession."

In the strength of these promises he adopts Joseph's two sons, so that they may share interitance with his own posterity: "Ephraim and Manasseh shall be mine, as Reuben and Simeon are." In making the pledge he names the younger son first. And since these are grandsons of Rachel, he is reminded of her: "When I came from Paddan, Rachel to my sorrow died . . . on the way . . . and I buried her there . . . in the land of Canaan." His repetition of the name of Canaan sounds out his longing for that land.

Now Joseph brings his sons closer, placing Ephraim at Israel's left hand, and Manasseh at his right. But Jacob crosses his hands to give the blessing, placing his right hand on the head of Ephraim, though he is younger, and his left on Manasseh's head, although Manasseh is the firstborn:

> The God before whom my fathers
> Abraham and Isaac walked,
> the God who has led me all my life long
> to this day . . . bless the lads;
> and in them let my name be perpetuated,
> and the name of my fathers.

By telling how God has led him all his life, he evokes a shepherd's gentleness and strength, and especially God's fidelity. The thought of God as shepherd, and of Israel's leaders as reflecting this image, is frequent in scripture. Samson, David, and Amos will all boast of their barehanded killing of lions to protect their sheep, and the Psalmist will immortalize the thought of the Lord's loving care in his famous poem: "The Lord is my shepherd." In this blessing, and in the oracle which follows, later history is placed on Israel's lips. By naming Ephraim first, he for one thing is accounting for that tribe's powerful place, long years after, in northern Canaan.

The writer now has Jacob speak an oracle which lists the twelve tribes named for his sons, so emphasizing the promise of a numerous posterity; he describes the places which they will own in the promised land, thus recalling the promise of a land to be their possession, and in the part devoted to Joseph he mentions the close relationship with God which is the third of the great promises given by the Lord. Similar lists with variations appear in Moses' speech at the end of Deuteronomy, and in Deborah's victory song in Judges. Scholars are agreed that these blessings are woven from very ancient poetic fragments, but their total meanings remain in part obscure and a subject for speculation.

In mysterious poetry enriched with images of water and weapons, clothes and food and animals, he hints at the past of his sons, their present characteristics, and their future destiny. Reuben, the firstborn, "unstable as water," hears only harsh words because he desecrated family solidarity by appropriating his father's wife: "You went up to your father's bed . . . you shall not have pre-eminence." Simeon and Levi, too, are cursed because of their cruelty at Shechem, when they defended their sister Dinah:

> Cursed be their anger, for it is fierce;
>   and their wrath, for it is cruel!
> I will divide them in Jacob
>   and scatter them in Israel.

By the time of Moses, Simeon will be dropped from the roster of Jacob's sons, and the position of Levi will be changed. This tribe, appointed as priests by Moses, will hold no grant of land.

Judah, the tribe from which David will spring, and from whom the Jews get their name, will fare better. He is a "lion's whelp," and "who dares rouse him up?":

> The scepter shall not depart from Judah,
>   nor the ruler's staff from between his feet,
> until he comes to whom it belongs;
>   and to him shall be the obedience of the peoples.

These lines have been widely read as a dim prophecy of the savior who will rise from Jesse's root and be the offspring of David, ruling all nations. To him, by association, the images belong:

> He washes his garments in wine
> and his vesture in the blood of grapes;
> his eyes shall be red with wine,
> and his teeth white with milk.

The description, whatever its symbolism, might well have inspired phrases of the much later Song of Songs.

From Judah, the oracle goes on to name Zebulun and his place "at the shore of the sea"; Issachar, the "strong ass" who slaves at heavy work; Dan, the "serpent in the way . . . that bites the horse's heels"—unseating his enemies, perhaps. Gad, Asher, Naphtali follow, with about ten words apiece foretelling victory for Gad, rich food for Asher, and freedom for Naphtali, "a hind let loose."

To Joseph, however, is given the most lyrical prophecy. He is a "fruitful bough by a spring," a strong archer whose bow remains unmoved. His help comes:

> by the hands of the Mighty One of Jacob
> (by the name of the Shepherd, the Rock of Israel).

He will receive blessings "of heaven above," "of the deep that couches beneath," beyond the limit of "the eternal mountains." He whose early dreams foretold fruitful prosperity, and power symbolized by sheaves of grain, is seen by the old father as "separate from his brothers," able to rule over them.

In such a way, the early blessing given to Jacob by Isaac, his father, is passed on to Joseph, who will know fruitfulness of earth, and "blessings of the breasts and of the womb," and his brothers shall, as he dreamed in his boyhood, "bow down before him."

Last comes the youngest of the sons: "Benjamin is a ravenous wolf, in the morning devouring the prey, and at even dividing the spoil." The words foreshadow the prowess in war later showed by the tribe of Benjamin, especially during the days of Saul, Israel's first king and a member of that family.

With all his affairs in order, Jacob is "gathered to his people" in death and buried with the pomp befitting a great and honorable patriarch, a man whose life slowly transformed him into Israel, one who prevails with God. All Egypt mourns him, and Joseph goes with a funeral cortege to Canaan to bury "him in the cave of the field . . . to the east of Mamre, which Abraham bought . . . from Ephron the Hittite, to possess as a burying place."

Then Joseph returns to Egypt where his brothers are saying, "It may be that Joseph will hate us and pay us back for all the evil which we did to him." But he reassures them, "Fear not . . . you meant evil against me; but God meant it for good . . . that many people should be kept alive. . . . So do not fear; I will provide for you and your little ones." They remain in Egypt, and when Joseph comes to die he repeats to them the promises made to his forefathers:

> God will visit you, and bring you up out of this land
> to the land which he swore to Abraham, to Isaac, and to Jacob.

Then Joseph takes "an oath of the sons of Israel, saying, 'God will visit you, and you shall carry up my bones from here.' "

Centuries afterwards his wish is carried out by Moses, who at the exodus from Egypt, remembers to take with him the body of Joseph. This Moses, when his turn comes to die, repeats Jacob's blessings on the tribe of Joseph—blessings which recall the images of Joseph's early dreams:

> Blessed by the Lord be his land,
>   with the choicest gifts of heaven above . . .
> with the choicest fruits of the sun,
>   and rich yield of the months,
> with the finest produce of ancient mountains,
>   and the abundance of the everlasting hills. . . .
> (DEUT. 33:13–15)

His dream of sheaves, fulfilled in Egypt, will find richer completion in the prosperous fields which his tribe will own in the land of promise. As long as the "everlasting hills" shall stand, his story, shaped by marvelous artistry and high patriotism, but above all by devoted commitment to the God of Israel, shall ring in Israel's memory.

After Joseph, who has brought his people into Egypt, they will stay there for four hundred years. Of this long time the Bible says only that the Israelites grew "fruitful and increased greatly . . . they grew exceedingly strong." Then arose a new king "who did not know Joseph" (Ex. 1:7–8). Fearing them the Egyptians begin to oppress them, until at last God sends a deliverer in Moses to set them free from slavery and lead them to the borders of that land so long promised.

Moses' last words about Joseph, mentioning "ancient mountains," and "everlasting hills," set the key for his own life. In Egypt, the lowland, the people will come down to the lowest point of their early history—into a slavery they will never forget. Moses will lead them to freedom across a high arid plateau. Joseph, for the most part, has not been aware how the Lord was using him as an instrument; Moses will always know. His will be courage unshakable as solid bulk of mountains; awe at God's high transcendence and man's small stature; wide vision like a view from mountaintops.

Beyond all this, his place on the heights of mountains is a point of intersection of earth with sky, of man with the Lord, and so he becomes a mediator, a man standing between humanity and divinity, fighting to lift up mankind, and to draw down mercy from God. His story begins in Exodus, the next book of the Bible.

Journey Toward the Promises

CHAPTER EIGHT

Moses: Man of Mountains

It is one thing to see the land of peace from a wooded ridge and another to tread the road that leads to it.
(St. Augustine)

Abraham and Jacob have wandered with their sheep over level plateaus; Joseph has ruled in the lowlands of Egypt. Now comes Moses whose true place is on mountains. From high peaks where he is at home—feet steady on solid rock, head haloed by deep sky—he listens to the voice of God, pleads with heaven, surveys earth unrolled to far horizons, and strides down toward people who lift their eyes to see him tower between heaven and hard rocks.

Four books are dominated by him: Exodus, Leviticus, Numbers, Deuteronomy; but they are not pure biography since his life has significance beyond his single self; he is founder of a nation that has influenced the world out of all proportion to its size or wealth, and shaper of a faith that has changed history. Exodus is partly narrative, giving the wonderful story of God's revelation of himself to Moses, and his intervention by means of this chosen leader to save captive Israel. With chapter 20 and the climactic reception of the decalogue, Exodus changes to a presentation of laws, the ordering of a constitution which helped to unify a scattered people.

Next Leviticus describes the liturgy designed for the honor of Yahweh; his must be a royal worship recognizing his transcendence as well as his intimate concern with the people whom he rules as king. After this, Numbers tells of Moses' work in organizing the young nation, while Deuteronomy presents magnificent orations placed by early writers on his lips as farewell speeches. This practice of attributing appropriate words to heroes was a common custom among ancient historians; an example has already appeared in Jacob's oracles. Here the speeches give, without doubt, a true picture of Moses' thoughts and personality, though he may not have actually said all the words. Scholars are still engaged in attempts to discover more about the historical person of Moses as distinguished from what he became in later tradition. Each has its own kind of truth.

Since interest in the present chapter is mainly on the human and literary aspects of Moses' life, certain passages which reveal him most vividly are selected—Exodus 1–21; 32–33; Numbers 11–14; the beginning and end of Deuteronomy. Shaping Moses' life is a design, three times repeated, of lowland events climaxing on mountaintops: his infancy and youth are set in rich Nile marshes, then he flees to the desert, living there a while as shepherd before he climbs the peak of Horeb (also called Sinai) to receive and respond to a momentous call from Yahweh. This call raises him to lonely eminence above the people who are to crowd the land below him.

In the second part Moses returns to Egypt to struggle with Pharaoh, leads his people through waters into wilderness, where he becomes their shepherd, and ascends again the mountain of his first vision to accept a vocation for Israel. During the third part he displays noteworthy leadership by learning to delegate authority, coping with rebellion, and bringing a conquering nation to the borders of the promised land, where from his last high place he makes his farewell, and dies lonely on the mountaintop. Here the Lord buries him, and "no man knows the place of his burial to this day" (Deut. 34:6).

From Nile and desert he goes to receive his mountain call; across the same desert he travels to the same mountain to hear Israel's call; through further wilderness he leads his people until he climbs the mountaintop from which he hears God's last call and goes forth to death. Such is the pattern.

Down by the Nile water,
Below the palace, where the steps left off,
In the mild, shallow water, stiff with reeds.[62]

Moses' story opens near the Nile where his people, now grown numerous since the days of Jacob and Joseph, are feared and oppressed by their Egyptian overlords, who make "their lives bitter with hard service, in mortar and brick." Moreover, a cruel edict stands against them, for Pharaoh has given orders: "Every son that is born to the Hebrews you shall cast into the Nile."

During this crisis a woman of the tribe of Levi bears a son: seeing that he is "a goodly child, she [hides] him three months." When she can conceal him no longer, she takes "a basket made of bulrushes," daubs it with pitch, and placing the child in it, she sets it among "the reeds at the river's brink."

Sluggish in its backwater, the river flows around the miniature Noah's ark. Moses' mother sets his sister Miriam to watch, and soon, says the story, an Egyptian princess, in a quiet place at the water's edge, comes upon the basket. A modern poet tells the scene:

Neither the circle of the fish's splash
Nor the crane's rusty cry
Troubled the sleeping reaches of the stream
which brought the child where Pharoah's daughter stood,
Who smiled to watch him while he slept.[63]

Pharaoh's daughter feels pity, but the reader is aware of irony here. Her people are killing the children of Israel, but in the future this Israelite boy will be involved with the death of Egypt's sons.

Another touch of irony appears in the fact that the boy's sister comes out of hiding and is sent to find a nurse, but the one she brings is the child's own mother who thought she had lost him. The story, besides, reverses the pattern found in most tales of lost children. Usually a royal infant is found by poor people, and after many adventures restored to his kingdom. Moses, on the contrary, is child of an enslaved family, adopted by royalty, and choosing, when he is grown, to leave the kingdom and throw in his lot with his own unfortunate people.

Who shall ascend the hill of the Lord?
And who shall stand in his holy place?
(Ps. 24)

The life of Moses has begun with his rescue by a princess; soon he will set out on a career of rescuing others, acting with sympathy and decisiveness. He is a man with a tremendous sense of responsibility, one who finds himself called to assume care for a childish and irresponsible multitude. The first scene of his adulthood occurs when he sees "an Egyptian beating a Hebrew, one of his people." Looking about fearfully, "and seeing no one," he kills the Egyptian and buries him there "in the sand." A non-biblical tradition relates that the man he defended was Joshua who later succeeded him as leader.

The incident reveals a personality conflict in the great Moses, a fear of consequences to himself. Many times he is to suffer such fear. His weakness throws into relief Yahweh's sovereign choice, his power to transform the man he calls. From another point of view, the reader is drawn to admire the objectivity of the writer, who admires Moses, yet does not hide his faults.

On the next day Moses tries another rescue, intervening between two Hebrews who have come to blows. Angered, the assailant asks, "Do you mean to kill me as you killed the Egyptian?" Then finding his deed strangely come to light, he grows afraid and flees the country. Just as his days alternate between level lands and high peaks, so his character and moods shift between fear and courage, despondency and exaltation.

He arrives in the land of Midian, and works another rescue. Resting near a well, he encounters the daughters of a man named Jethro (also called Reuel). Hostile shepherds try to interfere with their flocks, but Moses drives the men away, and Jethro offers him grateful hospitality. Moses remains there, marries one of the daughters, and begins to enjoy a lasting friendship with the stalwart Jethro.

The young Moses, used to the bustle and luxury of Egypt's court, finds new life as shepherd of Jethro's sheep. "Leading his flock to the west side of the wilderness," he learns a love of high and lonely places. One day he comes to "Horeb, the mountain of God," where he will be transformed into a shepherd of Yahweh's people, and on another momentous day, leading them, he will return to this same mountain. During his days on the windy plateau, his people in the lowland are "groaning under their bondage," and crying "out for help," but God hears them and remembers "his covenant with Abraham, with Isaac, and with Jacob." Heaven is concerned about happenings on earth and will lean down to Moses on a mountain.

> The word of God falls on the field
> of the heart
> and grows there like a seed
> (VON BALTHASAR)

Guarding his sheep there on Horeb, Moses suddenly sees flame rise in a bush, yet the bush does not burn. He approaches, and from the bush the Lord speaks his name—destiny calls out. The man hears an invitation to a lifetime of rescue, which will be effected not by his own power, but in the strength of God. "Through the entire tradition regarding Moses' call appears an attitude which [puts God] to the fore as the real doer of what is done. Moses' 'Who am I?' is met with no assurance that he is just the man for the task but only with the promise: 'Certainly, I will be with thee.' . . . And the amazing thing is that he was able to keep himself in the background, to stamp the movement which he initiated with the divine name and not his own . . . so that Yahweh got credit for it all."[64]

But first Moses learns the infinite distance between himself and divinity when God speaks to him from the flaming bush: "Moses, Moses!"

"Here am I"—his answer characterizes his continuing attitude of readiness toward God.

Then the Lord tells him: "Do not come near; put off your shoes from your feet, for the place on which you are standing is holy ground." And he goes on, "I am the God of your father, the God of Abraham, the God of Isaac, and the God of Jacob." Overcome by awe, Moses hides his face, for he is "afraid to look at God."

The Lord, however, intends deeds of mercy: "I have seen the affliction of my people who are in Egypt, and have heard their cry. . . . I know their sufferings, and have come down to deliver them out of the hand of the Egyptians, and to bring them . . . to a good and broad land, a land flowing with milk and honey."

> Come, I will send you to Pharaoh,
> that you may bring forth my people,
> the sons of Israel, out of Egypt.

Henceforward Moses' compassion for the poor and his sense of responsibility will find full scope. Still, he has not yet the solid strength of mountain bulk. As any man nerving himself for a heroic task, he at first weighs the obstacles. He tells God he is no leader but a fugitive from Pharaoh's justice; he does not even know the Lord's true name; he will not know how to persuade the Hebrew leaders of the genuineness of his mission.

One by one the Lord gives answers: he will become a leader because he is chosen; he will announce the Lord's own mysterious name which is I AM WHO AM; he will prove his mission by working three wonders. These will mark his authority and at the same time symbolize dependence on God—for power of leadership, for physical strength, for all that supports life.

First, at the Lord's command he casts his staff, which signifies the shepherding of sheep and even a kingly scepter, to the ground; it becomes a serpent and Moses shrinks back from it in physical fear. The scepter has turned limp and useless—no one rules sheep or men with a staff that bends. "Put out your hand," says the Lord, "and take it by the tail," and obedience causes it to stiffen and become a staff again. So Moses' leadership will be strengthened by Yahweh. The serpent, moreover, a prominent symbol in the idolatrous rites of surrounding nations, is here nullified by divine power and human obedience.

Next he must put his hand into his tunic, only to draw it out covered with leprosy. Physical horror must have struck him, and a shrinking from the isolation which would follow upon the disease, along with a sharpened sense of man's precarious hold on life. The sweep of the lonely wind of death turns him cold. But God tells him to repeat the gesture, and his hand is healed. The lesson of his dependence on God even for existence has struck home.

As a last sign, the Lord tells him, "Take some water from the Nile and pour it upon the dry ground; and the water . . . will become blood," which signifies death when it is poured out. Egypt, until now, has shed the blood of Hebrews; the waters of Nile, lifeblood of that land, through Moses' action will turn to blood and fail to support life; and worse still, blood will deluge Egypt, when in punishment for Pharaoh's resistance to God all the firstborn sons of Egypt shall die.

Still Moses hesitates, arguing that he is a man of little eloquence, "slow of speech and of tongue," but he is overruled, and trudges down the mountain to begin his dreaded task. His hand is laid in the great hand of Yahweh, and though he may feel joyless and ashen with fear, he must go on. He carries a staff that marks him as ruler, yet his rule is not his own; he is rather Yahweh's instrument, a "staff" by which God works to make his plans effective. Moses certainly felt the human frustrations of his role, the clash between opposing tides of feeling, yet to the end he is Yahweh's man.

> Go down Moses, 'way down Egypt land,
> Tell old Pharaoh let my people go
> (NEGRO SPIRITUAL.)

Moses now takes leave of his father-in-law and sets out for Egypt carrying his staff. On the way he meets Aaron, his brother, who goes with him to encounter Israel's leaders. Exodus makes little of the efforts needed to persuade them to strike out for freedom, yet Moses cannot have succeeded easily. To challenge the world power of Egypt was a daring gesture for a helpless people.

Mildly he presents the plan to Pharaoh: "Thus says the Lord, the God of Israel, 'Let my people go, that they may hold a feast to me in the wilderness.' " Pharaoh, of course, refuses:

> Who is the Lord, that I should heed his voice
> and let Israel go?
> I do not know the Lord, and moreover
> I will not let Israel go.

And he commands the taskmasters of the public works to oppress them more grievously: "You shall no longer give the people straw to make bricks, as heretofore; let them go and gather straw for themselves! But the number of bricks which they made heretofore you shall lay upon them, you shall by no means lessen it; for they are idle; therefore they cry, 'Let us go and offer sacrifice to our God.' Let heavier work be laid upon [them] and pay no regard to lying words."

Driven desperate, the men defy Moses until he is hemmed in all around—by God's inexorable purpose, by Pharaoh's resistance, by the people's resentment. But instead of heeding his own anguish he prays: "O Lord, why hast thou done evil to this people? Why didst thou ever send me? For since I came to Pharaoh . . . he has done evil to this people, and thou hast not delivered thy people." Already he is beginning his work as mediator, his lifelong task of bringing together Yahweh and his people, a vocation symbolized by his habit of standing on high mountains between heaven and earth. Here, too, has begun his continuing dialogue with God, that astonishingly familiar interchange which is not matched again until the Bible tells of David, the favored friend of the Lord.

In answer to his plea, the God of Israel repeats to him the promises given to Abraham, Isaac, Jacob—promises that his people shall come to a land of their own, that they shall have sons to possess the land, that they shall stand in a relationship of intimacy to the mighty Lord who leads them.

> I have heard the groaning of the people . . .
> and have remembered my covenant.
>
> I am the Lord . . . and I will redeem you
> with an outstretched arm . . .
> and I will take you for my people,
> and I will be your God. . . .
>
> I will bring you into the land . . .
> I will give it to you for a possession.
> I am the Lord.

As a first step in his plan, the Lord places power in Moses' hands, instructing him to bring plagues upon stubborn Egypt: four will come by means of living things—frogs, gnats, flies, locusts; three because elements are disturbed—water turns to blood, fierce hail falls, darkness covers earth; two by disease—pestilence on beasts, boils on men; and one by a mysterious sword of death in the hands of the Lord's angel.

Literary interest attaches to the plagues because of the varying human reactions of Pharaoh's magicians who can duplicate only a few of Moses' signs; of Pharaoh himself who refuses and consents and refuses again—incurring a plague with each refusal; of Moses who argues adroitly and ever more convincingly.

Pharaoh asks why the people must go into the desert, why not sacrifice here at home? Moses replies that the Israelites sacrifice animals which Egypt holds sacred—"Will they not stone us?" Next the king consents to let the men go, but women and children must remain. Moses' response never wavers: "We will go with our young and our old . . . with our sons and daughters and with our flocks and our herds."

At this Pharaoh grows desperate, "The Lord be with you, if ever I let you and your little ones go! Look, you have some evil purpose in mind." More plagues fall; Pharaoh again consents—but only if they will leave flocks and herds behind. Moses argues, "Our cattle also must go with us; not a hoof shall be left behind, for we must take of them to serve the Lord our God, and we do not know with what we must serve the Lord until we arrive there." He is a master of reasoning, and Pharaoh, defeated, but not convinced, drives him out of the court. The scene is set for the last, most terrible plague.

In telling it, the narrative functions in double fashion, describing how Israel acts in the emergency and how their deeds become a ritual of remembrance. Being sure now that the Lord's power will set them on the road to freedom, they kill a lamb and prepare to eat their last meal in Egypt. An angel of death is on his way, and so they sprinkle their doorposts with the lamb's blood, as a sign that their households are to be spared. The telling rises then to majestic and tragic poetry:

> At midnight the Lord smote all the first-born
> in the land of Egypt,
> from the first-born of Pharaoh who sat on his throne
> to the first-born of the captive who was in the dungeon,
> and all the first-born of the cattle. . . .
>
> And there was a great cry in Egypt,
> for there was not a house where one was not dead.

Through all the countryside sounds the rising lamentation, but where the Israelites dwell all is quiet, because the Lord sees to it that not one dog shall howl there to announce a death.

With a man dead in every house, the Egyptians have no time to hold back the people. They urge them to leave, press jewels upon them as they stand at a wayfarer's meal, staves in hand for the journey, clothes girt about them, ready for swift movement.

The dough not used at this hasty supper is picked up in its vessels without waiting for leaven to make it rise, and to this day at the Passover festival the Jewish people eat matzoth, which is bread without leavening, along with lamb roasted over a fire, and bitter herbs to remind themselves of their sorrow during the leavetaking and hardships of the journey.

Certainly, now that the time of farewell has come, they must feel an inner conflict, that duality which is a universal human emotion. In every goodbye, every time of parting, man feels a kind of release, and at the same time a kind of torment. This mixture of feelings applies to the exodus itself. Probably, for the Israelites that morning of departure, it was hard to decide if this land were prison or home.

This land, which has cut down their pride by ancient sorrows and forced them to unwilling work, has become their own. The anguish they have suffered here has in a sense endeared it to them. Their own past pulls them back to the Nile, and they look to the future with dread. Out beyond them, there is only the desert of freedom, and this too invites while it repels them. As modern philosophy insists, "Freedom is terror," and this journey out of fertile Egypt into the wilderness is a frightening plunge into a world without security. Still, they go on, and setting out in the dark they take along a part of the past, for they carry the bones of Joseph.

> I said, "I will water my orchard
> and drench my garden plot";
> and lo, my canal became a river,
> and my river became a sea.
> (SIRACH 24:31)

In flight they come to a body of water. Scholars say that this was not, as so long translated, the Red Sea, but an arm of waters named the Reed Sea because of sedges in its shallow places. However that may be, they look back from shore and discover the Egyptians close in pursuit, for Pharaoh has again changed his mind. Seeing their fear, Moses stretches his staff over the waters, and the Israelites march "into the midst of the sea on dry ground, the waters being a wall to them on their right hand and on their left." The writer, with a strong sense of the dramatic, raises the scene to epic heights. No words are strong enough to carry his admiration of the Lord's great works on Israel's behalf. "And the Lord went before them by day in a pillar of cloud to lead them . . . and by night in a pillar of fire to give them light, that they might travel by day and by night."

When the pursuers follow, the waters wash back upon "all Pharaoh's horses, his chariots, and his horsemen." This triumph of the Lord and his people is so important that it is told first in prose and then heightened by an ancient triumph song which recounts the event, opening with a shout of praise from the multitude.

> I will sing to the Lord, for he has triumphed gloriously;
> the horse and his rider he has thrown into the sea.

Then the prophetess Miriam, sister of Moses and Aaron, takes "a timbrel in her hand," while all the women follow her, dancing, and the song plays over two themes—of gratitude to the Lord and fierce rejoicing over the fall of foes. Choruses of men and women may have sung alternately. From one side, perhaps, comes the expression of wondering praise:

> The Lord is my strength and my song,
>   and he has become my salvation,
> this is my God, and I will praise him,
>   my father's God, and I will exalt him.

As the women's lighter melody naming God's mercies dies away, the crash of the men's heavier voices may have taken up the theme of vengeance:

> Pharaoh's chariots and his host he cast into the sea . . .
> The floods cover them;
>   they went down into the depths like a stone. . . .

Thou sendest forth thy fury,
it consumes them like stubble.
At the blast of thy nostrils the waters piled up,
the floods stood up in a heap.

The enemy said, "I will pursue, I will overtake . . .
my hand shall destroy them."

But quickly come rescue and rejoicing, for the Lord has mercy and protects his people:

Thou didst blow with thy wind,
the sea covered them;
they sank as lead in the mighty waters.

Who is like thee, O Lord, among the gods. . . .
terrible in glorious deeds, doing wonders?

Because of this wonder, the people learn to fear the Lord, and to put their trust in him and in his servant Moses. It makes no difference to their faith whether the deed was purely miraculous, or was a providential timing of the sudden floods which happen often in desert lands.

So has come a second step in their deliverance. At first an angel of death had passed over the houses of Egypt, killing their first-born, but sparing those houses marked with the blood of the sacrificial lamb; now the people themselves pass over waters of danger and enter into freedom. Both events are kept in remembrance to this day during the Passover festival.

Waters of separation have made leavetaking complete, and the Lord goes before them again in his signs of a pillar of cloud by day, a pillar of fire by night. Many years later, the door of Solomon's temple will open between two free-standing pillars. Art history conjectures that these stood for the pillars of cloud and of fire that led Israel in the exodus.

Now the name of one of those ways was Danger . . .
which led him into a wide field, full of dark mountains
(BUNYAN, *Pilgrim's Progress*)

No strictly chronological account is given of the years in the desert, but rather the journey is shown in vivid incidents whereby

Moses proves himself a true shepherd who provides and rules. Some of his deeds making provision for water, food, and safety may be told here before the people come to the mountain of the Law. After that, Moses becomes more than ever the strong ruler working to lift a whole people toward a superhuman ideal, learning techniques of government, leading the way to victory, quelling rebellion, and leaving them ready to march into the land of promise. But first he must care for physical needs; this he does by his own wisdom and by calling upon God.

The first necessity in the desert is water, and several picturesque scenes have to do with the finding of water. Once, after traveling "three days in the wilderness" and finding no water, the people grow desperate. They find a stream but it is too bitter to drink, so they name the place Mara, which means bitterness. They cry out in their thirst, and the Lord shows Moses a tree whose wood will turn the waters sweet. It is a memorable symbol, this, of tree branches that purify waters.

The march continues southward through the desert, and Moses leads them to new waters at the oasis of Elim, "where there were twelve springs of water and seventy palm trees; and they encamped there by the water." With the careful counting of trees and setting up of shelter the phrases convey a sense of relief and coolness.

Their rest, however, is short-lived, for they press on, and somewhere along the road Moses is confronted with a mysterious test, whether of his patience or his faith, the narrative does not make clear. He is ordered by Yahweh to strike a rock and water will spring from it. He strikes it not once but twice, speaking at the same time in anger, "Hear now, you rebels; shall we bring forth water for you out of this rock?" Whether the two strokes mean hesitation or wrath, he has committed a fault, and the Lord speaks: "Because you did not believe in me, to sanctify me in the eyes of the people of Israel, therefore you shall not bring this assembly into the land which I have given them" (Num. 20:10–12). It is a stern sentence. Never shall Moses' feet walk those hills, nor descend the cleft of Jordan; never shall he feel the land's pastures rich beneath him. This deprivation will add a note of pathos to the end of his life.

Still, through Yahweh's wonderworking power Moses continues to provide, giving food as well as water. When the people suffer hunger they complain:

> Would that we had died by the hand of the Lord
>   in the land of Egypt,
> when we sat by the fleshpots and ate bread
>   to the full;
> for you have brought us out into this wilderness
>   to kill this whole assembly with hunger.

Patiently the Lord answers them, "Behold, I will rain down bread from heaven for you." So Moses and Aaron tell the people, "At evening you shall know that it was the Lord who brought you out of the land of Egypt . . . and you shall see the glory of the Lord, because he has heard your murmurings, [giving] you in the evening flesh to eat and in the morning bread to the full."

Then "in the evening quails [come] up and cover the camp; and in the morning . . . when the dew [has] gone . . . there [is] on the face of the wilderness a fine, flake-like thing, fine as hoarfrost on the ground." This the people gather and grind between millstones, and cook in cakes, "and the taste of it was like the taste of cakes baked with oil" (Num. 11:8). They call it *manna*, which according to some commentators means "What is it?" And their wonderment over these signs of God's care is great. For a while they are content, but when they grow tired of the manna they complain again:

> O that we had meat to eat!
> We remember the fish we ate in Egypt for nothing,
>   the cucumbers, the melons, the leeks,
>   the onions, and the garlic. . . .
>
> But now . . . there is nothing at all
>   but this manna to look at.
>
> (NUM. 11:4–6)

Fish and onions and garlic—these are the memories of Egypt. But the land they long for is one flowing with milk and honey. The words communicate different feelings about the two places.

Their discontent grows too much for Moses, and with that freedom which marks his conversations with the Lord, he bursts out:

Why hast thou dealt ill with thy servant?
And why [dost thou] lay the burden of all this people
upon me?
Did I conceive all this people?
Did I bring them forth, that thou shouldst say to me,
"Carry them in your bosom, as a nurse carries
the sucking child,
to the land which thou didst swear to give their
fathers?

(NUM. 11:12)

To this the Lord makes no direct response, and Moses does not always feel this way about the people, for at the end of his life he talks in different tones—celebrating the manna, reminding Israel of God's wonders, and trying to insure their fidelity:

Take heed lest you forget the Lord your God....
who brought you out of the land of Egypt,
out of the house of bondage,
who led you through the great and terrible wilderness,
with its fiery serpents and scorpions...
who brought you water out of the flinty rock,
who fed you in the wilderness with manna....
(DEUT. 8:11 ff.)

His care is always for this stubborn, rebellious people—finding water for them, and food. Upon occasion he is also called to heal them and to guard against invasion. Once when they have been complaining, the Lord grows so angry he sends poisonous serpents among them, so that many die. They come to Moses saying, "We have sinned . . . pray to the Lord, that he take away the serpents from us." Then their leader makes "a bronze serpent," sets it "on a pole," and if a serpent has bitten any man, he is to "look at the bronze serpent and live" (Num. 21:5 ff.). Here the ambivalent symbol seems to stand for Yahweh's power over man's health.

Besides these dangers, the hostile Amalekites offer battle and Israel for the first time goes to war. Though Moses is a man of decision and courage, yet he appoints another, the young fighting man Joshua, to lead the army, while he himself goes up a mountain to mediate between heaven and earth. On his hillside, overlooking the battle, he raises his arms in prayer, overshadowing the people with protecting presence and pleading with God for them. Or it is possible that his upraised arms were directing the battle. When his arms tire, they are held up by Aaron, his brother, and Hur, the son of Jethro, "so that his hands [are] steady until the going down of the sun," enabling Israel to win victory by the power of the Lord's right hand. Always when Moses stations himself on a mountain, he is trying to pull heaven and earth closer together.

> He made him hear his voice,
> and led him into the thick darkness,
> and gave him . . . the law of life
> and knowledge.
>
> (SIRACH 45:5)

Southward again the people tend, toward that rocky peak where Moses heard his own call. Here he accepts for his people a new responsibility, calling on them to pledge lasting fidelity to a law given by God, to make a promise which will haunt them forever whether they follow or fail. Though the narrative shows a certain confusion owing to varied traditions gathered in it, yet it can be seen to build suspense and solemnity by having Moses ascend the mountain three times before he actually receives the law, and three times afterwards as if he were reluctant to leave the holy place. In the first three he moves to follow God's initiative, in the last three he climbs on his own.

Sinai, also called Horeb, is wreathed in smoke and flame, and he goes up once to learn that there must be mutual faithfulness between Yahweh and his people; again to have the Lord guarantee his position as spokesman; and a third time to carry back a warning that the people must respect the holiness of this place; after such preparation God gives Moses the tables of the law.

On the first ascent, the Lord reminds Moses that his providence has carried this people as if on eagle's wings—maybe Moses' eyes are at this moment actually caught by the sweep of an eagle around the crags. Until now, God's choice of Israel has been gratuitous—they have not earned his favor, nor been asked to prove loyalty by specific obedience. Now he calls them to respond:

You have seen what I did to the Egyptians,
 and how I bore you on eagles' wings
 and brought you to myself.

Now therefore, if you will obey my voice
 and keep my covenant,
you shall be my own possession among all peoples . . .
 a kingdom of priests and a holy nation.
(Ex. 19:4–6)

To this the people, hearing Moses speak for the Lord, respond with one voice, "All that the Lord has spoken, we will do." Their promise, freely given, is a permanent commitment.

A second time Moses goes up to bring back "the words of the people to the Lord," and God promises to speak to him from "a thick cloud," so that "the people may hear when I speak with you . . . and believe you forever." Now, says he, "Go to the people and consecrate them . . . let them wash their garments, and be ready by the third day. [Tell them], 'Take heed that you do not go up into the mountain' . . . whoever touches the mountain shall be put to death."

This message, too, he carries down, and "on the morning of the third day," there are "thunders and lightnings, and a thick cloud upon the mountain" so that all the people tremble. But Moses leads them "out of the camp to meet God" who speaks to him there, and summons him to the top of the mountain for the third time.

After all this preparation, Moses must have expected some great revelation, but God at first merely repeats the earlier warning:

Go down and warn the people,
lest they break through to the Lord to gaze
and many of them perish.

With characteristic freedom he replies: "The people cannot come up . . . for thou thyself didst charge us, saying, 'Set bounds about the mountain, and consecrate it.' " As at the burning bush, so here again, the mystery must be reverenced by separation, by awe and respect for holiness.

" 'Go down,' answers the Lord, 'and come up bringing Aaron

with you.' So Moses went down to the people and told them."

Then without transition the narrative shows him for the fourth and central time on the heights. Apparently he has sent Aaron down again to care for the people. Here Moses receives from the Lord the tables of that law, whose core is the ten commandments, and whose precepts are to govern humankind's relationships to God and to men. The code appears in Exodus 20, and is summed up by the Lord in the two great commandments: to love the Lord wholly, and love one's neighbor as oneself.

The people have pledged their obedience; the law shows them how to carry out the pledge. It is a law of freedom, a framework for life within which men may arrange the details of their days. This pledge on Sinai along with the giving of the decalogue, makes the third in the series of five salvation events. First came the promises made to Abraham—God's initiative in the covenant; then his practical carrying out of his pledge by the exodus, the deliverance into freedom; now the promises are extended to the whole people, they pledge returning fidelity, and are given workable rules for carrying out their promise.

Since the Lord will remain with this people, they desire some tangible sign of his presence, and much of the rest of Exodus, along with nearly the whole of Leviticus, is taken up with provisions for the ritual of public worship. A noteworthy aspect is the building of the ark of the covenant, which is described in Exodus 25 as a chest or box of acacia wood, which grows near Sinai, a little more than 3 × 2 × 2 feet, plated inside and out with pure gold, and having four gold rings at the corners through which poles were thrust for carrying it.

The account is a compilation of details from different ages. In the wilderness this ark is housed in a simple leather tent, and often carried before the people into battle. In the days of the temple it becomes a chest having winged figures called cherubim at each end, and kept in the inner sanctuary, called the holy of holies. These cherubim are not representations of God, but are rather thought of as supports of the invisible God, and they resemble those hieratic beast figures used in Assyria and elsewhere to uphold the thrones of their powerful rulers. The presence of the ark indicates that Yahweh is Israel's king.

From Moses' vision of unearthly majesty and power on the

mountain, where he now stays for forty days and forty nights, the writer in Exodus 32 shifts to a scene in the valley below, where the people are in trouble. Because Moses delays they gather around Aaron saying, "Up, make us gods, who shall go before us; as for this Moses, the man who brought us up out of Egypt, we do not know what has become of him." It is startling to see how the writers of the Bible never conceal the faults of their people. Such an attiude is unknown in the histories of contemporaneous Egypt, Assyria, Babylonia, whose histories are filled with great exploits, and seldom mention failings at all. They have nothing like the psychological understanding of the Hebrews.

Aaron makes no objection, calls for jewelry, and from it fashions a gold image which they fall to worshiping. This golden calf may have been a representation of Yahweh himself, and not a false god, but still the writers condemn any worship which resembles the idolatrous rites of the surrounding peoples.

Seeing their infidelity, the Lord of the mountain says to Moses: "This is a stiff-necked people; now therefore let me alone, that my wrath may burn hot against them." His words indicate a recognition of Moses' power as mediator; it is as if God cannot punish the people so long as Moses defends them. Then the Lord calls for an act of supreme devotion. He offers to substitute Moses' own sons as his chosen people instead of Israel; he says he will make them a great nation. In the light of the long tradition of promises indicating the gift of a numerous posterity as one of Israel's dearest hopes, Moses' renunciation is amazing.

He refuses to forsake Israel or to consent that his sons shall replace them:

> Why does thy wrath burn hot against thy people? . . .
> Why should the Egyptians say, "With evil intent
> did he bring them forth,
> to slay them in the mountains"?

And he goes on to remind the Lord of his covenant: "Remember Abraham, Isaac, and Israel, thy servants, to whom thou didst swear . . . 'I will multiply your descendants as the stars of heaven, and all this land that I have promised I will give to them.' " Then the Lord repents, and Moses comes down from the mountain carrying the tables of the law.

As he draws near the calf and the dancing his wrath flares up. He throws the tables down, breaking them on the rocks, and then taking the calf, he melts it in the fire, grinds it to powder, puts it into water, and makes the Israelites drink. Probably the act is intended as a trial by ordeal, and the worst offenders expected to find themselves poisoned by the drink.

It must have been an impressive scene—the flicker of the sacrificial fires meeting and matching the flaming radiance around Moses' head, and the rage of his gestures answered by the terrified flight of the dancing crowds. In his anger, Moses rails against Aaron, and calls upon his own tribe of Levi to punish the worst offenders with death. It may be that their support at this time won them their later honor as the priestly tribe.

Three times Moses has ascended in preparation, and on the fourth journey he has received the law. Three times now he goes up: as mediator to win pardon, as close friend of God privileged to see his glory, as a host who invites others to God's dwelling place. In the three preliminary ascents of the mountain, he had climbed at God's invitation. Now with a friend's intimacy, he himself chooses, in each of these incidents, to go up and meet God.

In spite of the people's defection, Moses' love for them remains steadfast, and he turns to the mountain again, begging pardon for them from God: "This people have sinned a great sin; they have made for themselves gods of gold. But now, if thou wilt, forgive their sin—and if not, blot me, I pray thee, out of thy book which thou hast written." To such lengths does he go—first giving up opportunity for his sons' heritage, and now sacrificing his own claim to God's favor by offering to have his name erased, for Israel's sake, from the list of God's friends. The Lord is moved to pardon, and the pattern is set for Israel's history: a story of repeated rise and fall in which they rebel and are punished; they repent and are forgiven, until an overwhelming impression emerges of the enduring patience of Yahweh with this perverse yet strangely loyal people.

Moses himself, all the while, grows in compassion for them and intimacy with the Lord. In a beautiful scene, he asks a favor for himself—that God will give him a sight of divine glory. And the Lord says:

Behold, there is a place by me where you shall stand
upon the rock;
and while my glory passes by I will put you
in a cleft of the rock,
and I will cover you with my hand until I have passed by;
Then I will take away my hand,
and you shall see my back;
but my face shall not be seen.

Like a loving father with a young son God has made Moses ready, placing the man's feet on solid mountain, standing him, as one might steady a child, in a cleft where he will not fall, and shielding him with his hand lest he be dazzled by the light. Moses can look up only after God has passed by. Because no man can see God's face and live, Moses will see only the back of God's glory—a mysterious phrase—that will be enough for his joy.

One other mysterious scene takes place before the people leave the mountain. It is Moses' last ascent of Sinai. This time it sounds as if the Lord makes a concession and allows human beings to look upon him and still not die.

Moses invites Aaron and seventy elders, appointed earlier to help him, to come up the mountain. He is enough at home with God to extend such an invitation. On the heights they see "the God of Israel; and there [is] under his feet as it were a pavement of sapphire stone, like the very heaven for clearness." Everything is shining glory in the Lord's own kingly palace. And all marvel, because God does "not lay his hand on the chief men . . . they beheld God, and ate and drank" (Ex. 24:9–11). Even though the Bible does not say they looked upon his very face, still the writer shows his awe at their experience here.

When Moses comes down from the mountain after such con verse, he does not know that his face has become radiant, but the people are dazzled, so that he must put a veil over his face when he talks to them. Supported now by God's intimate friendship, and bearing a newly carved copy of the law, Moses prepares to lead the people on, following the pillar of cloud. It is a new exodus, a departure from the mountain where they have met the Lord, a journey into a fierce and trackless desert.

> Moses was a man set apart . . . by a consuming sense of the presence and the reality of God, [and] he was a man among men in his assumption of responsibility.[65]

God goes before them as a cloud by day, a fire by night. They rebel, yet are irrevocably his; they find fault with Moses, yet trust him to the end. Through the years he increases in stature, never despairing, never growing satisfied to save a selected remnant, but fighting to lift all Israel to his own austere level of faith. As they go, he shows leadership by wise sharing of authority, coping with rebellion, and welding the people into unity. At the borders of Canaan he leaves them ready to fight for the land.

One of the gifts of a true leader is the ability to recognize the qualities of others, and to trust subordinates. Moses, earlier, has taken Aaron as a helper, and appointed Joshua to lead the armies against Amalek. He bestows generous praise on his helpers; for example, when he is teaching the people to beautify the tent of worship. Then he introduces a craftsman by telling of his accomplishments: "See, the Lord has called by name Bezalel the son of Uri . . . has filled him with . . . ability, with intelligence . . . and with all craftsmanship, to devise artistic designs, to work in gold and silver and bronze" (Ex. 35:30–32). Such scenes show his nobility, his lack of anxiety about his own honor, his care for the people's good and for Yahweh's honor.

He can also listen to advice from others. Once while the Israelites are encamped close to God's mountain, Jethro, his father-in-law, comes to visit. During his days there, Jethro sees all that Moses is doing for the people, and inquires: "Why do you sit alone, and all the people stand about you from morning till evening?" He is about to give Moses a lesson in the efficient delegation of authority.

"When they have a dispute," he says, "they come to me and I decide between a man and his neighbor, and I make them know the statutes of God and his decisions."

"What you are doing is not good. You and the people with you will wear yourselves out. . . . Listen now to my voice. . . . Choose able men from all the people . . . men who are trustworthy . . . and place [them] over the people. . . . Every great matter they shall bring to you, but any small matter they shall decide themselves . . . and they will bear the burden with you . . . and all this people will go to their place in peace" (Ex. 18).

With good grace Moses obeys. The scene shows his devotion to the people, his humble good sense in taking advice, the tact and wisdom of Jethro, and the warmth of their relationship. Jealousy finds no home in Moses.

His openheartedness appears clearly in a scene that takes place after he has chosen his helpers. Upon these men, as upon Moses, the spirit of the Lord rests. Two of them, however, show little docility, for when Moses summons them to the tent of meeting, they remain instead at the encampment and begin to prophesy without leave. This is reported, but Moses, instead of being angry, is glad:

> Are you jealous for my sake?
> Would that all the Lord's people were prophets,
> that the Lord would put his spirit upon them!
> (NUM. 11:29)

If they bring praise to God and help to the people, this is all that matters. He does not resent their disobeying his own orders.

> Lo, the wicked bend the bow,
> they have fitted their arrow to the string,
> to shoot in the dark at the upright
> of heart. . . .
> (Ps. 11:2)

Moses' humility, however, is not weakness. At least three times he quells rebellion with a strong hand, and twice inspires victories that find long celebration in Israel's tradition. His family rebels, three of his company defy him to his face, and the leaders of ten tribes revolt.

Once through envy his sister Miriam, along with Aaron, lodges two complaints—that Moses has married a foreigner, a Cushite woman, and that he has set himself up as sole ruler: "Has the Lord indeed spoken only through Moses? Has he not spoken through us also?"

"Now the man Moses was very meek," and slow to take offense

at slights. Because only his own honor is at stake he makes no protest, but the Lord vindicates him:

> Hear my words: if there is a propret among you,
> I the Lord make myself known to him in a vision,
> I speak with him in a dream.
> Not so with my servant Moses;
> he is entrusted with all my house.
> With him I speak . . . clearly,
> and not in dark speech.

And sternly addressing the culprits, God asks: "Why, then, were you not afraid to speak against my servant Moses?" (Num. 12).

Then, in punishment, Miriam, who must have been the instigator, become a leper, "as white as snow," so that Aaron is moved to plead for Moses' intercession: "Do not punish us because we have done foolishly and have sinned. Let her not be as one dead, of whom the flesh is half consumed when he comes out of his mother's womb." And bearing no grudge, Moses cries to the Lord, so that after seven days she is healed.

Another rebellion is followed by fearful disaster. Three men named Korah, Dathan, and Abiram, driven by ambition, call an assembly and accuse Moses and Aaron:

> You have gone too far!
> For all the congregation are holy, every one of them,
> and the Lord is among them;
> why then do you exalt yourselves above the assembly
> of the Lord?
>
> (Num. 16:3)

Now they are challenging not merely Moses' reputation, but his integrity—accusing him of self-seeking and misusing God's trust. He therefore turns for help to the Lord:

> Do not respect their offering.
> I have not taken one ass from them,
> and I have not harmed one of them.

Then calling an assembly of his own, he warns the crowds, "Get away from about the dwelling of Korah, Dathan, and Abiram . . . lest you be swept away with all their sins."

So Korah, Dathan, Abiram, with their families and followers, stand before their tents, with Israel facing them, and the bleak mountains standing guard. And Moses gives his answer:

If the Lord creates something new,
and the ground opens its mouth,
and swallows them up,
with all that belongs to them,
And they go down alive into Sheol.

Then you shall know that these men
have despised the Lord.

At his word the ground opens, and they go down "alive into Sheol; and the earth closed over them." So swift is the vengeance that vindicates the friend of God.

A more widespread revolt, motivated by fear, brings about a tragic reversal in Israel's fortune. It happens when they have come to the eastern border of Canaan. Moses chooses scouts, a man from each tribe, to explore the land: "Go up into the Negeb yonder, and . . . the hill country, and see what the land is, and whether the cities . . . are camps or strongholds, and whether the land is rich or poor, and whether there is wood in it or not. Be of good courage, and bring some of the fruit of the land." So they first set foot on the promised land at the "season of the first ripe grapes" (Num. 13).

They penetrate as far as Hebron, "and cut down from there a branch with a single cluster of grapes, and they carried it on a pole between two of them"—food enough for giants. "The land," they tell the people, "flows with milk and honey, and this is its fruit. Yet the people who dwell in the land are strong," like giants, beside them "we seemed to ourselves like grasshoppers."

Such words terrify the people. Though Moses assures them that the Lord has given the land, and now is the time to win it, yet their faith falters. Caleb and Joshua, alone among the twelve scouts, remain loyal. They urge immediate attack, but still the people balk. Fearing for themselves and their children, they even threaten to stone Moses and his two helpers.

Then God loses patience and says to Moses, "How long shall [they] murmur against me. Say to them, 'As I live . . . not one shall come into the land where I swore that I would make you dwell, except Caleb . . . and Joshua . . . But your little ones, who you said would become a prey, I will bring in, and they shall know the land. . . . But as for you, [you] shall be shepherds in the wilderness forty years."

Moses rails at their faults, begs the Lord to spare them, and when, too late, they muster to attack, he sees them suffer grave defeat, and hears them sentenced to forty years more in the desert. This generation will not enter the land; it will be given to their children—those children for whose sake they did not obey. This is the people's testing place, and they fail. It is the greatest setback of the long journey, comparable to the setback Moses met when he failed his test at the striking of the rock in order to obtain water. He cannot go into the land; neither, now, can the people who are alive at this time.

> All these are ours
> And we are the People of Heaven. Tells us no lies
> On our noons made loud by abolished clans.[66]

Rebellions are plentiful, but successes come too. Yahweh and Moses keep faith, and so in their own way do these strange and fickle people. Therefore the Lord prospers them. Numbers 22–24 shows how they looked to an alien king, Balak of Moab, and Balaam, his hired prophet. Israel is a horde that will devour Moab "as the ox licks up the grass of the field." This crowd of slaves brought out of Egypt has become a conquering nation. The masterly story of Balaam tells how he tried, at Balak's insistence, to lay a curse on Israel, but the Lord made him bless them instead. But since it is a fully developed short story, it will be treated by itself in the next chapter.

Two victories, over Og, the king of Bashan, and Sihon, Amorite king of Heshbon on the high plateau fifteen miles east of Jordan mouth, show that Balak of Moab has grounds for his fear. Og is memorable for his gigantic "bedstead of iron." "Nine cubits was its length, and four cubits its breadth." His defeat is swift and Israel takes his lands. The details of his great size show the people's fear beforehand and their pride after victory.

The battle with Sihon lives in tradition especially because of a song, a victory chant which Sihon had earlier used when he defeated Moab. Now Israel, having conquered Sihon in his turn, uses his own words to taunt him:

Come to Heshbon, let it be built
let the city of Sihon be established.
For the fire went forth from Heshbon,
flame from the city of Sihon.
It devoured Ar of Moab,
the lords of the heights of Arnon.

The spirited phrases make the modern reader regret that the ancient martial melody is lost. By singing of Sihon's former greatness, Israel magnifies its own victory. As Sihon used to shout woe upon his foes, so now woe is his from the Israelites:

Woe to you, O Moab!
You are undone, O people of Chemosh!
He has made his sons fugitives,
and his daughters captives. . . .
So their posterity perished,
from Heshbon, as far as Dibon,
and we laid waste until fire spread
to Medeba.

Even the place names have a fierce incantatory magic. Israel is so proud of the victory and the song, that the names of Sihon and Heshbon sound through at least fifteen other chapters in the Bible. Echoes of it ring out in Deuteronomy, Joshua, Judges, Jeremiah, Psalms, Esther, Judith, and other books.

Moses' work is nearly finished now. Two vivid pictures sum up his accomplishments—at the beginning, a slave nation under Egyptian taskmasters; at the end, an irresistible people about to make themselves masters of the land so long promised. But though they are grown strong, still Moses will not leave them untended, as sheep without a shepherd. He therefore calls several solemn assemblies, resigning his leadership into the hands of Joshua, his helper, and speaking his last counsels in words of noble farewell.

> What a man he must have been who wrought the pattern and stamped it upon a few thousand half-nomads more than three millennia ago.[67]

These last counsels and blessings are embodied in the book of Deuteronomy, where some of the most superb examples of ancient oratory appear. The book is made of three (or some say four) orations attributed to Moses, and appendices containing his famous song, his final blessing, and the stark words describing the tragedy and triumph of his death.

Deuteronomy's power to move hearts appears in a highly dramatic incident (2 Kings 22 ff.) during the reign of King Josiah, long after Moses. The people had fallen into idolatry and Josiah did not know how to win them back to their faith. One day men working in the temple found a book of law which undoubtedly contained much of what is now Deuteronomy. Josiah called the people together and had the book read aloud. Its words set off a sudden and widespread reform; it was as if the great leader Moses himself spoke to his people again, and his voice could still reach their hearts.

If such results came from a mere reading of Moses' words, what enthusiasm must have filled the people who heard him in person! It is easy to picture him in a characteristic stance high on the plateau east of Jordan, looking down upon the listening people. Deuteronomy suggests at least three such assemblies with speeches which emphasize first the past (1:1–4:43), then the present (4:44, 26, 28), finally the future (29–30). A long section of laws appears in the second speech, and a miscellany is gathered at the end.

The first oration, reviewing Israel's history since the exodus, reminds them that the Lord has kept his promises, has carried his people through the desert "as a man bears his son, in all the way that you went" (Deut. 1:31). The second calls on them now to obey the law whose primary note is love:

> Hear, O Israel: The Lord our God is one Lord;
> And you shall love the Lord your God with all your heart,
>   and with all your soul,
>   and with all your might.
> And these words . . . shall be upon your heart . . .
> And you shall write them on the doorposts of your house
>   and on your gates.
>
> (Deut. 6:4–9)

The gathering of laws at the heart of this section (12–26) is expressed in the forms of liturgy, aimed at repetition so that God's message should remain in mind.

This second speech ends with twelve curses intended for those who do not keep the law, and to these the people are to answer *Amen.* Then comes a series of blessings pronounced in the voice of Moses. They contrast the serving of the Lord in joy and abundance with the serving of evil in hunger and thirst. The choice is clear:

> Behold, I set before you this day
> a blessing and a curse:
> the blessing, if you obey the commandments
> of the Lord your God . . .
> and the curse if you do not obey.
> (DEUT. 11:26–28)

"And you shall rejoice before the Lord your God, you and your sons and your daughters." Remember what he did "to the Egyptian army," to Sihon and Og, and remain faithful.

Gradually a change has come about in the revelation which shapes Israel's life—a shift towards ethics, toward moral responsibility. With Abraham, Isaac, Jacob, it was enough that they should worship the Lord as their own God. No code of laws was set up, beyond the ordinary rules needed for family and tribal life in Bedouin encampments. The Lord had promised to bless these people, not for their merits, but purely out of his free choice, because they were his.

After Moses, they have the law, with its emphasis on blessings that result from fidelity. If they obey, then God will "give rain . . . in its season, the early rain and the later rain." Bible writers linger over the word *rain* as if, in this dry land, even the name brought refreshment.

> For the land which you are going over to possess
> is a land of hills and valleys, which drinks water
> by the rain from heaven,
> A land which the Lord your God cares for. . . .
>
> It is not like the land of Egypt . . .
> where you sowed your seed
> and watered it . . . like a garden
> of vegetables.
> (DEUT. 11:10 ff.)

Because the promised land is watered by rain from heaven, not, as with the overflow of the Nile, by rivers of earth, therefore its prosperity depends directly on God—that God to whom they have sworn loyalty. He will give fruitfulness from the sky in rainfall if they keep their oath.

The third oration (Deut. 29–30) stresses the days to come. Future generations will rise against Israel if they fail, yet if they return to the Lord and heed his voice, he will bring them home again; though they be driven to the farthest corner of the world, even from there the Lord will gather them. Plainly, the writer puts later events into the mouth of Moses. The people after him do fall away, and lose the land of promise, and then are brought home again after their chastisement. Here too begins a theme which the prophets later develop—the thought that Israel's misfortunes are its own fault. No other nation has ever shown such candor in recounting its own history.

After this last speech, the final chapters of Deuteronomy present a song attributed to Moses, his blessing on the tribes, and his death. Though the song (32:1–32:47) was written after his time, perhaps about 1060 B.C. during the reign of Saul, yet Moses' thoughts are believable here, and the writer leads one to see him singing before all the people about the mercies of God.

There he stands on Nebo, the peak of Pisgah, that rises east of Jericho, city of palms. Looking westward past their lifted faces at the green of that city deep in Jordan's cleft, he sings his triple theme: of Yahweh the Rock who sends rain to make earth fruitful; of the people who have spurned their saving Rock; of the divine power which routs enemies and calls his people back to himself. Back and forth the thought swings, like a pendulum swaying between God and man; moving from joyous praise to lament for rebellion, to the return of joy after sorrow.

The song is didactic, but strong, enthusiastic, and full of insight. It "is a justification of Yahweh's dealings with Israel, but it is also an ode celebrating Yahweh's . . . triumph over His (and Israel's) enemies."[68] In a cosmic sweep, Moses calls on all creation to listen:

> Give ear, O heaven, and I will speak;
> and let the earth hear the words of my mouth.
> May my teaching drop as the rain,
> my speech distil as the dew.

Then his vision pictures Yahweh as a strong rock, like the impregnable bluff on which Jerusalem stands. He sees, too, the waste places transformed by God into a fruitfulness rich as Jericho's tropical green before him:

> Ascribe greatness to our God!
> The Rock, his work is perfect. . . .
> He found him in a desert land,
> and in the howling waste of the wilderness;
> He encircled him, he cared for him,
> he kept him as the apple of his eye.
>
> Like an eagle that stirs up its nest,
> that flutters over its young,
> spreading out its wings, catching them,
> bearing them on its pinions,
> the Lord alone did lead him. . . .
> and he made him suck honey out of the rock.

Next, in part two of the song he shifts to biting irony, using an untranslatable word, a kind of pet name for Israel: "But Jeshurun waxed fat, and kicked. . . . You were unmindful of the Rock that begot you, and you forgot the God who gave you birth."

For this infidelity the Lord will send warring enemies to wreak punishment, and will ravage the fruitful land by fire, "For a fire is kindled by my anger, and it burns to the depths of Sheol . . . and sets on fire the foundations of the mountains."

> And I will send the teeth of beasts against them,
> with venom of crawling things of the dust.

Such will be the result of their forgetting God's law.

Finally, the third part of the song mourns the fact that Israel is slow to see God's finger in her misfortunes, slow to repent, until the Lord brings her back to himself. The images of fruitfulness return, but in distorted form:

> For their vine comes from the vine of Sodom,
> and from the fields of Gomorrah;
> their grapes are grapes of poison,
> their clusters are bitter;
> their wine is . . . the cruel venom of asps.

But the Lord will "have compassion on his servants," and suddenly his divine voice speaks, calling Israel to listen:

> See now that I, even I, am he,
> and there is no god beside me;
> I kill and I make alive;
> I wound and I heal.

All days and all events are in his hand. Therefore, concludes the song in a paean of praise:

> Praise his people, O you nations;
> for he avenges the blood of his servants,
> and takes vengeance on his adversaries,
> and makes expiation for the land of his people.

In its beginning the song called on the heavens and the whole cosmos to listen, now these heavens and all creation are to sing out, echoing Moses' voice in triumphant music.

Again, as in the exodus, Moses' words put before the people the peril of freedom, the need for commitment. Their God values free choice above all. Whether they find good fortune or ill, rain for their crops or the bright sword of fire, they are free.

Looking his last at this free people, Moses bestows his final blessings. Like the oracles of Jacob, they are a poetic description of the later history of the tribes, and were probably used in after times for sacred processions to or in the temple. In such a scene, "as the tribes pass by they hear the oracles of blessing concerning themselves, so that the occasion is a kind of cultic review of Israel." [69]

An introduction to the oracle (Deut. 33:2–5) sings the glory of the Lord who "came from Sinai, and dawned from Seir upon us; he shone forth from Mount Paran," accompanied by "ten thousands of holy ones, with flaming fire at his right hand." Then come blessings on each of ten tribes—Simeon and Issachar are not mentioned, perhaps because they early lost tribal identity. A comparison with Jacob's oracle (Gen. 49) reveals a change in the position of Levi, the tribe of Moses. In Genesis, Simeon and Levi were cursed for their cruelty to Shechem, here Levi has become the priestly tribe entrusted with the law, with sacrifice, and with determining the Lord's will for petitioners.

The most generous blessing goes to Joseph, whose sons Ephraim and Manasseh founded two tribes. Some phrases are obscure, and a few words may have been lost, yet the blessings are full of beauty and power, especially in the pure realization of God's majesty, his awe-inspiring transcendence, coupled with his immanence, his daily and intimate concern with all that affects his people:

> There is none like God, O Jeshurun,
> who rides through the heavens to your help,
> and in his majesty through the skies.
> The eternal God is your dwelling place,
> and underneath are the everlasting arms. . . .
> Happy are you, O Israel! Who is like you,
> a people saved by the Lord, the shield of your help.

Moses stands on the mountain to sing, and names three great mountains in his song—Sinai, and Seir, and Mount Paran. Now from his mountain lookout, God shows him a sweeping view of the ideal boundaries of the promised land, from Dan in the north to the Mediterranean on the west, from the badlands of the Negeb, and tropical Jericho at his feet, to the southern end of the Dead Sea.

But, says the Lord, though "this is the land of which I swore to Abraham, to Isaac, and to Jacob, 'I will give it to your descendants,' " and "I have let you see it with your eyes. . . . you shall not go over there." The remembrance of his fault at Meribath-Cades, when he struck twice the rock that flowed with water, has haunted Moses' speech. It occurs at least six times in Deuteronomy, and merges in his words with the people's failure when the scouts returned with their tales of giants in the land. Now that fault must be expiated.

From the heights of lyric exultation in the song, the writing drops down to simple bare prose, a powerful way to tell of Moses' solitary journey and death. In four steps he goes to meet that doom which is also his triumph: climbing his last mountain—Nebo, the headland of Pisgah; taking his last long look over the land he can ever enter; dying his lonely death there on the stark mountain peak; being buried there "in the valley in the land of Moab opposite Beth-peor." But "no man knows the place of his burial to this day." So he leaves the people below to mourn for their great hero.

> And there has not arisen a prophet since in Israel like Moses,
> whom the Lord knew face to face,
> none like him for all the signs and the wonders
> which the Lord sent him to do in the land of Egypt . . .
> and all the great and terrible deeds which Moses wrought
> in the sight of all Israel.

Swept at times by impulse as mountain peaks are swept by winds, yet steadfast as those pure bones of mountain forms, the pyramids of Egypt where he began, Moses stands alone in grandeur; alone in his wide view of the people's future and his vision of a redeeming God who works through man; alone in his passionate appeals to the people to keep Yahweh's covenant of faith and his law of moral rectitude; alone on mountains poised between heaven and earth.

He lived a mystery of separation, climbing high, standing on peaks to meet God, finding there a vision of order and fruitfulness, becoming a mediator, a protector of the valleys below as mountains shield the land from storms. Moses, more than any other, is a man of mountain peril and mountain glory.

CHAPTER NINE

Balaam: A Man in a Corner

THE noble courage of Moses, the unforgettable power of his life, contrast strangely with the comic figure of Balaam (Num. 22–24) who appears suddenly during Israel's wilderness journey while Moses is still alive. Balaam tries to do evil and finds himself forced to do good. He is driven into a corner by Yahweh's unrelenting love for these people. At the same time he is pushed into physical corners by a serious angel and a stubborn donkey.

For all its grave import, the Bible is full of such comic episodes. Jonah, for example, skulks under a gourd vine, wanting the Lord to destroy a whole city just to save face for his prophet; Christ stops under a famous tree with large leaves to peer up at the rich man hidden there, and the crowd halts too and looks up, as crowds will when someone stops to stare. And then Zaccheus, the man short of stature, forgets all his dignity and scrambles down before the gathering. As Chaucer says, "men must not make earnest of game," not be too stodgy to laugh when laughter is in order, nor to delight in fantasy when the fanciful invites response. It is a recognition of truth.

Chagall's pictures, for instance, are full of the Bible, full of reverence, yet in his dream world donkeys sail through the air lightly as clouds and men ride with ease on the backs of serene-looking roosters. And another Jewish artist, Shalom Moskovitz (See *Horizon*, July 1961), who lives now in Galilee, touches Old Testament stories with humor. In one picture he portrays with naive seriousness the slaying of Egypt's firstborn, man and beast. They lie in neat rows, all dead but for one donkey who slips off the left edge of the picture alive.

An older artist in the Bible's book of Numbers uses a folk

story about a talking donkey and the soothsayer Balaam to tell of God's care for Israel. The story was already old when he adapted it to his purposes. The people are making their difficult journey across the Sinai desert, crossing a land edged and guarded by forbidding mountains. Sudden as a wedge of sky through a mountain gap, this story lights the road. The poet Hopkins has a phrase for such swift shafting of light. He says: "Sky betweenpie mountains lights a lovely mile." Triangular between dark peaks the clear blue shines down.

The short tale tells how the neighbors feared the prosperous Israelites, whom Yahweh's power and Moses' leadership have shaped into a mighty people. Balak, a Moabite king, therefore sends for the soothsayer Balaam to curse them. Balaam is willing but the Lord resists him, and he knows his curse is ineffectual without God's ratification. Exquisite artistry appears in the story's shaping. It falls into three parts in a two, three, four pattern: two embassies which reveal human motives in humorous fashion; three halts on a journey caused by a talking donkey who is surprisingly matter of fact about such fantastic powers; four visions of Israel's greatness phrased in majestic poetry by the reluctant prophet.

The first part gives a humorous view of two men who think money is exceedingly important. Balak, king of Moab, is a man with a gift for metaphor who believes money can buy anything, even a curse for his enemies. Balaam is a non-Hebrew prophet, a soothsayer who would like to sell his curse if only the Lord would let him. Because of this conflict, he finds himself continually hemmed in, driven into corners.

At the beginning Balak appears, a frantic little man, looking out over the plains at the Israelite camp. As he looks, he keeps thinking of the people as a powerful and threatening beast: "This horde will now lick up all that is round about us, as the ox licks up the grass of the field." Because they "cover the face of the earth," and are settling down opposite Moab, he sends the first embassy to Balaam: "Come now, curse this people for me, since they are too mighty for me."

So the chiefs of Moab set out "with the fees for divination in their hand" and come to Balaam. They are welcomed with oriental leisure and hospitality: they must stay the night. Meanwhile, Balaam will consult the Lord. The storyteller, then, in simple fashion, pictures the Lord coming to ask Balaam what these men want. He explains carefully, and is told: "You shall not go with them; you shall not curse the people, for they are blessed."

Reluctantly he tells the messengers that the Lord will not allow him to go. Balak, the king, when they return, is not discouraged. He merely thinks this is a way of striking a better bargain. He sends another embassy, "more in number and more honorable than they," saying, "Let nothing hinder you from coming to me; for I will surely do you great honor, and whatever you say to me I will do; come, curse this people for me."

But Balaam answers, "Though Balak were to give me his house full of silver and gold, I could not go beyond the command of the Lord." His speech shows his regret at refusing a tidy profit. He translates Balak's offer of reward into terms of gold and silver, which were not named in the message. Still, he pleads again, and this time the Lord, like a parent giving in to a child's insistence, says he may go. So he saddles his donkey and sets out. Then begins one of the famous comic journeys of literature. Since the messengers do not witness it, one gathers that they probably went on ahead with their swift camels. The story plays on the notion that the beast sees better, is wiser than his master. On the way, Balaam is hedged into narrower and narrower places.

As he rides, an angel, whom he cannot see, stands in the way. The ass, however, sees the angel and edging away from the road takes to the open fields. It is a space wider than the path. Balaam, at this, beats "the ass, to turn her into the road."

Next the angel chooses a smaller space in which to accost them, "a narrow path between the vineyards, with a wall on either side. . . . When the ass [sees] the angel of the Lord, she [pushes] against the wall, and [presses] Balaam's foot against the wall." Again he beats her forward.

At last the angel moves to a "narrow place, where there [is] no way to turn either to the right or to the left." It is the tightest corner of all. They are wedged in, and since they cannot get out the ass lies down under her rider. The reader responds with amused sympathy for both man and beast when Balaam falls into a rage and beats her "with his staff."

But now, says the storyteller, the Lord endows the animal with speech, and she remarks without rancor: "What have I done to you, that you have struck me these three times?" The innocent question calls for a chuckle—one would think even an ass would know what she has done to make Balaam angry.

Without showing any surprise at the donkey's power of speech, Balaam tells her: "Because you have made sport of me. I wish I had a sword in my hand, for then I would kill you."

Still she answers peaceably, recalling their long and amicable life together, "Am I not your ass, upon which you have ridden all your life long to this day? Was I ever accustomed to do so to you?"

"No," says he. But we hear no more of what he might have said, because suddenly his eyes are opened and he at last sees the angel whom the ass has seen all along. The angel's first words reproach him for beating the animal: "Why have you struck your ass these three times? . . . If she had not turned aside from me . . . I would have slain you and let her live." It seems to be a reference to Balaam's threat to use his sword on the beast.

"I have sinned," he admits, "for I did not know that thou didst stand in the road." Humbly he tells of his own blindness, and by implication the better vision of his donkey. Besides this irony, another lies in the fact that the reader knows Balaam will soon be unable to speak the curse he wishes to, while the donkey has been given speech.

Balaam even offers to go home again now, but the angel tells him to go on, warning him, however, that he may speak "only the word which I bid you." It might seem that Balaam has suffered enough reproaches from the ass and the angel, but when he arrives the king scolds him too, and as might have been expected, he talks about money: "Why did you not come to me? Am I not able to honor you?"

The prophet, however, answers only that he is here now, and adds uneasily that he still can say nothing except what the Lord allows. It sounds again as if he would like to comply and so earn Balak's gold, but he doubts his power to do it. Nevertheless, he will try.

Because Balaam is willing to barter he seems to think the Lord can be bribed to change his mind. Plainly he has been told that he is not to curse this people, still before the first three attempts to do just that, he has Balak raise "seven altars, and provide . . . seven bulls and seven rams" for sacrifice. Then he goes off to see what God will say.

The words the Lord puts four times into his mouth show an ascending pattern of: 1) statement of purpose, followed by blessing of Israel in—2) the past; 3) the present; 4) the future. He begins by announcing that he is not going to curse a people whom the Lord does not condemn.

> From Aram Balak has brought me,
> the king of Moab from the eastern mountains:
> "Come, curse Jacob for me,
> and come, denounce Israel!"
> How can I curse whom God has not cursed?
> How can I denounce whom the Lord has not denounced?

And he falls to praising the Israelites encamped below him:

> From the top of the mountains I see him,
> from the hills I behold him;
> lo, a people dwelling alone,
> and not reckoning itself among the nations!
> Who can count the dust of Jacob,
> or number the fourth part of Israel?

"What have you done to me?" cries Balak. "I took you to curse my enemies, and behold, you have [blessed] them." Still he feels that Balaam may have been overcome by the wide view of Israel's strength: "Come with me to another place, from which you may see them; you shall see only the nearest of them, and shall not see them all. . . . And he took him to the . . . top of Pisgah." Here sacrifices are offered as before, and when Balaam prays the Lord puts "a word in his month," saying, "Return to Balak, and thus shall you speak." He begins to see that he cannot change the Lord's mind for him.

> Rise, Balak, and hear;
> hearken to me, O son of Zippor:
> God is not man, that he should lie,
> or a son of man, that he should repent.

Then in his second blessing he reviews the glories of Israel's history:

> He has not beheld misfortune in Jacob;
> nor has he seen trouble in Israel.
> The Lord their God is with them,
> and the shout of a king is among them.
> God brings them out of Egypt;
> they have as it were the horns of the wild ox.

Here is the early metaphor repeated, while Balaam thinks of Israel's past, of her glorious deliverance from Egypt. These people are like the wild ox; or rather, an even more powerful beast: "As a lioness it rises up and as a lion it lifts itself; it does not lie down till it devours the prey, and drinks the blood of the slain."

Understandably, Balak grows impatient. "Neither curse them at all, nor bless them at all." If he cannot curse, let him at least not shower blessings on them. But he will try one more view. There is some truth in his suppositions. A change in one's position, in one's point of view, will often alter one's actions. "Come now, I will take you to another place; perhaps it will please God that you may curse them from there." He is not so sure now; he says "perhaps."

They go through the same sacrificial preliminaries, but now Balaam, who could not see an angel plain on his path, realizes that his vision has strengthened. He does not go, "as at other times, to look for omens," but looks out at Israel "encamping tribe by tribe," and speaks boldly: "The oracle of Balaam the son of Beor, the oracle of the man whose eye is opened . . . who hears the words of God [and] sees the vision of the Almighty."

What he sees is the present glory of Israel, the majesty of God's people. His words are famous. In them he shares his broad vision from this wide and windy mountain of "Peor, that overlooks the desert":

> How fair are your tents, O Jacob,
> your encampments, O Israel!
> Like valleys that stretch afar,
> like gardens beside a river,
> like aloes that the Lord has planted,
> like cedar trees beside the waters.

He is looking out toward the desert, and so all these images of cool and fructifying waters become more refreshing. The sensation is like that evoked in T. S. Eliot's "Journey of the Magi," when the wise men, after traveling hard roads in the "very dead of winter," come down

> to a temperate valley,
> Wet, below the snow line, smelling of vegetation;
> With a running stream and a water mill beating
> the darkness.

Then the prophet repeats the images of the wild ox and the lioness, concluding with: "Blessed be every one who blesses you, and cursed be every one who curses you."

At this "Balak's anger [is] kindled against Balaam, and he [strikes] his hands together." All his money and trouble have gone for nothing. "I called you to curse my enemies, and behold, you have blessed them these three times. . . . Now flee to your place." "I said, 'I will certainly honor you,' but the Lord has held you back from honor."

And it is clear that Balaam is still regretting the lost rewards, for even as he insists that he could not do anything "beyond the word of the Lord," he reiterates his earlier speech about money: "Did I not tell your messengers . . . 'If Balak should give me his house full of silver and gold, I would not be able . . . to do either good or bad of my own will; what the Lord speaks, that will I speak?' "

Then for good measure he speaks a last prophecy, talking this time about Israel's future:

> A star shall come forth out of Jacob,
> and a scepter shall rise out of Israel. . . .
> By Jacob shall dominion be exercised,
> and the survivors of cities be destroyed!
> Enduring is your dwelling place,
> and your nest is set in the rock.

The star and the staff or stem from Israel's root are enshrined in the Christmas liturgy, as prophecies of the savior to come, and so Balaam, for all his human cupidity, is immortalized in his own words.

After this the story ends swiftly: "Balaam rose, and went back to his place; and Balak also went his way." So they vanish—two men brought to life by a superb storyteller, and a donkey who charms those who hear her speak. With humorous insight into psychology, folklore fantasy, and high poetry, the story's purpose is fulfilled. The Lord, indeed, has a care for Israel; no man may lay a curse on these people. Jacob shall "crush the forehead of Moab" and all his enemies. This tale has served as an interlude. In the next chapter some of Balaam's prophecies of victory find fulfillment, for the mighty leader, Joshua, sets forth to battle and wins for Israel a place in the promised land.

Winning the Country

CHAPTER TEN

Joshua: Courage and the Clash of Arms

In . . . phrases that glorify the defeat of an enemy there is a strong and heady wine. . . . Much of the Old Testament is a sort of dual epic of invasion and defence.[70]

MOSES is dead. The people stand, poised like a wave before its fall, on the eastern edge of the promised land. In front of them lie hills which break and tumble to the north-south cut of Jordan, then rise abruptly on its western side to form the central mountain country. This is turn eases down into foothills which level out to form the Mediterranean coastal plain. It is a rough land, this one so long promised by the Lord, and its five lengthwise strips of terrain are further broken across by secondary earth faults shaping pockets where small kingdoms shelter. Such land contours would make any sweep of conquest unlikely, yet the book of Joshua, which glorifies national history, shows the people thundering across the jagged landscape like waves pouring westward toward the sea.

This is epic glorification, and Joshua, an Ephraimite, the leader left by Moses, is an epic hero. He shows little of the psychological complexity of Moses, but thinks in singleminded terms of war and of Yahweh as God of war. Epic heroes stride in seven-league boots, living lives of large gesture under wide skies. Epic materials —and this is true of Joshua—spring from diverse sources cherished in national tradition; epic singers telescope or expand incidents with literary freedom, making little of defeat and much of victory, pausing to develop trivial happenings into vivid semblance of life and relegating important events to a sentence; epic is filled with a sense of the marvelous. All this is true of Joshua's book, which presents an idealized history in heightened narrative.

Of Joshua as a human being we see only a profile, a silhouette. Painters say that objects reveal themselves in three ways—by silhouette, by light and shadow, by color. With Moses, lights and shadows played over the complexity of his character, revealing and concealing. One saw him, for example, taken up into a dark cloud to meet the Lord, but never found out how he felt about his visions, what was his human response to them. Much of his life is lived in regions beyond human words. Jacob is a different case; he has appeared in bold colors and vivid incident. Though complex in character, his life is not as enigmatic as that of Moses. David will be one of the richest studies, combining subtle shades and flaunting colors with the play of light and shadow. Joshua, however, stands stark against harsh outlines of jagged rocks, armed for war, committed to his own vision of Yahweh as Lord of battles, and to his own mission of securing the promised land for Israel.

The book of Joshua is divided into three sections: the conquest (chap. 1–12); the division of the land (13–21); Joshua's last messages (22–24). Its purpose is twofold: to demonstrate Yahweh's faithfulness to his promises, and to show Joshua's worth as successor to Moses. For the first, the book's main subject matter is the winning and settling of the land promised by the Lord, and its whole narrative is infused with the biblical view of Yahweh as Lord of history, shaping human events to his own ends. All that happens is his direct doing, and indirect, secondary causes are passed over. This is most important in understanding the book. If a storm hinders an enemy, Yahweh is at work; if Joshua sees need to destroy a city, the ban is Yahweh's order; if the hours of daylight last long enough to suffice for victory, then Yahweh has slowed down the sun.

To carry out his second aim, the writer shows Joshua as a man of stature, first by naming courage as his dominant trait, and second by patterning many incidents of his life after the doings of Moses, that greater man. As Norman K. Gottwald says in *A Light to the Nations*, "The student of Joshua's life cannot fail to be impressed by the many similarities to the life of Moses. Moses crossed the Reed Sea; Joshua the Jordan. Moses sent spies ahead to Hebron. Joshua dispatched spies to Jericho. Moses instituted circumcision at Sinai, and Joshua at Gilgal. Moses celebrated the Passover in Egypt, and Joshua at Gilgal. Moses gave the law at Sinai, and Joshua at Ebal. Moses officiated at the covenant at Sinai, and Joshua enjoined the covenant at Shechem. . . . Moses 'took off his shoes' before the burning bush, and Joshua removed his sandals in the presence of the sword-bearing messenger of God."[71]

Still, Joshua's call is specific to him, unique to his personality and circumstances; his life is given to war and to distributing the spoils of war. Herein he is his own man and Yahweh's, not an echo of Moses. The warrior stands alone. His doings begin in Exodus and Numbers, and his life falls into a pattern marked off by recurring ceremonies: 1) his personal apprenticeship under Moses followed by his call; 2) two preparations for invasions and a Passover celebration; 3) two battles and a covenant renewal; 4) two large-scale campaigns, the division of the land, and a dedication ceremony performed by the Transjordan tribes; 5) two farewell speeches attributed to Joshua, climaxing with his people's renewed consecration to Yahweh. The story ends with a short account of his death and burial, and the burial of the bones of Joseph at Shechem—the last event bringing the long exile of Jacob's sons full circle, with Joseph the first to go to Egypt, brought home again.

Moses first saw God in solitude;
Joshua in fire and thunder.

Joshua is made ready for his life's work by an apprenticeship to courage: he faces human foes, natural dangers, and the mystery of God. In each early appearance he is involved with war or exercising bravery in some way, and his life's commitment is to Yahweh as God of war. At Rephidim, in the first battle after Egypt, he engages Amalek in conflict, while Moses on a mountain prays with outstretched arms (Ex. 17:9 ff.). At Sinai, he ascends the holy mountain and sees Moses called, amid fire, thunder, and earthquake, into the "glory of the Lord" whose face no man can look on and live (Ex. 24:13 ff.).

Later when he descends the mountain with Moses and hears Israel celebrating its worship of the golden calf, he, like a true warrior, says these are sounds of battle, but Moses interprets them as revelry (Ex. 32:17 ff.). Again in the meeting tent, after Moses has spoken with God, the young Joshua is so struck with awe that he will not move out of the tent (Ex. 11:28 ff.). Finally, when Moses sends twelve scouts ahead into Canaan, ten of them return and instigate panic in the people. They say that giants live in the land. Only Joshua and Caleb urge the immediate attack which Yahweh wills and Moses commands. But the Israelites in their fear will not move until it is too late, then tardily they attack, suffer defeat, and for cowardice and rebellion are sentenced to wander another forty years in the desert. Courage, then, marked by steadfastness and zeal—such are Joshua's virtues, and his dominant interests are Yahweh and warfare.

> Let each man march to the drummer he hears
> (THOREAU)

Joshua's call is spoken by Moses in words of poetry. He summons the young man, and "in the sight of all" names him leader. The call is framed between exhortations to courage:

> Be strong and of good courage;
> for you shall go with this people
> into the land which the Lord has sworn
> to their fathers to give them;
> and you shall put them in possession of it.
>
> It is the Lord who goes before you;
> he will be with you, he will not fail you
> or forsake you;
> Do not fear or be dismayed.
> (DEUT. 31:7–8)

Then Joshua is filled with wisdom because Moses has laid hands upon him. Therefore "the people of Israel [obey] him, and [do] as the Lord" has commanded (Deut. 34:9). And after Moses' death God is lavish in repeating his promises to this new leader:

Moses my servant is dead;
now therefore arise, go over this Jordan,
into the land I am giving . . . to the people of Israel.

Every place that the sole of your foot will tread upon
I have given to you,
as I promised Moses.

(Jos. 1:2–3)

Three times God repeats the call to bravery, telling Joshua to "be strong and of good courage" in winning the land, in obeying the book of the law, and in putting all his trust in the Lord: "I will be with you; I will not fail you or forsake you. . . . Only be strong and very courageous." Joshua has his call and his reasons for courage. Immediately he acts.

I looked over Jordan and what did I see
comin' for to carry me home . . .
(Negro Spiritual)

By two steps he makes ready for invasion, then he pauses for worship. This pattern he will follow again and again. His first act is to follow Moses' example and his own early experience as a spy by sending two spies to explore Jericho, for that city lies across Israel's intended path. The writer tells their adventures in lively fashion, expanding the scene in epic style, and furnishing an image of a dangling scarlet rope that teases men's imaginations to this day.

The scouts take refuge with a harlot named Rahab, a resourceful woman with an eye out for her family's safety. Her house forms an actual part of Jericho's wall, which was no neat strong rampant, but rough earthworks piled between houses already built. Now it is "told the king of Jericho," that these aliens are in his land. He has reason for worry. These Israelites have defeated Sihon and Og, and the news has preceded them; they have frightened Balak, king of Moab, so severely that he has called in the prophet Balaam to curse them.

Jericho's ruler, therefore, sends messengers bidding Rahab to put out the visitors. Instead, with her spirit of independence, and her intuition of Israel's coming victories, she hustles them up to her flat Palestinian roof, and hides them "with the stalks of flax which she had laid in order on the roof" to dry. Then she goes down to confront the pursuers while, on the sunny roof, snug under the flax, the men grow drowsy. But before they can sleep, she comes back to them saying:

> I know that the Lord has given you the land,
> and that the fear of you has fallen upon us. . . .
>
> For we have heard how the Lord
> dried up the water of the Red Sea before you . . .
> and what you did to the two kings . . . Sihon and Og. . . .
>
> And as soon as we heard it, our hearts melted,
> and there was no courage left in any man.

"Now then, swear to me by the Lord that as I have dealt kindly with you, you also will deal kindly with my father's house, and give me a sure sign [that you will] deliver our lives from death."

"Our life for yours! If you do not tell this business of ours, then we will deal kindly and faithfully with you when the Lord gives us the land." Then she lets them "down by a rope through the window, for her house was built into the wall, so that she dwelt in the wall." As they go, the men tell her—and the effect is as though she leans out the window to hear their parting orders:

> When we come into the land,
> you shall bind this scarlet cord
> in the window through which you let us down. . . .
> If a hand is laid upon any one who is with you
> in the house,
> his blood shall be on our head.

"According to your words, so be it," she says, and when they are gone she ties "the scarlet cord in the window." The rope by which they have climbed to safety will become a sign of protection to their rescuer. Its vivid color hanging loose against the wall, along with the sense of sleep settling over the hidden spies on the roof—such sensuous details linger in memory. They are the stuff of literature. One wonders, too, how much of the later victory is owing to Rahab. She not only shelters the spies, but sends them back to Joshua convinced that Israel is unconquerable.

Upon their return, Joshua promises to abide by the pledge given to Rahab. Then like Moses crossing the Red Sea, he mobilizes the people to cross the Jordan and take possession of the land. Even those to whom Moses had given the lands of Sihon and Og, land east of Jordan—the Reubenites, Gadites, and half the tribe of Manasseh, are called on to help in the westering movement. Joshua's daring knows no doubts. He is sure that "the Lord will do wonders" among the people.

He gives orders that the ark of the covenant is to be carried first, and "when the soles of the feet of the priests who bear the ark of the Lord . . . rest in the waters of the Jordan," it ceases to flow. "The waters coming down from above stood and rose up in a heap . . . and those flowing toward the sea of the Arabah, the Salt Sea, were wholly cut off." Then the people cross on dry ground and stand opposite Jericho. Clearly the wonders of the exodus are recalled, and when all reach the shore, twelve memorial stones are set up, with Joshua making their significance clear:

> When your children ask in time to come,
> "What do these stones mean to you?"
> then you shall tell them that the waters of the Jordan
> were cut off before the ark of the covenant.
>
> So these stones shall be to the people of Israel
> a memorial forever.

His instructions foreshadow future family rituals like those which commemorate the Passover, with questions to be asked by children and answered by their fathers, in order to keep alive the memory of the wonders worked by Yahweh for his people.

The two events of the spies with Rahab and the crossing of the Jordan are followed by a double ceremony of consecration: of the people and of the fruits of earth. First the Lord says to Joshua:

> Make flint knives
> and circumcise the people of Israel
> again the second time.

The knives of stone are interesting to archeologists as indicating the stage of Israel's culture in this thirteenth century B.C., and the rite must be accomplished this second time because though "all the males of the people who came out of Egypt" were circumcised, "yet all the people that were born . . . in the wilderness" were not so dedicated to God. A new generation has grown up and must be dedicated anew.

This is a pledge and sign of freedom, a reversal of the slavery of Egypt. "This day," says the Lord, "I have rolled away the reproach of Egypt from you." And so the place is called Gilgal, a name that means a "reversal," or a "turning around," a "rolling away."

In a mood of joyful thanksgiving, the people then celebrate the first Passover in Canaan, eating of "the produce of the land, unleavened cakes and parched grain." And the writer, with his flair for the dramatic, adds:

> And the manna ceased on the morrow . . .
> and the people of Israel had manna no more
> but ate of the fruit of the land of Canaan.

Epic style is clear: it is as if the manna has been falling all this time and now suddenly it stops.

Then just as suddenly comes a strange scene, without preparation or clear purpose in the narrative, the only direct vision attributed to Joshua. While he is near Jericho he raises his eyes and one stands "before him with his drawn sword in his hand."

Fearlessly Joshua accosts him: "Are you for us, or for our adversaries?"

And the visitor replies laconically, "No; but as commander of the army of the Lord I have now come."

Joshua falls prostrate, asking, "What does my Lord bid his servant?" Doubtless he expects some portentous message. But all he hears is a direct echo of Moses' early call:

> Put off your shoes from your feet;
> for the place where you stand is holy.

"And Joshua did so." So the incident ends, leaving the reader to wonder about its significance. Obviously, it shows Joshua's echoing of Moses' life, but surely a heavenly visitant must have brought some other news.

> Joshua fit the battle of Jericho
> and the walls come a' tumblin' down
> (NEGRO SPIRITUAL)

After this vision, Joshua begins his actual work by conquering two cities, Jericho and Ai, and then celebrating these first victories by a ceremony of sacrifices on Mount Ebal. The siege of Jericho is full of picturesque activity, while that of Ai has a number of interesting sidelights.

At Jericho the Lord tells Joshua:

> You shall march around the city,
> all the men of war going around the city once.
> Thus shall you do for six days.
>
> And seven priests shall bear seven trumpets
> of rams' horns before the ark;
> and on the seventh day you shall march
> around the city seven times,
> the priests blowing the trumpets.

Their blast shall be a signal for "all the people" to "shout with a great shout." Then "the wall of the city will fall down flat."

Several interesting things happen here in the way the story is told. The words quoted above intimate that the marching is done in silence until the seventh circling of the seventh day, then the noise is to break out; but a later passage says, "the trumpets blew continually," though the people did not shout or make any noise until the signal. Scholars agree that these and similar discrepancies rise from the welding together of more than one tradition.

Just before the great commotion, Joshua gives his orders:

> Shout; for the Lord has given you the city.
> And the city and all that is within it
> shall be devoted to the Lord for destruction.
>
> Only Rahab the harlot
> and all who are with her in her house shall live,
> because she hid the messengers that were sent.

> But keep yourselves from the things devoted to destruction . . .
> all siver and gold are sacred to the Lord.

Here is a clear instance of Joshua's idea of Yahweh as God of war; soon an occasion will show the misery that comes to those who disobey the ban. But first comes triumph:

> So the people shouted,
> and the trumpets were blown . . .
> and the wall fell down flat,
> so that the people went up into the city,
> every man straight before him.

Like all wars, it is dreadful in its bloodshed, yet to this people who still remember days of slavery, it is a moment for national pride and exultation.

Meanwhile Joshua has not forgotten Rahab. The two spies are sent to bring out "Rahab . . . and all her kindred, and set them outside the camp of Israel." And she dwells "in Israel to this day, because she hid the messengers . . . and sent to spy out Jericho." Later on it appears that she became famous for her marriage to Salmon the Judean from whose line the Messiah came. Both Ruth (4:18–22) and Matthew (1:5) renew her memory.

Recent archeology has shown that the walls of Jericho did fall—from whatever cause: natural event directed by God, storming by Joshua, or directly supernatural intervention. Such is not the case with the next city of Ai, whose name means "The Ruin." It was already a ruin in the days of Joshua, and Professor W. F. Albright of Johns Hopkins University, one of the greatest archeologists, suggests that the city actually attacked by Joshua after Jericho was not Ai, but Bethel which lies nearby. Because of the name "The Ruin," the account may have become transferred in the telling.[72]

The first attack on Ai results in failure. Thirty-six Israelites are killed, and the army flees, so that "the hearts of the people [melt and become] as water." Joshua, like Moses in similar moments, turns in desperation to the Lord. The answer is that Israel has sinned.

They have transgressed my covenant
which I commanded them;
they have stolen and lied,
and put [some of the devoted things]
among their own stuff.

Joshua must discover and punish those who are guilty.

Then comes a dreadful lottery: tribes, clans, families, individuals are singled out in turn until the culprit stands forth—he who has "done a shameful thing in Israel." Like Korah, Dathan, and Abiram, in the time of Moses, he must be executed. But unlike them, this Achan the son of Carmi, shows a humble honesty that wins sympathy; and unlike them no earthquake comes to swallow him up:

Of a truth I have sinned, [he says],
and this is what I did:
when I saw among the spoil a beautiful mantle from Shinar,
and two hundred shekels of silver, and a bar of gold . . .
I coveted them . . . and they are hidden
in the earth inside my tent,
with the silver underneath.

When the things are found as he has said, then "all Israel [stones] him with stones," and raise over him "a great heap of stones that remains to this day."

With the ban removed, Joshua again rallies his men, planning his strategy with cunning. He picks out "thirty thousand mighty men of valor" and gives instructions to "lie in ambush against the city, behind it"—west of it. Meanwhile Joshua with another force will advance from another side. "And when they come out against us, as before, we shall flee before them; and they will come out after us, till we have drawn them away from the city." Then "you shall rise up from the ambush, and seize the city." The ruse succeeds; Ai is taken, and it is time for another ceremony.

Joshua builds "an altar in Mount Ebal to the Lord, the God of Israel . . . an altar of unhewn stones, upon which no man has lifted an iron tool." The writer remarks that this was in keeping with the law of Moses, but one is tempted to see a relationship between the lack of iron tools here, and the use of the stone knives in the earlier scene of circumcision. On the altar they place offerings, and there Joshua inscribes "upon the stones a copy of the law of Moses."

"And all Israel, sojourner as well as homeborn . . . stood on opposite sides of the ark . . . half of them in front of Mount Gerizim and half of them in front of Mount Ebal." And then were "read all the words of the law, the blessing and the curse, according to all that is written in the book of the law." The people are being reminded of the conditions of their consecration. Soon, with one voice, they will renew their binding pledge.

> So they fought on and the iron tumult
> went up into the brazen sky
> through the barren bright air.[73]

Now in quick succession the book tells of two great campaigns in the south and in the north, but these are preceded by the only touch of humor in the book. This section will end, after the division of the conquered lands, by the building of an unusual altar on the bank of the Jordan. The humorous incident is the Gibeonite conspiracy.

Frightened by the victory at Ai, these close neighbors of the fallen city plan a crafty trick. They make ready provisions, and take "worn-out sacks upon their asses, and wine-skins, worn-out and torn and mended, with worn-out patched sandals on their feet . . . and all their provisions . . . dry and moldy." With these stage trappings they plan to fool Joshua into believing they have come from some far-off place.

Arriving at Gilgal, no great distance, they announce to Joshua, "We have come from a far country; so now make a covenant with us." Then showing their provisions they go on, "Here is our bread; it was still warm when we took it from our houses . . . but now, behold, it is dry and moldy; these wineskins were new when we filled them, and behold, they are burst; and these garments and shoes of ours are worn out from the very long journey.

"From a very far country your servants have come, because of the name of the Lord your God; for we have heard . . . all that he did in Egypt, and all that he did to the two kings . . .

Sihon the king of Heshbon, and Og king of Bashan." The nicely climaxing speech is aimed, not only to win sympathy, but more to prove that they come from a place so far that the Israelites would have no wish to conquer it.

"So the men [partake] of their provisions, and [do] not ask direction from the Lord." By this the reader is alerted to the foolishness of their act. So "Joshua [makes] peace with them, and . . . a covenant with them." This oath will, years later in David's time, have terrible consequences for the sons of Saul, Israel's first king.

But trouble is closer than that. Within three days the Israelites learn that these people are from nearby—their city may well have been next along the victorious route. Still, an oath sworn in the name of Yahweh may not be revoked. They can never attack this territory. They do, however, claim some vengeance by forcing the Gibeonites to work for Israel, making them "hewers of wood and drawers of water for all the congregation." The phrase has become a catchword in the English language—"hewers of wood and drawers of water."

Quickly the truth of the alliance is put to the test. Israel is committed to defending this crew of Gibeonites. "Adonizedek king of Jerusalem," hearing how Joshua has taken Ai, and "how the inhabitants of Gibeon [have] made peace with Israel" grows fearful because Gibeon is "a great city, like one of the royal cities, and because it was greater than Ai, and all its men were mighty." He therefore, in his fear, allies himself with four neighboring kings and lays siege to Gibeon.

A desperate message reaches Joshua, and he makes a surprise attack at night. Its terror is conveniently reinforced by a storm—for "the Lord [throws] great stones from heaven upon them as far as Azekah . . . there were more who died because of the hailstones than the men of Israel killed with the sword." The victory is Yahweh's. More will be heard in the book of Judges about this defeated Adonizedek.

Before the battle is over, however, Joshua begins to fear that it will be only a partial success, and so he asks that daylight may last long enough to bring complete victory. His prayer is embedded in one of those ancient and beautiful song fragments we have seen before in songs like Lamech's in Genesis, or the

Song of the Well in Numbers (21:17–18). Joshua prays "in the sight of Israel,"

> "Sun, stand thou still at Gibeon,
> and thou Moon in the valley of Aijalon."
> And the sun stood still, and the moon stayed,
> until the nation took vengeance
> on their enemies.

This is poetry. The cadences sing their way into memory with the music of ancient place names.

But some later and more prosaic editor took the poetry for fact and so he goes solemnly on, "The sun stayed in the midst of heaven, and did not hasten to go down for about a whole day. There has been no day like it before or since." His words, as De Vault says in his commentary on Joshua, "have caused no little trouble to readers in the past. . . . Happily [the pseudo-scientific explanations] are being replaced by a sane exegesis which recognizes the passage for what it is—a highly poetic version of an emotionally charged cry of [Joshua], who hoped for time, for daylight, in which to crush the enemy utterly. The enemy was crushed, so the time was granted, and this is expressed poetically in verse 13a, prosaically in 13b."[74] Joshua concludes his victory by executing the five warring kings, and then moves on to the conquest of southern Canaan in the first of two sustained campaigns.

The account is scarcely more than a listing of victories in which the vanquished are all put to the sword. Joshua probably did kill many inhabitants of these towns, but certainly not all, for the land remained populated by nations who continued to harass Israel.

After the southern successes he seems to have moved through central Canaan (which later came to be named Samaria) without trouble. It is thought that there may have been kinfolk of the Israelites living there—men perhaps who never moved to Egypt, or who had returned at an earlier time. Such people would easily have allied themselves with the newcomers. Whatever the reason, Joshua is soon found in the north at Merom facing a hostile coalition of kings with "a great host, in number like the sand that is upon the seashore, with very many horses and chariots."

The Israelites have not yet learned to manage horses and chariots, so after the battle, they hamstring "their horses, and [burn] their chariots with fire." Again a series of victories is enumerated—some of them probably won after the days of Joshua, but such telescoping of time is common in epic-history. So "Joshua took all that land, the hill country, and all the Negeb and . . . the hill country of Israel and its lowland from Mount Halak, that rises toward Seir, as far as Baal-gad in the valley of Lebanon below Mount Hermon. . . . So Joshua took the whole land, according to all that the Lord had spoken to Moses." And Joshua "gave it for an inheritance to Israel." The section closes with this survey of the lands and peoples conquered, remarking, however, that some survived "in Gaza, in Gath, and in Ashdod." Then follows a long list of all the conquered kings from Sihon and Og to the foreign king at Gilgal, and includes even the king of Jerusalem, though his city was not taken until the time of David.

> . . . The mountains shall drip sweet wine,
> and all the hills shall flow with it.
> I will restore the fortunes of my people Israel,
> and they shall rebuild the ruined cities
> and inhabit them. . . .
>
> (AMOS 9:13–14)

It is time for Joshua to assign the land to the different tribes. The whole portion of Judges from chapter 13 on is full of interest for the historian and archeologist, but it is not literature. A quick survey of the most important locations will suffice here. East of Jordan, the tribes of Reuben, Gad, and half the tribe of Manasseh are settled. A very large section in the south comes by lot to Judah. This will be David's tribe and country, holding leadership in the south and becoming eventually an independent country.

The strongest tribe to the north turns out to be Ephraim, with the warlike Benjamin placed between Ephraim and Judah. Israel's first king will be a man of Benjamin. And after Solomon this northern section will break away from Judah and will be named Israel. In 721 B.C. it will fall before Sargon II of Assyria, and its people carried into captivity. Hence will arise the name, "the lost tribes of Israel." The conquerors will replace those deported, and the mixed group that results will later be known as Samaritans.

To Levi, no expanse of territory is given because their energies are to be consecrated to the service of Yahweh rather than to winning and defending land, but cities within other tribes' possessions are given to them. They therefore do not count as one of the twelve tribes in this case, and the sons of Joseph are divided into two—Ephraim and Manasseh—to make the number complete. These are given independent holdings. This loose confederation of tribes brought together for purposes of defense and worship is sometimes named an amphictyony, and resembles the alliances of some of Israel's neighbors.

The section on the division of the land comes to an end with the ceremony described in Joshua 22. He praises the Transjordan tribes and sends them home:

> You have not forsaken your brethren these many days . . .
> but have been careful to keep the charge
> of the Lord your God. . . .
> Therefore turn and go to your home in the land
> where your possession lies, which Moses . . . gave you.
> Take good care to observe . . . the law . . .
> to love the Lord your God, and to walk in all his ways.

They start off, but in their zeal they perform an act of worship that nearly sets off a civil war.

At the Jordan they build an "altar of great size." The other tribes, hearing of it, assemble "to make war against them." But someone's common sense prevails and an embassy is sent to inquire into the meaning of this altar:

> What is this treachery . . .
> against the God of Israel?
> Have we not had enough of the sin at Peor
> that you must [build] yourselves an altar . . .
> in rebellion against the Lord?

Peaceably the Transjordanites give answer: "The Mighty One, God, the Lord! He knows; and let Israel itself know! . . . We did it from fear that in time to come your children might say to our children, 'What have you to do with the Lord, the God of Israel? For the Lord has made the Jordan a boundary between us and you . . . you have no portion in the Lord.' " They have only been trying to guard their share in Israel's worship, and do not intend the place as a rival shrine. One striking thing here, as in the scene where Joshua led them through Jordan dry shod, is the people's concern for their children—for the future. There must be no cutting off of their descendants from Israel's heritage. The other tribes respond to this reasonable answer with good grace, and the rift is healed.

> Though he heap up silver like dust,
> and pile up clothing like clay;
> he may pile it up, but the just will
> wear it,
> the innocent will divide the silver.
> (Job 27:16–17)

With the same legal formula as that used by Isaac in giving his last blessing to Jacob, a formula which indicates the desire to make one's last will, Joshua now gives his final message to the people. The Lord says to him, "You are old and advanced in years." And Joshua summons all Israel and repeats the words. Then he goes on, in chapter 23, to assure them that if they remain loyal to the Lord he will drive out those nations which remain in the land. But if they abandon him, they can know for certain that the Lord will no longer be their defense.

> But these nations . . . shall be a snare
> and a trap for you,
> a scourge on your sides, and thorns in your eyes,
> till you perish from off this good land.

The alternatives sound like the ritual curses and blessings invoked by Moses in Deuteronomy.

The next chapter is an even older farewell speech. In it Joshua is seen as surveying history from the days of "Terah, the father of Abraham and of Nahor, [who] served other gods," to Isaac, Jacob, Esau, Moses, Aaron and the wonders worked at the Red Sea. He reminds them of Balaam who was forced to bless them, and ends with their recent victories in Canaan.

After such preparation he calls on them to ratify their commitment to the God who fulfills his promises by giving them "a land on which you had not labored," and letting them "eat the fruit of vineyards and oliveyards which you did not plant."

> Now therefore fear the Lord,
> 	and serve him in sincerity and faithfulness;
> put away the gods which your fathers served beyond the River.

But "if you be unwilling to serve the Lord, choose this day whom you will serve. . . . As for me and my house, we will serve the Lord."

Fervently they respond:

> Far be it from us
> that we should forsake the Lord . . .
> who brought us and our fathers
> up from the land of Egypt,
> out of the house of bondage.

Then Joshua takes "a great stone" and sets "it up there under the oak in the sanctuary of the Lord," saying, "This stone shall be a witness against us; for it has heard all the words of the Lord which he spoke to us."

"After these things Joshua . . . the servant of the Lord" dies. And they bury him "in the hill country of Ephraim, north of the mountain of Gaash." And "the bones of Joseph which the people of Israel brought up from Egypt were buried at Shechem, in the portion of ground which Jacob bought from the sons of Hamor." So the long exile which began with Joseph is ended, the journey has come full circle from this land, into slavery, and back again in freedom.

At the end of Joshua's book there is a feeling of great accomplishment. His early hopes, like the wide vision of Moses, showed him all the land—its length from Lebanon in the north to the glitter of the Dead Sea in the south; from the eastern mountains where he looked over Canaan to the Mediterranean's edge. His story has moved in a crescendo of success. After hearing his life call to courage, he has planned his march like a master of strategy. Care and determination mark his sending of spies and crossing of Jordan; courage and canny calculation bring his victories. These victories grow progressively more important. Single cities are taken first, then the whole of the southland, and afterwards the northern expanse. Once occupied, the land is justly portioned out and its defense and cultivation entrusted to separate tribes, who must clear out the remaining pockets of resistance.

With a clear conscience Joshua can bid Israel remain faithful. His own loyalty to Yahweh as God of power, a soldier's God, has never wavered. His fidelity has been plain to the people's sight, not only in his life's work, but also in the ceremonies of worship he has carried out at every major turning point of his career.

The sense of accomplishment in the book is a part of the triumphant unity attained in epic writing. Joshua's victories are heightened in the telling. Judges, the next book of the Bible, shows that victories were often won piecemeal, that after Joshua much work remained until the land could belong fully to the people.

CHAPTER ELEVEN

Kaleidoscope of Judges

After Joshua's death Israel faces a transition period, and some of the most picturesque characters in scripture have their day. Judges, the book which tells of them—a kind of anthology—collects a number of the Bible's liveliest tales. As Judges says, "In those days there was no king in Israel; every man did what was right in his own eyes" (17:6). And often what these men thought right was bizarre—not to say barbaric. For these years of the twelfth and eleventh centuries B.C. are unsettled and uncertain, and the leaders violently individual. Each fights in his way and place to win or to protect some portion of the land, but no single figure emerges with power enough to unify all the tribes.

By describing these chaotic attempts to secure and settle Canaan, the book of Judges aims to show Yahweh's fidelity to a backsliding people. This is the main point of the introduction (1–3). The body of the book (4–16) tells of twelve leaders, twelve military chieftains from different tribes and localities. Six are merely mentioned. All are chosen by God in some emergency and given specific work to do. The last chapters (17–21), which are not closely related to the other material, detail two sinister incidents in the tribal histories of Dan and Benjamin.

Since these last are of more interest as history than as literature, they will not be included here, nor will those judges who appear only as names. Two men, moreover, Gideon and Samson, are centers of developed short stories, and so will be treated laters in Chapters XII and XIII. The rest of the vivid fragments will furnish the substance of this chapter, and since it must be a gathering of bits and pieces, of kaleidoscopic glimpses, it will be somewhat fragmentary in nature. It will conclude with a fairly extended treatment of Deborah and her admirable victory song (4–5), even though she appears early in Judges.

The introductory lesson is put into the mouth of the Lord; God has been a father to Israel, but the people have strayed from his paths:

> I brought you up from Egypt,
> and brought you into the land
> which I swore to give to your fathers.
>
> I said "I will never break my covenant with you,
> and you shall make no covenant
> with the inhabitants of this land;
> you shall break down their altars."
>
> But you have not obeyed my command. . . .
> So now I say, I will not drive them out . . .
> but they shall become adversaries to you,
> and their gods shall be a snare to you.

Upon hearing these threats, the people weep aloud in repentance. Then the Lord raises up "judges [to save] them out of the power of those who plundered them." These men are not judges in any modern sense of the term, but are chieftains and military leaders, heroes in war.

To reinforce his lesson of the fierceness of God's wrath and the fidelity of his love, the writer infuses his stories with his own strong faith, showing in them a pattern of rebellion, consequent misfortune, repentance, and rescue. The people fall into idolatry and are punished by their enemies who act as instruments in God's hands; they repent, cry out to God, and he saves them by means of chosen leaders called judges. Writers inspired by such a purpose of showing God's fidelity are called deuteronomic because they follow the spirit of Deuteronomy, that book of fervent orations aimed at arousing total commitment to Yahweh.

Measure for measure
must be answered
(HENRY VI, ACT 2)

The first unique individual in Judges is not a judge at all but an enemy king, Adonibezek, who has been captured by the tribesmen of Judah. They "cut off his thumbs and his great toes," and he responds with dignity and wry humor;

> Seventy kings with their thumbs and their great toes cut off
> used to pick up scraps under my table;
> as I have done, so God has requited me.

Enemy though he is, he calls up admiration for his courage, his keen-eyed recognition that he has got what he meted out to others, and his cleverness in boasting of his former prowess even while he surrenders to misfortune—he has served not one, but seventy kings as he is now being served. The economy of writing which brings a man alive in three lines is admirable.

Next comes a family interplay of personalities which throws a new light on Caleb, the old warrior who had stood by Joshua in the incident of the twelve spies sent by Moses. Seasoned fighter as he is, he surrenders quickly when moved by love for his daughter Achsah. He has bestowed her as bride on Othoniel, a young soldier who becomes a judge. With her he has given some land as a dowry, but she wants something else and knows how to obtain it. After her wedding, she comes to her father, and as she alights "from her ass," Caleb asks her, "What do you wish?" The story does not tell how he knew she wanted a favor, but she must have given some sign.

Immediately she makes use of the sympathy she has gained, "Give me a present," she says, "since you have set me in the land of the Negeb, give me also springs of water." So Caleb gives her "the upper springs and the lower springs." This is a generous gift in a land of little water. Most interesting here is the father-daughter relationship, the first one dramatized in the Bible. Soon Judges will show another father and daughter in a more tragic situation.

That thou mayst know him perfectly, he's one
Of a left-handed making

(Beaumont and Fletcher)

Then during the days of Eglon, king of Moab, "a very fat man," comes the Benjaminite called Ehud. He was "a left-handed man," and the point of the story hangs on the seemingly insignificant detail. Eglon, because of the people's sins, has "defeated Israel," and taken "possession of the city of palms," a name used for Jericho, and Ehud is assigned to carry tribute to him. He prepares "a sword with two edges, a cubit in length," and girds it "on his right thigh under his clothes." Because he is left-handed, the dagger hangs on the right side where, presumably, Eglon's guards will not search.

When he arrives, he says he brings a message for the king alone, and so contrives that the courtiers be sent away. Then Ehud comes to him as he sits "alone in his cool roof chamber." There "with his left hand," Ehud draws "the sword from his right thigh," and thrusts "it into his belly; and the hilt also [goes] in after the blade, and the fat [closes] over the blade." The realistic details could be matched in Homer's *Iliad* or an Anglo-Saxon war song of blood and murder.

Ehud then goes out, locking the doors behind him, and Eglon's servants hesitate for a long time before they enter. When they do find courage, they discover the king dead. Ehud, meanwhile, has made use of the delay. He has "sounded the trumpet in the hill country of Ephraim," shouting, "Follow after me; for the Lord has given your enemies the Moabites into your hand." His coup succeeds, Moab is quelled, and the land has "rest for eighty years." Since forty years is an indefinitely long time in biblical speech, doubling it to eighty gives duration to this peace in the land of Ephraim.

After Ehud's death, however, Ephraim in the central highlands is beset by the Canaanite king Jabin, and his general Sisera. The prophetess Deborah and Barak the judge are called to the rescue. Their story with its ancient battle song will be treated later. So will the story of Gideon which comes next. Gideon's sons, after him, become involved in the ruling of Israel, and one of them, Jotham, tells a fable, which is famous because this form is unusual in the Bible.

A fable is a brief tale told to point a moral. The characters are animals or inanimate objects gifted with speech.

Gideon has "seventy sons," a number which indicates that he was a prosperous man with a large harem. One is Abimelech, a wicked man, who wants to be king, though his father after a notable victory over Midian had explicitly refused the kingship, saying that the Lord alone ruled Israel. Abimelech goes "to his mother's kinsmen" and wins an alliance with them, then he hires "worthless and reckless fellows," and going to "his father's house at Ophrah," slays his brothers "upon one stone." The writer says nothing of any resistance they may have offered. The tale sounds as if Abimelech stood there the whole day and sheared off heads as fast as he could lift his sword—sixty-eight of them, for Jotham, the youngest son of Gideon, escapes, and Abimelech is made a local king at Shechem.

Then Jotham goes and stands "on the top of Mount Gerizim," and shouts down his fable to the people below, "Listen to me, you men of Shechem":

> The trees once went forth to anoint a king over them;
> And they said to the olive tree, "Reign over us."
>
> But the olive tree said to them,
> "Shall I leave my fatness, by which gods and men are honored,
> and go to sway over the trees?

The olive is wise enough to value fruitfulness more than pomp, and shows it by characterizing this kind of leadership as an empty gesture, as a purposeless swaying over other trees. The moral is, of course, that no productive citizen would want to be king.

The trees next approach the fig, but she will not surrender her "sweetness . . . and good fruit" in order to "sway over the trees." Nor will the vine consent to give up the task of making "wine which cheers gods and men, and go to sway over the trees." The repetition, as in most fables, drives the lesson home.

At last the trees seek out the unprofitable bramble, fit only to light a fire under a pot, and the bramble answers:

If in good faith you are anointing me king over you,
then come and take refuge in my shade;
but if not, let fire come out of the bramble
and devour the cedars of Lebanon.

Here there is no question of fruit. All the thorn has to offer is a scanty shade, which appears thinner by contrast with the mighty cedars of Lebanon which the bramble itself has mentioned. Jotham is implying that its words are as foolish as its hunger for power.

Besides, the bramble has invoked fire, and through fire, destruction is to come. With bitter irony Jotham concludes his fable:

My father fought for you, and risked his life . . .
if you then have acted in good faith and honor . . .
then rejoice in Abimelech, and let him also rejoice in you.

But if not, let fire come out from Abimelech,
and devour the citizens of Shechem.

He has now invoked fire directly as well as in the words of the bramble. And fire comes. After three years the people rebel against their king; they go "out into the field [to gather] the grapes," to tread them out and hold festival. There they eat and drink and curse Abimelech: "Who is Abimelech, and who are we of Shechem, that we should serve him?"

But the rebellion begun this day fails, and the citizens take refuge in the "Tower of Shechem . . . the stronghold of the house of El-berith." So Abimelech goes up to "Mount Zalmon, he and all the men that were with him; and Abimelech [takes] an axe" and cuts down "a bundle of brushwood" as kindling for the fire he intends. He places the brushwood at the foot of the crypt and sets it blazing, so that "about a thousand men and women" perish.

Moreover, Abimelech's own end also comes because of another fire. In Thebez of Canaan stands a strong tower, and he attacks it, and draws "near to the door of the tower to burn it with fire."

But "a certain woman," looking down at the aggressor, casts "an upper millstone upon Abimelech's head, and [crushes] his skull." Then he calls upon "his armor-bearer," saying, "Draw your sword and kill me, lest men say of me, 'a woman killed him.'" So his attendant runs him through and he dies. Such is the end of the bloodthirsty Abimelech, son of Gideon. The story is memorable, not so much for its bloody deeds, as for its shaping of Jotham's fable which progresses through the refusals of the fruitful trees, to consent by the most worthless plant, to the final working out of destruction by fires which were foretold.

> Destined by the fates
> to die by my father's hand,
> to come, behind the horses of delight,
> not to marriage, but to woe and horror
> (EURIPIDES, *Iphigenia in Tauris*)

After Abimelech comes Jephthah, whose tragedy is like that of Agamemnon, king of the Greeks before the walls of Troy. The king was constrained by a goddess to offer his young daughter Iphigenia in sacrifice. Only so could he win favoring winds to get his war fleet to Troy. Jephthah, motivated by a similar desire for victory, offers a similar sacrifice.

This Gileadite Jephthah, "the son of a harlot," had been driven away by his brothers. But when the Ammonites press hard upon the people, the elders of Gilead go "to bring Jephthah from the land of Tob." He must have been mighty in battle for them to seek him out after banishing him. After some argument he consents to head their forces, and begins by sending a message to the Ammonites, offering peaceful coexistence. "Will you not possess what Chemosh your god gives you to possess? And all that the Lord our God has dispossessed before us, we will possess." But they pay no heed, and Jephthah in his zeal is moved to pronounce a fateful vow to the Lord:

> If thou wilt give the Ammonites into my hand,
> then whoever comes forth from the doors of my house
> to meet me, when I return victorious . . .
> shall be the Lord's, and I will offer him up
> for a burnt offering.

With mistaken fervor, he hopes thus to force Yahweh to do his will. It is an attempt at magic, a bribe offered to divinity.

It is hard for individuals in Israel to be purged of the ancient evil of child sacrifice. Yet God, whom he importunes, has shown long ago with Abraham and Isaac, that he desires no such gift.

His promise given, Jephthah goes ahead and inflicts a severe defeat upon the enemy, and comes home. At this point the narrative becomes charged with powerful emotion:

> Jephthah came to his home at Mispah;
> and behold his daughter came out to meet him
> with timbrels and with dances.
>
> She was his only child;
> beside her he had neither son nor daughter.

When he sees her, he rends his garments in grief:

> Alas, my daughter! you have brought me very low,
> and you have become the cause of great trouble to me;
> for I have opened my mouth to the Lord,
> and I cannot take back my vow.

Her answer shows an astonishing obedience in such a crisis, "My father . . . do to me according to what has gone forth from your mouth." And now she pleads for one favor, "Let me alone two months, that I may go and wander on the mountains, and bewail my virginity, I and my companions." She is grieved most of all because she must die a maiden, having given no sons to carry on the family and add to Israel's strength.

"At the end of two months" she returns "to her father" who does "with her according to his vow." Then comes a strange sentence. "And it became a custom in Israel that the daughters of Israel went year by year to lament the daughter of Jephthah the Gileadite four days in the year." One is tempted to see in the practice a modification of idolatrous festivities honoring the gods of fertility. Such festivals were common among the neighboring Canaanites, and the fact that this is a mourning rite for one who died without children suggests the connection.

One other noteworthy incident links itself with Jephthah's name—a happening that has given a catchword to the English language. During a civil war, Jephthah's men, opposing Ephraim, have seized the fords of Jordan. When any man tries to cross at the ford they ask, "Are you an Ephraimite?"

If he answers, "No!" they order him to say the word *shibboleth*, which means merely "an ear of corn." But Ephraimites are unable to pronounce the *sh* sound, and betray themselves by saying *sibboleth*. Then they are slain. From this, English has adopted the word *shibboleth*, meaning any characteristic or oddity setting a man apart from his fellows. As John Cleveland, a satiric poet who died in 1658, puts it:

> They had a Shibboleth to discover them,
> he who pronounced *Brot* and *Cawse*
> for *Bread* and *Cheese*
> had his head lopt off.

So, too, the Ephraimites, marked by oddity of speech, had their heads "lopt off."

Next in Judges comes Samson, but he will be treated in a separate chapter. To round off this one, the story of Deborah, from chapters 4 and 5, has been chosen. Like the account of the Red Sea crossing, which was told first in prose and then in Miriam's antiphonal song, or like Joshua's cry to the sun and moon, so also the adventures of Deborah, that lioness among women, are told in prose of excellent historical worth, and then in the magnificent Song of Deborah, which may well be contemporaneous with the events it describes.

> Night roared. . . .
> Till a lioness arose breasting the babble;
> A prophetess towered in the tumult.[75]

In chapter 4 of Judges, it appears that Israel, after the peace following upon Ehud's victory, again offends the Lord and is again beset by the inimical Canaanites. In particular, Sisera, a powerful leader, terrifies them with his nine hundred iron chariots.

At this time the prophetess Deborah was judging in Israel. In the hill country of Ephraim, about eight miles north of Jerusalem, which was still an enemy fortress, she has her place under a palm named Deborah's tree. In her heart dwells the compassion of Moses and the courage of Joshua, so that the misery of her countrymen becomes unbearable to her. She sends word north to Barak of Naphtali, telling him that the Lord commands him, "Go, gather your men at Mount Tabor." There God will give Sisera into his hand. Like Isaiah and Jeremiah and the great prophets of later times, she speaks in the name and with the power of the Lord.

Some of the reverence she evokes appears in his answer: "If you will go with me, I will go; but if you will not go with me, I will not go." Her reply is abrupt and forthright:

> I will surely go with you;
> nevertheless, the road on which you are going
> will not lead to your glory,
> for the Lord will sell Sisera
> into the hand of a woman.

Deborah's cryptic speech is noteworthy. She says the glory will go to a woman, leaving Barak to suppose she means herself, but she does not. Another woman, Jael, the wife of Heber, will vanquish Sisera. Still Deborah does not explain.

The prose account goes soberly on to tell how the army of Sisera falls beneath the sword, but he himself flees on foot. He comes "to the tent of Jael, the wife of Heber the Kenite," whose husband is at peace with the foe. Her loyalty, however, belongs to Israel. She welcomes him, "Turn aside, my lord, turn aside to me; have no fear." Her reassurances are so fulsome that they should have warned the man. She offers him a place to rest and milk to drink. Then when he is asleep she takes a tent peg and mallet, and drives "the peg into his temple, till it [goes] down into the ground, as he [is] lying fast asleep from weariness. So he [dies]."

Such are the bare bones of the story, told with the prose continuity of history. But in Judges 5 these happenings appear as poetry, in the ancient and fierce, but beautiful, Song of Deborah, made up of outlines and luminous points, of the concentration and lyric movement of poetry. Its archaic vocabulary and syntax indicate such early composition that scholars believe it to be contemporary with the events it narrates.

As a song of exultant patriotism and of praise to Israel's God, it presents seven swift scenes of a mighty contest in which stars and rivers fight beside human warriors. Each scene flames to a dramatic climax of its own; the whole forms a wonderful unity built concentrically, with three scenes of preparation, then the call and response of the tribes at the center in scene four, and the battle with its results in the last three pictures.

An introduction announces the theme of praise, then the pictures flash in vivid life before the viewer who sees: 1) the Lord in majesty; 2) Israel in desolation; 3) her leaders oblivious of danger; 4) the tribes called to war, with those who come and those who delay; 5) the clash of battle joined; 6) Jael, instrument of rescue; 7) Sisera's mother, image of desolation.

First comes the introduction to Deborah's song:

> Hear, O kings; give ear, O princes;
> to the Lord I will sing,
> I will make melody to the Lord the God of Israel.

Then quickly the first picture follows—of the Lord's power and his mindfulness of his people:

> Lord, when thou didst go forth from Seir . . .
> the earth trembled, and the heavens dropped
> yea, the clouds dropped water.
> The mountains quaked before the Lord,
> yon Sinai before the Lord, the God of Israel.

It recalls the vision of Moses on Sinai when the Lord appeared in thunder and fire as a figure of invincible power. It also looks forward to scene five when the Lord will again harness nature's violence to his use.

In contrast with the power of God, the second scene shows Israel, in days of slavery, so that caravans which bring prosperity have ceased, and travelers are not safe from banditry but must keep "to the byways."

> In the days of Jael, caravans ceased
>   and travelers kept to the byways.
> When new gods were chosen,
>   then war was in the gates.
> Was shield or spear to be seen
>   among forty thousand in Israel?
> My heart goes out to the commanders of Israel.

Because they have followed after false gods, they are stripped of strength, left weaponless with war at the gates.

Meanwhile in the third vision, the leaders are blind to their country's overhanging doom. They ride out in trappings of luxury, heedless of the people's straits.

> Tell of it, you who ride on tawny asses,
> you who sit on rich carpets
> and you who walk by the way.
>
> To the sound of musicians at the watering places,
> there they repeat the triumphs of the Lord,
> the triumphs of his peasantry in Israel.

Tawny asses and rich carpets are not for fighting. These men are too sunk in luxury to unify Israel or to remember "the triumphs of the Lord." Then as though the "musicians at the watering places" were all to strike their strings at once, Deborah sounds the battle cry which stands at the center of the poem.

Once it has been heard, the tribes are forced to decide for or against Deborah and the cause of freedom:

> Awake, awake, Deborah!
> Awake, awake, utter a song!
> Arise, Barak, lead away your captives,
> O son of Abinoam.

Barak has reason for courage. The princes of Ephraim, Benjamin, Machir, Zebulun, Issachar, and Naphtali are with him. Still Gilead, Reuben, Dan, and Asher hesitate:

> Why [do] you tarry among the sheepfolds [Reuben],
> to hear the piping for the flocks?
>
> Gilead stayed beyond the Jordan;
> and Dan, why [does] he abide with the ships?
>
> Asher [sits] still at the coast of the sea,
> settling down by his landings.

In contrast to this lethargy, the song swings back in exultant praise of two loyal tribes:

> Zebulun is a people that jeoparded their lives to the death;
> Naphtali, too, on the heights of the field.

With praise for the courageous, and invective against those who hesitate, the poem has come to its center, the actual clash of battle.

The kings of Canaan come to war, only to go down in disgrace. "At Taanach, by the waters of Megiddo, they got no spoils of silver," because

> From heaven fought the stars,
> from their courses they fought against Sisera.

The heavens in their disturbance start a storm which sets the flash floods of the desert washing down the valleys. "The torrent Kishon swept them away, the onrushing torrent, the torrent Kishon." Perhaps Deborah, knowing the land and its sudden storms, has waited for this moment—waited until the nine hundred chariots of Sisera are made useless by mud and flooding waters:

> Then loud beat the horses' hoofs
> with the galloping, galloping of his steeds.

Nothing else is shown of the battle; nothing more is needed.

So far, one of the main artistic principles of the poem has been contrast. The power of Yahweh in his storms and the helplessness of Israel in desolation; the poverty of a land where caravans cannot come, and the luxury of the leaders with their white asses and saddlecloths; the zeal of some tribes and the apathy of others—each balances the other. This stately progress is broken by bursts of emotion, exhortations to action, sharp addresses of praise and scorn, and sharply contrasted pictures. Two of these appear in the concluding sections.

Here at the end the poem moves from armies of nameless men to two individualized women: Jael in her tent, and the mother of Sisera in her palace. Gestures may have introduced the new theme, for it comes with sudden words:

> Most blessed of women be Jael . . .
> of tent-dwelling women most blessed.
> He asked water and she gave him milk,
> she brought him curds in a lordly bowl.

The irony is terrible when the ruthless Jael offers milk, the food of children, to the enemy. With a leap from the hospitable matron to the fierce avenger, the poem exults in her deed:

> She put her hand to the tent peg
>   and her right hand to the workmen's mallet;
> she struck Sisera a blow,
>   she crushed his head,
>   she shattered and pierced his temple.
> He sank, he fell, he lay still at her feet.

But sudden as shifting of torchlight comes the last picture—of Sisera's mother, who does not know her son is dead. The song makes good use of the ironic situation, as this nameless woman watches for her son who will not return.

> Out of the window she peered,
>   the mother of Sisera gazed through the lattice:
> "Why is his chariot so long in coming?
>   Why tarry the hoofbeats of his chariots?"

Here is economy and understatement like that of the English ballads with their tragic burdens.

In vain "her wisest ladies" waiting with her offer words of comfort—words she keeps repeating to herself:

> "Are they not finding and dividing the spoil?
>   A maiden or two for every man,
> spoil of dyed stuffs for Sisera,
>   spoil of dyed stuffs embroidered,
>   two pieces of dyed work
>   embroidered for my neck as spoil."

As the poem begins with the saddlecloths of Israel's nobles, their luxurious carpets, symbolizing their lack of power and leadership, so now it ends with the ornate spoils of "dyed stuffs" and embroidered shawls. They too signify loss, for they will never belong to Sisera, the dead leader of Canaan, nor to his mother, who stands in her window waiting for him.

As the song opens with the theme of praise to Yahweh, so now it closes on a similar note, using again an image of power taken from nature:

So perish all thine enemies, O Lord!
But thy friends be like the sun as he rises
in his might!

With earthquake and thunder the Lord comes at first, by stars out of order and waters flooding down desert ravines the enemy is beaten, now may the might of the Lord help his people as the sun does when it floods earth with light and heat.

Though the book of Judges may appear chaotic in its structure, and though it tells of an age of chaos, yet for all that, its human insights, its variety of human motives, its violent and vivid action, all work together to make it memorable. Here are people fully alive, abounding in energy, uniquely themselves with a cause to live and fight for. From the cunning Ehud to the satirical Jotham, from the tragedy of Jephthah to the exultant song of Deborah, there is variety and literary treasure.

As a revelation of Yahweh's faithfulness, and a view of history which might have been lost forever, the book is priceless. At this moment Israel is changing. They have been a people on the move, now they are making some first attempts at a settled life, at becoming a nation of landholders. But unity is needed for survival, and soon they will begin to look for a man strong enough to rule as king. Before that happens, however, the lives of two more judges must be surveyed.

This Chapter, in treating the shorter narratives of Judges, has been a piecemeal survey of a piecemeal but exciting book. Buried among its swift incident are two more stories—those of Gideon and Samson. They have been saved for treatment in the next Chapters, so that they may be seen as the artistic wholes they are. The robust and witty Gideon will be treated next, as he answers his call to rescue the people from another enemy, the savage Midianites.

CHAPTER TWELVE

Gideon's Trumpet Call

DEBORAH's song rings out in triumph to celebrate a victory; Gideon's trumpet blares defiance before battle. His trumpet makes a good symbol for this brash warrior. Like the trumpet's lighter music which is almost laughter, Gideon's story has its amusing aspects, and like the loud note of its challenge, his actions crash out in courage. One blast of his horn and he rallies a whole clan behind him. A shattering of earthen jars, the din of trumpets, a blaze of light, and his three hundred men conquer thousands of Midianites shouting, "A sword for the Lord and for Gideon!"

As with many people in the Bible, Gideon's is a story of vocation—of God's call to a human being. In this case it is an invitation to assume leadership and power, in order that through him God may rescue Israel. As always, the call comes in an individual way to one unique human being. Our interest in the development of Gideon follows the progress of his response to the call. Herein lies the secret of his transformation.

He begins as a farmer and becomes a warrior; he begins in obscurity and comes to fame; he begins in caution and is transformed into a fearless leader. This theme starts faintly with God's first call and Gideon's protest that he is too lowly a man to lead the armies. It wavers with Gideon's early hesitations and changes from a minor to a major key with the dream which influences him to fear no longer. It rings out with certainty through his victories and ends on a satisfying note when Gideon returns his power to the Lord from whom it came.

This man, chosen by the Lord for his saving work, has more than one dimension. In particular he unites the paradoxical qualities of caution and brashness, timidity and courage. As farmer he appears first, making his way toward the winepress, a spot where he can thresh his grain without interference from the Midianite conquerors who have been destroying Israel's crops. As warrior, later on, he threshes a different kind of crop —flays his enemies with thorns—a bloody threshing, as he himself names it. These two threshings frame the story and point up the two sides of Gideon's character.

In line with his two main qualities, the two natural elements of fire and water are used by the writer to vivify his meanings. Fire is a forceful, active symbol. Water is usually thought of as gentle and fructifying. Fire is never quiet. It thrusts and leaps and devours, as Gideon the warrior does. But water, while it too can destroy, is often found in quiet lakes and ponds, or falling in rain to make crops grow. In these aspects it mirrors the Gideon whose work is to cultivate the fruits of earth. These two images of fire and water occur, each three times, in meaningful progression, and like the first pastoral threshing and the last violent one, they shadow forth the two prominent elements in Gideon's personality.

Nothing is seen of him in Judges until, at chapter 6, an angel sits "under the oak at Ophrah, which [belongs] to Joash," Gideon's father. He is waiting for Gideon. When he comes the angel greets him with a compliment, "The Lord is with you, you mighty man of valor." One wonders if he smiled, for Gideon has chosen this spot in order to avoid trouble. He has come out to the winepress to save his wheat from the Midianites, a sensible precaution, but not one to earn him the name of "man of valor." This task of threshing befits Gideon the husbandman.

With natural logic, Gideon asks the angel: "If the Lord is with us, why has all this [oppression] befallen us? And where are all his wonderful deeds?" But the angel has his own logic. He tells Gideon to go himself and liberate the people: "Go in this might of yours and deliver Israel from the hand of Midian; do not I send you?" Gideon has his vocation now, and the angel's motive in referring to his "valor" is clear.

Yet the cautious side of the man is still uppermost. He asks for a proof, for a sign that this message is from the Lord. And then he does not wait to see what it will be. It is as though he has just remembered the courtesy owing to an angel. He starts away, abruptly ordering the angel, "Do not depart from here . . . until I come . . . and bring out my present, and set it before thee." This patient angel, who first waited for Gideon under the oak tree, now waits a long time while he prepares "a kid, and unleavened cakes." The meat he puts "in a basket, and the broth . . . in a pot," and brings them to the angel.

He is told to "Take the meat and the unleavened cakes, and put them on this rock, and pour the broth over them." Then comes the proof which was requested before. It is a sign in fire. The angel touches meat and bread with the tip of his staff and fire blazes out and consumes it all. The fire is an active principle which carries Gideon's worship upward to the Lord.

Soon Gideon hears an order to build his own fire as proof of his fealty to God. He is to destroy the woodland shrine of the false god, Baal. So with "ten men of his servants" to help him, he cuts down the sacred grove. "But because he [is] too afraid of his family and the men of the town to do it by day, he [does] it by night." Here is the hesitant Gideon once more. The wood from the grove he uses to build a fire for a new sacrifice to the Lord.

Next day, just as he has feared, there is trouble. The people resent the dishonor done to a god they wished to placate. But with the same kind of boldness in speech that the son has shown, Gideon's father defends him. To the people's protests, Joash the father retorts, "Will you contend for Baal? Or will you defend his cause? If he is a god, let him contend for himself." Evidently the people admire the aptness of the argument, for in remembrance of the father's quick speech the son receives a new name. They begin to call Gideon "Jerubbaal," which means, "Let Baal contend against him."

So far there have been two signs in fire, one miraculous, springing from the angel's staff, one purely natural, built by Gideon. Both have wafted his gifts to the Lord. But when the sign occurs again it will be an instrument of victory—the victory which is the Lord's gift to Gideon.

Soon, however, come the signs given in water. Gideon is still cautious, still asking for proof that his call comes from God. In answer to his prayer, he receives the famous and picturesque sign of the dew falling upon the fleece. In a strangely quiet and pastoral image for this noisy story, it stirs memories of the Advent response in the liturgy: "The Lord shall come down like rain upon the fleece." It is also reminiscent of the image in the lovely medieval poem:

> He cam also stille where his mother was
> As dew in Aprille that falleth on the gras.
> He cam also stille where his mother lay
> As dew in Aprille that falleth on the hay.

According to the conditions of his prayer, Gideon spreads a lamb's fleece upon the ground. Then the Lord sends dew to fall on the fleece while the ground around it remains dry. When Gideon awakes he wrings out the fleece and "wrung enough dew from the fleece to fill a bowl with water." On the following night the prayer and the sign given in water are reversed. The fleece remains dry and dew covers the ground.

After this the Lord takes the sign of water which Gideon had suggested and uses it to draw out from him a trust which is heroic. With a trumpet blast Gideon has gathered an army at his heels, and is encamped at the spring of Harod. Here the Lord remarks, "The people with you are too many for me to give the Midianites into their hand, lest Israel vaunt themselves . . . saying, 'My own hand has delivered me.' " So to safeguard God's honor and the people's trust in him, Gideon must send home all the soldiers who are afraid, and "twenty-two thousand returned, and ten thousand remained." But this army is still too large. Now comes the testing by water.

Gideon is told to have his men drink of a stream and then, "Everyone that laps the water with his tongue, as a dog laps, you shall set by himself; likewise every one that kneels down to drink." Those that lap, "putting their hands to their mouths," are three hundred men. All the rest kneel down to drink. Gideon, following God's orders, keeps the three hundred and sends the rest home. His army is depleted, but with this handful the Lord will give him victory. It is the second sign in water.

The successes which follow can be attributed to no one but the Lord. They consist largely in winning control of the "waters as far as Beth-barah, and also the Jordan." So it is that the sign of water, first used by Gideon to test the Lord in the scene with dew and fleece, then used by God to challenge Gideon's trust by cutting down the army, becomes finally the reward of waterways won by victory—a victory gained by more than human means.

Before the victory, however, Gideon, looking at his small army, needs reassurance. The Lord therefore sends him to hear the telling of a soldier's dream which will transform his hesitation into courage. "Go down," he says, to the camp of the Midianites at night. "But if you fear to go down," take with you, "Purah your servant. . . . And you shall hear what they say, and afterward your hands shall be strengthened."

This dream which Gideon overhears is the symbolic center of the account. Hitherto Gideon has been cautious and even fearful—at the threshing near the winepress, in his destroying of Baal's wood, in requiring the sign of dew and fleece. After the dream which pivots the story and Gideon's transformation, he becomes bold in deed as he has been in speech. The dream itself is abrupt and amusing as Gideon is, yet like him it also suggests destruction.

That night Gideon approaches the enemy camp. There the army lies "along the valley like locusts for multitude." And their camels are "without number, as the sand which is upon the seashores." Then in the stillness he overhears a sentry recounting a dream. "I dreamed a dream; and lo, a cake of barley bread tumbled into the camp of Midian, and came to the tent, and struck it so that it fell, and turned it upside down, so that the tent lay flat." Immediately his companion begins to interpret the dream—a universal human habit. "This is no other then the sword of Gideon, the son of Joash, a man of Israel; into his hand God has given Midian and all the host."

Of course the listening Gideon is overjoyed. He prostrates himself in awe, and then speeds back to camp with a rousing cry of, "Arise; for the Lord has given the host of Midian into your hand." He divides the men into three companies and provides them all with trumpets, and "empty jars, with torches inside the jars." No army ever carried stranger equipment—torches hidden in jars, and a noisemaker for every soldier. Quietly they surround the Midianites. They must have been skilled stalkers, for though they come "to the outskirts of the camp at the beginning of the middle watch, when they had just set the watch," so that these guards would be wide awake, still they are not detected.

When all are ready, Gideon gives the sign. They blow the trumpets and smash the jars, and every man stands with a torch in his left hand, and in his right the horn he is blowing, and the cry rings loud: "A sword for the Lord and for Gideon!" The scene is dramatic. In the stillness of the desert night all that crash and reverberation; in the dark of the sleeping camp that sudden flaming illumination. This shining of the burning torches, which must have seemed to the suddenly wakened soldiers like a world on fire, is the last of the fire images, and like the third appearance of water in the winning of the streams, it marks a scene of victory. From now on Gideon is all warrior, yet he keeps his farmer's speech of vintage and threshing, transferring it to the new context of war.

For example, when some allies of his from Ephraim, after the winning of the watercourses, begin to protest because he had not called them to share in the first victory, he appeases them by saying: "What have I done now in comparison with you? Is not the gleaning of the grapes of Ephraim better than the vintage of Abiezer?" Again, a little later when he has demanded food for his army from the men of Succoth, and they have refused him, he threatens vengeance by a cruel threshing: "When the Lord has given Zebah and Zalmunna into my hand, I will flail your flesh with the thorns of the wilderness." The pastoral implications of *gleaning*, *vintage*, and *flailing* add to the ferocity of effect.

Gideon, moreover, wants his son, Jether, to become as fierce a warrior as himself, for he presents two captives to the boy saying, "Rise, and slay them." But he is "afraid, because he [is] still a youth." The captive chieftains then show both compassion and courage. They say, "Rise yourself, and fall upon us; for as the man is, so is his strength." Do not, in other words, expect this deed of a mere boy. Gideon then puts them to death, and takes "the crescents" from the necks of their camels.

After these victories, the theme of power and of its use for the Lord's purposes comes to a climax and a reversal. The Israelites wish the man who has delivered them to rule as their king. But Gideon knows from whom his power has come and he will not arrogate to himself what belongs to the Lord. He refuses in noble words: "I will not rule over you, and my son will not rule over you; the Lord will rule over you." The power which God gave him at the time of his call is now returned to the Lord who is its source.

His gesture is followed by a kind of anti-climax which looks back to the scene where Gideon destroyed the shrine of Baal, and also looks forward to the renewed faithlessness of the people after his death. Gideon, seemingly without idolatrous intent, takes up a collection of jewelry and makes an image which he sets up in Ophrah. "And all Israel played the harlot after it there, and it became a snare to Gideon and to his family." However, this seems to be a temporary wavering, for the Bible says that it was only after Gideon was dead, that Israel "did not remember the Lord their God, who had rescued them," and began again to worship the Baals, the false gods. Like a good husbandman, as long as Gideon lives he protects God's field of Israel, and the land has rest.

In the theme of Gideon's vocation lies the suspense that holds interest. With Gideon's receiving of power the story begins, with its return to God, it ends. The harvest and vintage images frame the tale and show some of the complexity of Gideon's character. Moreover, the triple use of the symbols of fire and water enrich the account. They are universally meaningful, and in their way reveal the purpose of the inspired writer. Finally the centering of the story and of Gideon's change of character around the dream of the barley loaf gives balance to the structure.

For all the blare of his trumpets, Gideon himself might have been no more likely to save God's people than the loaf to demolish a tent. But God helps him to do the impossible. He might well have adopted the words Moses, earlier, spoke to the Israelites: "It was not because you were more in number than any other people that the Lord set his love upon you and chose you, for you were the fewest of peoples; but it is because the Lord loves you" (Deut. 7:7–8). Because the Lord loved him and called him, he came to his destined nobility. In the next chapter, Samson seems an even less likely man for God's work, yet he too is chosen, and in spite of all his faults he too accomplishes a great task and reaches nobility at the end of his life.

CHAPTER THIRTEEN

Samson's Raucous Riddles

GIDEON, with his mixed fear and brashness, seems an unlikely candidate for greatness, yet the Lord calls him and his response leads to a certain admirable stature. Samson, aside from his obvious physical strength, appears even less fit for a heroic role. Wonderment takes the observer again and again when he looks at those whom Yahweh calls: Jacob the trickster, Joseph a spoiled younger son, Jephthah who tries to please God by child sacrifice, and now Samson, a typical folk hero—strong armed, fond of feasting and women, addicted to horseplay, to practical jokes, and rough wit. He is Paul Bunyan, Jack the Giant Killer, and a kind of country Casanova, whose adventures were undoubtedly sung around campfires on festive evenings.

In the English review *Scripture* (July 1959), J. Blenkinsopp remarks that "these stories in their original form were by no means religious in character. They go back no doubt to bardic recitations" at feasts as in Homer, or at religious festivals "as in the case of the Philistines in the temple of Dagan." Their religious meaning is discoverable "not in the episodes themselves but in the context in which they were placed by the inspired editor."

The purpose here is to see both levels at once: Samson the folk hero, and Samson called by God to another heroism; his wordly deeds and his otherworldly transformation that happens because he stands one man alone against his country's enemies, the hostile Philistines. He reaches his full greatness, and even that is a riddle, is double leveled, at the end of his life when he kills himself along with thousands of Philistines. The final heroism preoccupies Milton when he writes *Samson Agonistes*, the most famous poem about this roistering man of God. But by centering on the last days of a Samson ennobled by suffering, Milton omits some fine contrasts which the Bible uses to good effect. Milton might have been enriched had he possessed some of the Bible writers' sense of humor. More shall be seen of Milton's Samson later on.

Meanwhile, before he becomes a hero, Samson is a boasting trickster who breaks promises made to Yahweh, falls helpless before the wiles of women, and brings both disaster and victory by his riddling ways. He delights in fooling others, but is blind when they betray and make a fool of him, and for all his conviviality he is a lonely man. His story is built in five parts: an introduction, three incidents centering around Samson's fondness for women and for jokes, and a conclusion where, by a simple trick, he carries out that heroic purpose toward which his life has been tending.

Let that archangel now, that perilous one
from beyond the stars,
step down.[76]

In the introduction, Samson's parents, before his birth, are told by a mysterious messenger from God that this son will "deliver Israel from the hand of the Philistines," who are now their greatest oppressors. This is his call and it is a lonely one—singlehanded he will spend his life harrying Israel's foes. As a preparation, the parents are to dedicate Samson as a Nazirite—pledging him to avoid unclean food, to refrain from strong drink, and to allow no razor to come near his head. Their promises play an important part in his destiny, especially the last, for it signifies a lifelong commitment to warfare. As Hastings remarks in *The Dictionary of the Bible*, "Those who dedicated themselves to [a] Holy War allowed their hair to grow."[77] Because Samson's hair was never to be cut, the implication is that he should never be done with fighting.

Is there not a woman among the daughters
of your kinsmen . . . that you must go to
take a wife from the uncircumsised Philistines?
(JG. 14:3)

The saga proper begins when a Philistine woman at Timnah takes Samson's eye and he goes home demanding that she be obtained as his bride: "Get her for me as my wife." That he wants her—to him this is reason enough, though his parents object to his union with an enemy Philistine. But the scripture writer remarks that they do not know God's plans, that by this marriage the Lord is "seeking an occasion against the Philistines." Yet Samson, though God has designs for him, is no saint, as his first breaking of his vow soon proves.

With his parents he sets out to do his wooing, and on a byway he meets a young lion that comes roaring to meet him. With bare hands he tears it to pieces and hurries back to his parents, telling them nothing of the adventure. His secrecy is significant in the light of what happens later.

Their errand prospers, and the trio return home to prepare for the new household. Later when they return to Timnah for the wedding, Samson turns off the path again to look at the lion he had left there. "And behold, there was a swarm of bees in the body of the lion, and honey." Though contact with a dead body renders food ritually unclean, and his vow forbids his eating it, still he takes a handful of the honey and savors it as he walks back to the main path. There he offers some to his father and mother, but without telling them "that he had taken the honey from the carcass of the lion." His vow is broken, his parents who made the pledge for him are ignorant of his failing, but he goes his way to celebrate his wedding with a feast. He even makes the adventure an occasion of entertainment there, and his riddling ways precipitate a first violent victory.

During the feast, thirty young Philistine men are his companions. Samson says to them, "Let me now put a riddle to you." If they guess its answer within seven days they will each receive a linen tunic and a new set of festal garments. "Put your riddle, that we may hear it," they say. So, thinking of his lion and honeycomb he says:

Out of the eater came something to eat.
Out of the strong came something sweet.

In its original language it is a rhymed riddle, full of sound echoes. Today it seems unfair in its conditions, for how can the young men guess its answer without having had previous knowledge of Samson's doings?

When by the seventh day his companions cannot find the answer, they go to Samson's bride:

Entice your husband to tell us what the riddle is,
lest we burn you and your father's house with fire.

Two foreshadowings of coming events are here: though the woman complies, yet her house and her family will indeed be burned; and later on Samson's enemies will gain information from another woman to his desolation.

The first bride now weeps and coaxes, saying to Samson, "You do not love me," until at last he tells her. She, of course, betrays him and the men come with their answer:

What is sweeter than honey?
What is stronger than a lion?

In a fury, Samson replies with more verbal jugglery:

If you had not plowed with my heifer,
you would not have found out my riddle.

And with that he goes down to Ashkelon, slays thirty men and takes their clothes to pay his debt. After this he returns home, leaving his wife to be given to another. But his anger is not yet burned out.

When wheat harvest time is come, Samson returns seeking his bride. But her father will not "allow him to go in." He says, "I really thought that you utterly hated her; so I gave her to your companion. Is not her younger sister fairer than she? Pray take her instead." The unfortunate Philistine father evokes sympathy as he tries to placate the fierce Samson.

Hearing these words Sampson goes out in a rage, catches three hundred foxes, and ties them tail to tail with torches between. Kindling the torches, he sets the foxes loose in "the standing grain of the Philistines, and [burns] up the shocks and the standing grain, as well as the olive orchards." The maddened Philistines hasten to burn the woman and her father alive, thus carrying out the threat they had earlier used to force her to betray Samson.

For revenge because of her death, Samson massacres so many Philistines that his own people, fearing reprisals, hand him over to the enemy. He, however, breaks loose and kills a thousand men with a bone he finds to hand, and celebrates his deed with a boast song:

With the jawbone of an ass,
heaps upon heaps,
with the jawbone of an ass
have I slain a thousand men.

His first riddle has brought a victory for Israel, disaster to the thirty men of Ashkelon, destruction upon fruitful fields, and death to the wife he chose.

Samson went to Gaza,
and there he saw a harlot,
and he went in to her.
(Jg. 16:1)

Samson's next trick is not verbal, but a deed of pure derring-do. Though it shows his weakness for women, it brings no catastrophe. He goes to Gaza, a city where he is destined much later to spend his last sorrowful days. As yet, though, he is lusty and boastful, and desirous of spending the night with a woman of the town. The Philistines, learning that he is within, surround the place and lie "in wait for him all night at the gate of the city." All night they wait saying—in the morning, "then we will kill him."

He, however, wakes at midnight, and rising he seizes "the doors of the gate of the city and the two posts." He hoists them "on his shoulders and [carries] them to the top of the hill that is before Hebron." What happens when the guards arise is not told, but they must have been astonished to find the gates gone, and Samson must have stalked up the hill with pride, looking down upon his baffled foes. Here, however, is another foreshadowing, another premonition of sorrows to come, for one day these gates of Gaza will close about him, and he, blind and helpless, will be unable to escape.

Tell me wherein your
great strength lies. . . .
(Jg. 16:6)

"After this he [loves] a woman in the valley of Sorek, whose name [is] Delilah. And the lords of the Philistines" come saying, "Entice him, and see wherein his great strength lies, and by what means we may overpower him, that we may bind him to subdue him; and we will each give you eleven hundred pieces of silver." The first bride was threatened with death; Delilah is offered a reward. Both ally themselves with their townsmen against Samson. For all his boastful self-confidence, Samson is a lonely figure, unable to hold the loyalty of women, and fighting his enemies singlehanded to the last. In this he is different from other leaders in Judges, who gather armies about them and fight at the head of their men.

In a series of temptations presented by Delilah, the story gathers suspense because of Samson's delight in walking along the edge of danger; he is so intoxicated with his own clever word play that he comes closer and closer to revealing the secret of his strength which rests in his uncut hair. Three times he lies to her; three times Delilah calls in his enemies to capture him; each time he blindly goes back to her and escapes by a narrower margin. The fourth time he tells the truth to his own undoing.

At first he says, "Bind me with seven fresh bowstrings which have not been dried, then I shall become weak, and be like any other man." Bowstrings do not look like hair, but both are strands from living bodies. Then he tells her, "Bind me with new ropes." These are closer to hair since rope is made of twisted cords like braids. In the third episode he actually mentions his hair, saying, "If you weave the seven locks of my head with the web and make it tight with the pin [of your loom], then I shall become weak." But when she calls his enemies, he rises to his feet pulling "away the pin, the loom, and the web."

At last, however, her persistence and persuasiveness prove too much for him. She torments him, vexing him "with her words day after day." In desperation he tells the truth—that he is a Nazirite consecrated to God. "A razor has never come upon my head . . . If I be shaved, then my strength will leave me." So Delilah bids him "sleep upon her knees; and she [calls] a man, and [has] him shave off the seven locks of his head."

Then the Philistine chieftains burst in. This time he tries in vain to escape. He does not realize that the Lord has "left him," because he has broken another condition of his vow. His first violation, committed when he ate honey from the lion's carcass, led to the first riddle with its resulting casualties. This time he makes his riddles first and so opens the way to the breaking of the pledge by which he was bound to keep his hair unshorn, and again disasters follow.

The troubles consequent upon the first riddle fell upon others; this catastrophe strikes Samson himself down, for the Philistines put out his eyes and carry him off to Gaza, binding him with bronze fetters, and putting him to grinding "at the mill in prison." But the incident ends on a note of hope for "the hair of his head," which signifies his strength, begins "to grow again after it has been shaved." These gates of Gaza, which in his pride he has carried away to the top of a hill, now close about him, and his humiliation is great, for he must work at tasks commonly given to slaves. It is the moment of his greatest weakness, and yet out of it will be born his greatest victory.

This is what Milton emphasizes when he names his great poem *Samson Agonistes*—Samson struggling or wrestling—by his title he focuses attention on the climactic moment when Samson will grasp and wrench the pillars of Dagon's temple. Milton's dramatic poem begins after Samson is blinded, and is primarily concerned with the end of his life and his great victory. Now it is that the old blind hero stands "eyeless in Gaza, at the mill with slaves," lamenting in some of the noblest lines ever written:

> O dark, dark, dark, amid the blaze of noon,
> Irrecoverably dark. . . .
> The Sun to me is dark
> And silent as the Moon,
> When she deserts the night,
> Hid in her vacant interlunar cave.

At this darkest moment, however, Samson will strike a blow for Yahweh and Israel, and face death with that courage which has never been lacking to him, going down alone among strangers, as he has been lonely all his life.

> Let me feel the pillars
> on which the house rests,
> that I may lean against them.
> (JG. 16:26)

Samson's strength has returned with the new growth of his hair, but his captors do not know it. One day they lead him out and force him to play the fool before them on the holiday of their god Dagon. Meanwhile they chant:

> Our god has given Samson our enemy
> into our hand,
> the ravager of our country,
> who has slain many of us.

During an interval, Samson asks the attendant who is leading him to guide his hands to the pillars that support the building, so that he may "lean against them." These are the last of his double-leveled words. His purpose is not, as he implies, to rest, but to do the most gigantic work of his life. The attendant, in all simplicity, does as Samson asks.

Now the temple is "full of men and women; all the lords of the Philistines [are] there, and on the roof . . . about three thousand men and women" looking on. A hush falls as the festive crowd awaits further entertainment. Then they hear Samson's shout:

> Strengthen me, I pray thee, only this once, O God,
> that I may be avenged upon the Philistines
> for one of my two eyes. . . .
> Let me die with the Philistines.

And with a mighty wrenching he shakes the pillars, and the temple falls "upon all the people." Milton dwells on the scene, saying, "as an eagle/His cloudless thunder bolted on their heads," and

> As with the force of winds and waters pent
> When mountains tremble . . .
> With horrible convulsion to and fro
> He tugged . . . till down they came, and drew
> The whole roof after them with burst of thunder
> Upon the heads of all who sat beneath.

The hero has met his destiny, and the Bible frames for him a laconic epitaph: "So the dead whom he slew at his death were more than those whom he had slain during his life."

His death is a fulfillment of his destiny even while it is in part a penalty for his own folly. Had he kept his Nazirite pledge, and been less susceptible to women's cajolery, he would not have come to prison. Had he responded differently to his call he might have paid a lesser price. But because he is himself and no other, his dying becomes both retribution and a triumph where all his personal characteristics play a part.

He has come to this moment because of his weakness for women, has prepared for it by a last play upon words when he persuaded his guide to let him rest against the pillars—though he exerted all his strength, yet in one sense he found against them his final rest, his destiny, won by physical prowess and courage to face death—his fall and fulfillment at once. From the beginning he walked through blunders and half-blind choices, and now in his physical blindness he blunders into greatness by helping to free his people from their enemies.

Soon after his story, the book of Ruth tells of a woman different from those Samson knew. Loving and loyal, she moves in a free commitment that "makes all her goings graces," as Hopkins says of those who are uniquely themselves. There could be no greater contrast to the characters in Samson's saga, yet through all this variety of free persons and their deeds of will and weakness, the Lord is guiding Israel to the fulfillment of his plans.

CHAPTER FOURTEEN

Ruth in Alien Fields

THE peaceful book of Ruth appears quietly between the violence of Judges' tales about Samson, Gideon, Jephthah, and the tragic predictions of Samuel. It was written fairly late in Israel's history, and may be something like a parable rather than strict history. It tells the adventures of a woman, and is the first narrative in the Bible to give a strong sense of a particular place: the village of Bethlehem with its atmosphere of friendly gossip, leisured courtesy, plentiful harvest. Here is one spot at least, in the promised land, where war seems far away.

From a barren desert road where Ruth makes her commitment, the story moves to fruitful harvest fields; from famine, exile, and death to plenty and homecoming and new life. Its theme is unusual—that of noble friendship between two women, and it gives a new turn to the traditional themes of the woman bereft of children and the stranger in a foreign land. To make the friendship more surprising, the woman loved with such loyal devotion is Ruth's mother-in-law—a relationship of trust fairly common in life, but unusual in literature. In renewing the older themes, the teller shows the childless woman not as heroine, but as a mother-in-law; and the stranger, not a Jew in exile, but an alien Moabite in the land of Israel. Moreover, with economy typical of the short story at its best, this one develops only three characters: Ruth, the stranger; Naomi, her dead husband's mother; and Boaz, the man who marries Ruth.

The name Bethlehem means House of Bread, and the lives of three beautiful women of the Bible are linked with it. It suggests the peace and plenty that go well with such women. First in time is Rachel who died young but held the heart of Jacob all his years. His last speech about her has been quoted before, but it bears repetition for its beauty and pathos. From his deathbed his old voice lingers over memories of her while Joseph her son listens:

For when I came from Paddan,
    Rachel to my sorrow died
in the land of Canaan on the way,
    when there was still some distance
    to go to Ephrath;
and I buried her there on the way to Ephrath
(that is, Bethlehem).

(GEN. 48:7)

Even after the years his repeated phrases and place names evoke his sense of loss. His Rachel must have been a woman worthy of affection, and for more than her beauty.

When Rachel is long gone, Bethlehem becomes home to Ruth, and later still to Mary who came "from Galilee, from the city of Nazareth, to Judea, to the city of David, which is called Bethlehem," as Luke says. She comes of the line of David who rose from Jacob's kindred, while Rachel was wife to Jacob himself, and Ruth, too, as the story tells, becomes part of David's family.

Between Rachel and Mary appears Ruth, born not of Israel, but of alien Moab, yet destined to bear a son who will become father to Jesse, the father of David. Her story is not one of great conflict or temptation; it tells little of politics or battles. Rather it is a romance such as women might tell during quiet afternoons at weaving or the baking of bread. It narrates a situation of choosing, of commitment, with the consequences that follow, and all is set against a background of harvest time and the reaping of barley in the fields of ancient Palestine.

After a short introduction, Ruth is seen freely choosing her destiny, making her leap into the dark; then come two sections telling how she copes with her new life and how it is made secure for her—each of these scenes centers around an interesting custom of her day and place. The conclusion shows how her destiny is fulfilled in the birth of a son. Five parts, then, shape the story: the preliminaries, a commitment, a new life, a new household, and a son to hold the future.

The introduction is a mere sketch of events leading up to the story. It tells how "in the days when the judges ruled," a man named Elimelech from Bethlehem of Judah "went to sojourn in the country of Moab," because "there was a famine in the land." Exile, and famine, such are the somber beginnings, and then comes another darker note, for there in Moab, Elimelech dies and "his two sons . . . Mahlon and Chilion." Then Naomi his wife is "bereft of her two sons and her husband." Still, she has living with her the two young wives of her sons—one called Orpah and the other Ruth. Hunger and homelessness and death serve as setting, yet the story, with its theme of Ruth's selfless devotion, moves forward into plenty and welcome and new life.

Widowed and childless, the desolate Naomi one day bids farewell to Moab and sets out homeward with her two daughters-in-law. For her it is a return from exile, but for them the road leads away from home. The journey is motivated by good news, for Naomi has heard that in Bethlehem the Lord has "visited his people and given them food." Bethlehem is once more the House of Bread.

As soon as she sets foot on the road that leads southward to Judah, she turns to her companions and in stately words encourages them to return, each to her own mother's house:

> Go, return each of you to her mother's house.
> May the Lord deal kindly with you,
> as you have dealt with the dead and with me.
>
> The Lord grant that you may find a home,
> Each of you in the house of her husband.

About two-thirds of the story is conversation, and much of its lasting appeal results from the beautiful language used by its people as they phrase good wishes for each other in words of noble dignity. Naomi ends her speech by giving the young women each a parting kiss, but they weep aloud, declaring that they "will return" with her to her people.

"Turn back, my daughters, why will you go with me? Have I yet sons in my womb that they may become your husbands? . . . No, my daughters, for it is exceedingly bitter to me for your sake that the hand of the Lord has gone forth against me." At this they weep more than ever, but then Orpah, good-willed but less steadfast than Ruth, kisses her mother-in-law and goes back. So the narrator disposes of one minor character and at the same time emphasizes the freedom of Ruth's choice. Certainly she must have been tempted to go home as she sees Orpah go.

In a poem called "Orpah Returns to Her People," John Hollander hears her saying:

> It is another country, surely,
> Whose road, toward the sun
> And toward fair bright fields of barley
> Glides behind limes, and is gone.

Momentarily she looks southward to shining fields ahead. But then, like a shadow over golden barley, comes her resolve:

> I'll return to our Northern river, sourly
> Rained and snowed upon.

And her thoughts continue: "Ruth will glean for a new master /When the fields are full," still, her resolve is taken:

> . . . No other's pasture,
> Can husband me ever. I must go
> Back home now, over stones and snow.[78]

The cold and snow she thinks of presage loneliness for her, and as she turns away the story quietly gathers suspense, leading the reader to ask: Will Ruth go along this road toward sunlight, or will she also turn "back home now, over stones and snow"? It is time for her commitment.

Naomi speaks again: "See, your sister-in-law has gone back to her people and to her gods; return after your sister-in-law." Her words show how complete the choice must be. If Ruth comes, she will be leaving not only her country and her people but the gods of her homeland too. The answer shows her awareness of these meanings. It rings out in speech whose cadences haunt our language:

> Entreat me not to leave you
>   or to return from following you;
> for where you go I will go,
>   and where you lodge I will lodge;

your people shall be my people,
 and your God my God.

Where you die I will die,
 and there will I be buried.
May the Lord do so to me and more also
 if even death parts me from you.

It is a moment of high resolve, of choice that will shape Ruth's future irrevocably. Plainly she has seen the alternative—acted out by Orpah, urged upon her by Naomi—and deliberately she has chosen a new land, another people, a God strange to her, and a grave for herself among all these.

After this Naomi objects no more. They go on together, and have scarce entered the bustling little town of Bethlehem before the news goes round, and all the women are asking, "Is this Naomi?" They gather around her here at the city gates and show their gladness, but Naomi has not forgotten her childless state. She tells them to call her no longer Naomi, which means beautiful or pleasant, but to call her Mara which means bitter, because the Lord has filled her with bitterness. Later on, at this gate, a ceremony fulfilled by a kinsman of hers, Boaz, will provide her with reasons for rejoicing. Then her lot will no longer be bitter.

> When you reap your harvest in your field,
> and have forgotten a sheaf in the field,
> you shall not go back to get it;
> it shall be for the sojourner,
> the fatherless, and the widow. . . .
> (DEUT. 24:19)

They arrive in Bethlehem "at the beginning of the barley harvest," and this provides an opportunity for livelihood. So Ruth the Moabite says to Naomi, "Let me go to the field, and glean among the ears of grain after him in whose sight I shall find favor." All her speeches, like Naomi's, are marked by courtesy. At this time it was a custom in Israel to allow the needy to follow the reapers in prosperous fields, gleaning the ears that were dropped. By happy chance or by good planning on Naomi's part, Ruth comes to the fields of Boaz, a kinsman of Elimelech, her father-in-law who is dead.

The kindness, courtesy, and susceptible heart of Boaz emerge in the next few scenes. He greets his reapers with a blessing, saying, "The Lord bless you!" and then asks about the young woman he sees among the gleaners. In so small a village he would know all but this stranger. When she is introduced, he provides for her:

> Now, listen, my daughter,
> do not go to glean in another field . . .
> but keep close to my maidens.
> Have I not charged the young men not to molest you?
> And when you are thirsty,
> go to the vessels and drink
> what the young men have drawn.

She reminds hims that she is an alien, but he shows that the news of her goodness has come to his ears:

> All that you have done for your mother-in-law
> since the death of your husband
> has been fully told me,
> and how you left your father and mother and your native land
> and came to a people that you did not know before.
>
> The Lord recompense you . . . and a full reward
> be given you by the Lord, the God of Israel,
> under whose wings you have come to take refuge.

And he invites her to share food, a universal sign of friendship. After the meal he quietly instructs his servants, "Let her glean even among the sheaves . . . and also pull out some from the bundles for her, and leave it for her to glean." He will go beyond the instructions of Deuteronomy which had commanded that forgotten sheaves be left for the alien and orphan. At evening, carrying a whole bushel of grain, she returns to Naomi, and brings her also some of the food that was left when she had finished her meal.

Naomi welcomes her with gladness and begins to lay new plans in accord with another custom in Israel. This Boaz is kinsman to Naomi's dead husband, and under the law he bears responsibility for Ruth, the young widow of Elimelech's son. He shall be reminded that he should provide a husband who will give her sons to carry on her first husband's name. In such a marriage, the first child was looked upon as the heir of the former husband, guaranteeing that his memory should not die out among the people and his property should be kept in the family.

This night Boaz will remain at his threshing floor, for the winnowing of barley will run late. Carefully Naomi instructs Ruth in the strange ritual. She is to dress in festive garments and go, taking care that Boaz does not see her:

> My daughter, should I not seek a home for you,
>   that it may be well with you?
> And is not Boaz our kinsman, with whose maidens you were?
> Wash therefore and anoint yourself,
>   and put on your best clothes and go down to the threshing
>   floor . . .
> But when he lies down, observe the place . . .
>   then, go and uncover his feet and lie down;
> and he will tell you what to do.

With quiet trust, Ruth carries out her mother-in-law's plan. At the threshing place, Boaz eats and drinks, and "his heart [is] merry." When he lies down "at the end of a heap of grain," then she softly uncovers his feet and lies down.

At midnight, however, "the man [is] startled," and turning over, sees the woman lying at his feet. "Who are you?" he asks.

"I am Ruth, your maidservant; spread your skirt over your maidservant, for you are next of kin." The gesture is a symbol of the protection he owes her.

"May you be blessed by the Lord, my daughter . . . do not fear, I will do for you all that you ask, for all my fellow townsmen know that you are a woman of worth." Momentarily all seems settled, but suspense grows again when Boaz remarks, "And now it is true that I am a near kinsman, yet there is a kinsman nearer than I. Remain this night, and in the morning, if he will do the part of the next of kin for you, well; let him do it; but if he is not willing . . . then, as the Lord lives, I will do the part of the next of kin for you. Lie down until the morning."

It must have been hard for her to sleep that night as she wondered about this unknown kinsman, and whether he would claim her as wife, or whether she would marry the kindly Boaz. One wonders, too, about Naomi's motives in sending her to Boaz. She must have felt he would make a better husband than the closer relative who had the prior claim; she must have had great trust in Boaz's ability to handle the situation.

With the first light, Boaz rises quietly, and with two gestures shows his courtesy once more. First he warns Ruth to let no one know she has been there, for fear her reputation should be injured, and then he gives her gifts to carry home: "Bring the mantle you are wearing and hold it out."

> And he [measures] out six measures of barley,
> and [lays] it upon her;
> then she [goes] into the city . . . to her mother-in-law.

In the sign of fruitful grain she will show Naomi that her errand has been fruitful.

Boaz goes and takes his seat at the gate of the city. This, as was seen in the story of Lot, is the place of business among these people. He waits there until this nameless kinsman passes by, and Boaz calls out: "Turn aside, friend; sit down here." Again there is a sense of leisure. The man is content to sit there and wait until Boaz shall take the initiative. Gradually he picks out "ten men of the elders of the city," and asks them to sit down.

With a good deal of tact he leads the gathering to his point of view. At first he says nothing of Ruth, but merely remarks that Naomi "is selling the parcel of land which belonged to our kinsman Elimelech."

> So I thought I would tell you of it, and say,
> buy it in the presence of those sitting here,
> and in the presence of the elders of my people.
> If you will redeem it, redeem it;
> but if you will not, tell me,
> [for] I come after you.

With renewed suspense the reader awaits the answer, and when it comes, hope begins to falter, for the man says, "I will redeem it."

Boaz, however, has another resource. He names the conditions of sale: according to the law, whoever buys the land must also take Ruth the Moabite, "the widow of the dead, in order to restore the name of the dead to his inheritance." This means that Ruth's sons will inherit the name and lands of her former husband, Mahlon. Hearing this, the kinsman thinks of the sons he already has: "I cannot redeem it for myself, lest I impair my own inheritance. Take my right of redemption yourself, for I cannot redeem it." He will not spend money for property which his older sons cannot inherit.

Now comes another old custom in Israel. "To confirm a transaction, the one drew off his sandal and gave it to the other, and this was the manner of attesting in Israel," as men today might shake hands over a bargain. With all dignity the ritual is followed and the contract ratified. Then Boaz reminds "the elders and all the people, 'You are witnesses this day that I have bought from the hand of Naomi all that belonged to Elimelech. . . . Also Ruth the Moabitess . . . to be my wife. . . . You are witnesses this day.' "

Then all at the gate reply:

> We are witnesses.
> May the Lord make the woman, who is coming into your house,
> like Rachel and Leah, who together built up the house of Israel.

"May you prosper in Ephrathah and be renowned in Bethlehem; and may your house be like the house of Perez, whom Tamar bore to Judah." With their blessing the scene ends, and the story moves toward its close.

So it is that Boaz claims Ruth and weds her, and in time she bears a son. As the story began with Naomi who knew famine and exile and death, so now it shows her provided for, and welcomed, and sharing the joy of Ruth and Boaz over the new life and hope that comes with the birth of a son. When young Obed is born, all the neighboring women who had rejoiced at Naomi's return to Bethlehem, now congratulate that good mother-in-law:

> Blessed be the Lord,
> who has not left you this day
> without next of kin. . . .

> He shall be to you a restorer of life
> and a nourisher of your old age.
> For your daughter-in-law who loves you,
> who is more to you than seven sons,
> has borne him.

Such fondness does Naomi show for the child that these neighbors smilingly remark that "A son has been born to Naomi." And "they named him Obed." All the attention is turned to Naomi and the child. Ruth remains contentedly in the background. And this young Obed, remarks the Bible, "was the father of Jesse, the father of David," the greatest king of Israel.

Peacefully the story ends. Ruth, the alien woman, is a stranger no longer, but has found a lasting home. Her early commitment, her leap into the unknown which meant acceptance of another people with other customs and a strange God, has brought her fulfillment. The destiny she chose, knowing its import, but foreseeing none of its actual circumstances, has brought her to a House of Bread, where beautiful speech is the rule, and beautiful customs are carried out in kindness by people of noble dignity.

It is no wonder that Ruth's story is one of the best loved in the Bible; hers is a memorable personality. Her free choice is the force which moves the story from its beginning in exile, famine, death, to plenty, and a new home, and a firstborn son. After this peace and joy, the Bible takes up the theme of the childless woman once again in the story of Samuel the prophet. This mother's longing, however, will be quickly fulfilled by the birth of her son, and then very soon move into scenes as dark as those at the beginning of Ruth.

To Jerusalem the Golden

CHAPTER FIFTEEN

Light and Shade for Samuel

THE close of Ruth leaves a sense of peace and fruition. Here is harvest. Here, too, is an end of one period of history. The mood of Ruth continues for a short space into the story of Samuel (I Sam. 1–7), yet the books of Samuel, being set in a world of war, are more like Judges than Ruth. The judges have risen from the natural situation. Each in his own territory has answered some need, has fought for part of the land, but enemies remain; the tribes are disunified. A new leader is needed—one who will be more than a local chieftain. Samuel, dedicated to Yahweh from youth, a prophet and judge, but not a man of war, brings the answer. He is handpicked by God to anoint two kings, Saul and David—one tragic, one gloriously successful.

The two books of Samuel, telling of Samuel himself, Saul, and David, contain some of the finest writing in the Bible or in any ancient literature, being famous for psychological understanding, convincing motivation, and rousing action. As for Samuel's story, the early part is beautifully developed, but later on the writer shows a tendency to summarize long years in a sentence. The narrative, too, woven of diversified materials, shows gaps and inconsistencies. It opens with a winning picture of the simple village home where Samuel is born, and goes on to tell of his boyhood at the shrine of Shiloh. Then he vanishes for forty years, and of that time the Bible says only that he lived at Ramah and traveled about judging and prophesying. Soon after, the account shifts to Samuel's old age and his anointing of Saul as king. Samuel's character, like his story, is marked by contradictions. At times he is affectionate and likeable, but again inhumanly harsh; now optimistic, now swept by dire pessimism. Some of these traits show up only later, after Saul takes the center of the stage. Though in part the variations may be owing to the fusing of different manuscripts, still Samuel's very inconsistencies make him seem all the more human.

The literary power of the account comes from its believable conversations with their turns of meaning, its unifying themes, and especially its artistry as worked out in scenes of contrasting light and darkness. In it the narrator's gift for communication and dialogue among his characters causes even insignificant events to take on dramatic power. Such exchanges of speech lend immediacy and urgency to events, as shall be seen. The reader then hears with his own ears and knows how the people feel.

Besides a flair for dialogue, the writer also shows his literary skill by means of several interwoven themes. One is the importance of sons: the longed-for child (as with Abraham and Sarah), the favored yet barren wife (as with Jacob and Rachel), the younger son as the chosen of Yahweh (as with Abel, Isaac, Jacob, Joseph). Wicked sons are also important: one set of them motivates the story, and a second group brings events full circle by setting in motion the tragedy of Saul. Yahweh's shrine at Shiloh and the ark of the covenant's holy power also preoccupy the writer, who employs incidental images of clothing and of blindness to good effect.

Above all, he is a master of contrast, as the structure shows. It moves through light and shade, through bright happenings followed by sorrow. Such differences are like heavy shadows cast across lighted fields, or recesses of darkness in buildings whose facades are illumined by sun. In all this a threefold architectural pattern of alternating light and darkness, joy and sorrow is discernible: first, the good son contrasted with wicked sons; second, a prophet's rise and reverence for Yahweh set against a priest's weakness leading to the loss of Yahweh's ark; and last, the return of the ark and a time of prosperity followed by new distress owing to the wickedness of Samuel's own sons. The design, patterned in contrasts, can be stated more simply as: good sons, wicked sons; good prophet, weak priest; peace, foreboding.

Samuel's birth and the days of his youth form the subject matter of the first section, which is made up of two conversations followed by the birth of a son, two more conversations of a different purpose and a song of thanksgiving. This part is then balanced by a section on Eli and the sacrilegious doings of his sons.

In the beginning "a certain man of Ramathaim-zophim of the hill country of Ephraim, whose name is Elkanah," appears. He has two wives, Hannah and Peninnah. Peninnah has children, but Hannah is childless. Each year they go "to worship and to sacrifice to the Lord of hosts at Shiloh," where Eli the priest and his two sons, Hophni and Phinehas, serve at the shrine. Elkanah loves Hannah greatly, but when the family goes on its pilgrimage, he must show Peninnah greater honor by giving portions of sacrificial meats to her "and to all her sons and daughters," while to Hannah he can give "only one portion." "And her rival used to provoke her sorely" because the Lord had made her childless.

So it is that Hannah weeps and cannot eat, and her husband takes the initiative in consoling her. Their conversation is marked by conjugal tenderness:

> Hannah, why do you weep?
> And why do you not eat?
> And why is your heart sad?
> Am I not more to you than ten sons?

His concern is plain, and her love for him is implicit in his confidence that he is dearer to her than many sons.

Still she is sorrowful, and at the shrine she prays to the Lord, weeping bitterly and offering a heartrending vow:

> O Lord of hosts . . . look on the affliction of thy maidservant,
> and remember me, [and] give to thy maidservant a son.
> Then I will give him to the Lord all the days of his life.

Even before her son is born, her grateful generosity plans to return him to God the giver. As she prays, Eli the priest notices that her lips move, and yet, contrary to the usual custom of praying aloud, her voice is not heard. In a scene that mingles comedy and pathos he takes her "to be a drunken woman," and the second conversation ensues, showing his misunderstanding:

How long will you be drunken?
Put away your wine from you.

Quietly Hannah replies,

No, my lord, I am a woman sorely troubled;
I have drunk neither wine nor strong drink,
but have been pouring out my soul before the Lord.

She does not tell the reason of her grief, and he sends her away with a blessing, "Go in peace, and the God of Israel grant your petition which you have made to him."

In both conversations so far, men have taken the initiative—first Elkanah, then Eli—while Hannah has been passive, her part merely to reply. After the birth of her child she will grow in self-assurance. Elkanah and his wives now return to Ramah, and there at last Hannah bears a son and calls him Samuel, for she says, "I have asked him of the Lord."

With the conversations after Samuel's birth, it is no longer Elkanah or Eli who will take the lead, but Hannah herself. Her first concern is to show that she remembers her vow. When her husband is ready to journey to Shiloh for the annual sacrifice, she does not wish to go. Decisively she tells him:

As soon as the child is weaned, I will bring him,
that he may appear in the presence of the Lord,
and abide there for ever.

Being a valiant woman, she faces openly all the implications of her offering. She herself will bring the child and offer him to Yahweh's service. Once that is done he will not return home again. And true to his great love for her, Elkanah consents, "Do what seems best to you . . . only, may the Lord establish his word."

When finally Samuel is old enough, she takes him to Shiloh, and with him, generous offerings of "a three-year-old bull, an ephah of flour, and a skin of wine." No longer is her gift, as in the beginning, but one poor portion. And meeting Eli, she once more opens the conversation in the fourth of these early speeches:

As you live, my lord, I am the woman
who was standing here in your presence praying to the Lord.
For this child I prayed;
and the Lord has granted me my petition . . .

therefore I have lent him to the Lord;
as long as he lives, he is lent to the Lord.

This time she willingly tells the favor she has asked, and then the Bible pictures her as breaking out in a triumphant hymn of praise.

Like Miriam's song of thankfulness after the Red Sea crossing, like Deborah's rejoicing after the defeat of Sisera, her song exalts the power and the mercy of God:

My heart exults in the Lord. . . .
There is none holy like the Lord . . .
there is no rock like our God.

Sorrow has surrendered like a beaten foe: "The bows of the mighty are broken, but the feeble gird on strength." Then in a pendulum movement of contrasts fitting well into this story built on contrasts of light and darkness, she sings of good and ill fortune, of riches and poverty reversed by the will of Yahweh:

Those who were full have hired themselves out for bread,
but those who were hungry have ceased to hunger.
The barren has borne seven,
but she who has many children is forlorn.

The days of all are in God's hands; he "kills and brings to life; he brings down to Sheol and raises up." Her next lines will be echoed many years later in Luke's gospel when Mary sings her joy at the coming birth of her son; clearly the Magnificat found in Luke is inspired by Hannah's words:

He raises the poor from the dust;
he lifts the needy from the ash heap,
to make them sit with princes
and inherit a seat of honor.

For the pillars of the earth are the Lord's,
and on them he has set the world.

So Hannah leaves Shiloh, and goes back to Ramah, leaving the child there to minister "to the Lord, in the presence of Eli the priest," and nothing is said of the sorrow she must have felt on coming back to her desolate house. In time, however, she is blessed with three sons and two daughters, so that her home is empty no more.

Samuel, meanwhile, ministers "before the Lord, a boy girded with a linen ephod," an apronlike garment, sign of his consecrated service. And every year Hannah "used to make for him a little robe and take it to him . . . when she went up with her husband to offer the yearly sacrifice." Both mentions of clothing are significant, the one indicating that Samuel belongs in a special way to the service of God, the other symbolizing Hannah's love. Her constancy is made clear by her gift; she must have experienced fresh joy and sorrow both, as each year she fashioned new garments larger than last year's to fit her growing son.

After all her joy, the pendulum swings to darker scenes, to Eli's sons who bring grief to their father and dishonor to the Lord. They are "worthless men" who have "no regard for the Lord." When people wish to offer sacrifice, these unworthy priests "come, while the meat [is] boiling, with a three-pronged fork . . . and thrust it into the pan," taking the choicest portions for themselves. They also lead women into prostitution in rites like those of nearby idolatrous tribes.

Eli now receives three warnings in an order of increasing urgency. At first the word about his sons' wickedness comes through rumor, then by a messenger sent from God, and finally by a vision given to Samuel, his helper. After the first, Eli attempts to turn his sons from their sins, but fails; after the second he does nothing, and the theme of his physical blindness appears. During the third warning, which is given to Samuel, the boy is shown as spiritually blind at first—not recognizing the revelations of the Lord—but growing into clearer sight with Eli's help. Still, Eli cannot change his sons, but his response shows his courage in facing misfortune and a great reverence for God.

Early in the account he keeps on hearing "all that his sons were doing to all Israel," and he reproves them, "My sons, it is no good report that I hear. . . . If a man sins against a man, God will mediate for him; but if a man sins against the Lord, who can intercede for him?" But they will not "listen to the voice of their father," and the writer contrasts their wickedness with the goodness of Samuel who grows "in favor with the Lord and with men."

Next a messenger of God comes saying, "Thus the Lord has said. . . . I promise that your house [shall be] cut off . . . so that there will not be an old man in your house":

And this which shall befall your two sons, Hophni and Phinehas,
shall be the sign to you:
both of them shall die on the same day.
And I will raise up . . . a faithful priest . . .
and I will build him a sure house.

Such is the second warning. It carries a prophecy of the coming rise of Samuel, who will succeed Eli as caretaker of the ark and offerer of sacrifice to God.

No improvement appears in the sons' conduct, and the last warning comes, not to Eli but to Samuel who is already becoming important at the shrine. The scene is one of the best known and most winning in scripture. As the writer remarks, "the word of the Lord was rare in those days," so that when he comes, his visit takes Samuel and Eli by surprise.

One night Eli is lying down in his place. His "eyesight had begun to grow dim, so that he could not see." On this evening "the lamp of God [has] not yet gone out." This is the second time his physical blindness is mentioned, with an implication of spiritual blindness underlying it, while the phrase about the lamp going out foreshadows another darkness—the coming destruction of the Shiloh shrine. Samuel, too, is blind at first to the identity of the divine voice. As he rests in his place of guardianship, where the ark of God is kept, Yahweh calls his name: "Samuel! Samuel!" And the boy jumps up and runs to Eli saying, "Here I am, for you called me."

"I did not call," says Eli, "lie down again." But no sooner is Samuel asleep than the Lord, seeming to enjoy the commotion he causes, calls again and the scene is repeated. For Samuel does "not yet know the Lord, and the word of the Lord [has] not yet been revealed to him."

Therefore when God calls him the third time, he runs again to Eli. This time the old man's eyes are opened and he tells Samuel to

Go, lie down; and if he calls you, you shall say,
"Speak, Lord, for thy servant hears."

Carefully Samuel obeys, and the Lord at last delivers his frightful message:

Behold, I am about to do a thing in Israel,
at which the two ears of every one that hears it will tingle.

On that day I will fulfill against Eli
all that I have spoken concerning his house. . . .
for the iniquity which he knew,
because his sons were blaspheming God,
and he did not restrain them.

All night Samuel keeps the message to himself, and rises early to open "the doors of the house of the Lord." But he is "afraid to tell the vision to Eli."

Then the old man proves his true worth. He insists that Samuel tell him all that the Lord has said. And the boy hides "nothing from him." When he has heard it all, he answers in noble words:

It is the Lord;
let him do what seems good to him.

But for a while the doom is delayed; Samuel grows, and the Lord is "with him and [lets] none of his words fall to the ground." So ends the first and most fully developed section of the story, which tells of Hannah and her good son Samuel; of Eli and his wicked sons, Hophni and Phinehas.

In the second section, bright events in the rise of Samuel are summarized in short fashion, then the writer, moving to his theme of wicked sons, begins to develop the doom that follows upon evil deeds. Little detail is used in telling of Samuel's prosperity. He is now a man, and "all Israel from Dan to Beer-sheba" knows he is "established as a prophet of the Lord," who continues to reveal himself in Shiloh. No mention is made of the way these visions come to public notice. The theme of Shiloh as Yahweh's chosen shrine, so prominent here, will make the next division of the story, when the shrine is devastated, all the more tragic.

Samuel's goodness also contrasts again with the phrase which tells of Eli's sons, saying that Eli is exceedingly old, and his sons keep right on making their conduct hateful before the Lord.

Because of their blasphemies, the Lord sends misfortune upon the whole people. Their enemies, the Philistines, long ago defeated by Samson, now muster against Israel for war. The fighting men encamp at Ebenezer, the Stone of Help, but there will be no help this time, for "about four thousand men" are slain "on the field of battle." In these straits, they send for "the ark of the covenant of the Lord of hosts . . . that he may come among us and save us from the power of our enemies." With it come Hophni and Phinehas, the two sons of Eli.

Its arrival rouses Israel, so that they give a great cheer, and the earth reechoes. The Philistines, listening, cry out: "Woe to us! Who can deliver us? . . . These are the gods who smote the Egyptians. . . . Take courage, and acquit yourselves like men, O Philistines, lest you become slaves to the Hebrews . . . acquit yourselves like men and fight."

They fight with such desperate courage that Israel flees in confusion, "every man to his home; and there [is] a very great slaughter." So complete is the rout that the ark of God is captured, and the two sons of Eli perish.

Back in the city, the old blind Eli is "sitting upon his seat by the road watching, for his heart [trembles] for the ark of God." Now a man of Benjamin comes running "with his clothes rent and . . . earth upon his head." Eli has heard the uproar, and waits in suspense, but the writer pauses to reiterate his earlier image of blindness—"Now Eli was ninety-eight years old and his eyes were set, so that he could not see." Then the runner bursts out with his tale:

> Israel has fled before the Philistines,
> and there has also been a great slaughter . . .
> and your two sons also, Hophni and Phinehas, are dead,
> and the ark of God has been captured.

His broken phrases give the sound of breathless haste. As if these things were not catastrophe enough, when the man mentions the ark of God, Eli falls "over backward from his seat by the side of the gate; and his neck [is] broken, and he [dies] for he [is] an old man, and heavy."

At the same time, Eli's daughter-in-law, wife of Phinehas, and now in her pregnancy, is struck with such grief that the pains of travail come upon her prematurely. "And about the time of her death the women attending her" say to her, "Fear not, for you have borne a son." But she neither answers nor gives heed. And she names "the child Ichabod, saying, 'The glory has departed from Israel, for the ark of God has been captured.' " The predicted doom has fallen, and the writer moves on, in the last of his paired scenes, to tell how the ark is saved, and how Samuel's sons, becoming wicked men, help to precipitate the tragic events of Saul's reign.

The triumphant Philistines carry away the ark "from Ebenezer to Ashdod." There they set it up in the house of Dagon—that god whose temple saw the death and triumph of Samson the strong man. But when the Philistines arise "early on the next morning," and go to their worship, there is Dagon "fallen face downward on the ground before the ark of the Lord." They "put him back in his place," but again on the next morning, "behold, Dagon had fallen . . . and the head of Dagon and both his hands were lying cut off upon the threshold." "This is why," remarks the writer, explaining a strange Philistine custom, "the priests of Dagon and all who enter the house of Dagon do not tread on the threshold of Dagon in Ashdod to this day."

Besides the fall of their idol, the ark also brings upon them plagues of mice that ravage the land, and of boils that infect the people. Seeing this they protest:

> The ark of the God of Israel
> must not remain with us;
> for his hand is heavy upon us
> and upon Dagon our god.

They move the ark to the city of Gath, but a great panic ensues, and the Lord afflicts "both young and old, so that tumors [break] out upon them." The same thing happens at Ekron, and the ark has been "in the country of the Philistines seven months," when they resolve to send it away, and with it a "guilt offering" of "five golden tumors and five golden mice." They hope by this to give glory to the God of Israel, and perhaps the Lord will lift his hand from them.

They are not ready to send it directly to Israel, but will leave its destination to chance or to providence. Accordingly they fetch "two milch cows upon which there has never come a yoke," hitch them to a cart, and "take their calves home, away from them." If the cows act according to their nature, they will refuse to leave the place where their calves are, but if they take to the road without coercion, the Philistines will know that Yahweh approves the move.

When the cows go "straight in the direction of Beth-shemesh along one highway, lowing as they [go], and turning neither to the right nor to the left," then the Philistines have their sign of approbation. The people of Beth-shemesh are reaping "their wheat harvest in the valley." Suddenly they lift up their eyes and see the ark, and come rejoicing to meet it. The animals stop near a huge stone in a field, so the men break up the wood of the cart and sacrifice the cows as a burnt offering, placing the golden objects on the stone as an altar.

Since the shrine of Shiloh was lost at the time the ark was taken and Eli died, a new home for it must now be found. The ark is therefore brought to Kiriath-jearim, "to the house of Abinadab on the hill; and they [consecrate] his son, Eleazar, to have charge of the ark of the Lord," and for twenty years the people worship there.

Then one day Samuel calls upon the house of Israel saying, "Gather all Israel at Mizpah, and I will pray to the Lord for you." Then the people fast and call upon God, and they grow strong. The Philistines draw near to attack, but "the Lord [thunders] with a mighty voice," and they are routed. And Israel pursues "the Philistines, and [smites] them, as far as below Beth-car." So Samuel takes a stone and sets it up "between Mizpah and Jesha-nah," and calls "its name Ebenezer, saying, 'The Lord has helped us.' "

During the ensuing years of peace, Samuel goes on his round of duty, "on a circuit year by year to Bethel, Gilgal, and Mizpah," judging Israel in all these places, and then returning home to Ramah.

Unlike the first two sections of the story where foreboding and the coming of doom have received the most attention, in this last scene the happier events have been described at length, while the events leading to the dark story of Saul will now be merely summarized by the biblical writer.

Samuel grows old, and unfortunately he establishes his sons Joel and Abijah as "judges over Israel." They perform their office in Beersheba, the southernmost town of Israel, some distance below Ramah, Samuel's home. These sons do not walk in Samuel's ways, but become grasping for gain by methods of violence, and by receiving bribes and perverting justice. Like

Eli's sons, they are wicked men, and like them they invite catastrophe. The story which began with an old priest's wicked sons, now ends with an old prophet's wicked heirs.

"Then all the elders of Israel" gather before Samuel at Ramah, and say to him:

> Behold, you are old and your sons
> do not walk in your ways;
> now appoint for us a king to govern us
> like all the nations.

But the thing displeases Samuel when they say, "Give us a king to govern us." The people, beset by enemies, feel the need for a political head, yet the prophet is reluctant to see them ruled by any king but Yahweh. He has chosen them, saved them from slavery in Egypt, protected them in the desert, brought them into a land of promise, yet they are not content with his rule.

When he prays, the Lord gives a grudging consent:

> Hearken to the voice of the people . . .
> for they have not rejected you,
> but they have rejected me
> from being king over them. . . .
>
> Now then, hearken to their voice;
> only you shall solemnly warn them,
> and show them the ways of the king
> who shall reign over them.

This is a moment of great importance, a turning point in Israel's history. And Samuel, in spite of his misgivings, is chosen to usher in the new period—the change from a nomadic life to a more orderly and settled existence. Henceforth Israel chooses to be ruled by kings. No longer will it depend upon local judges sprung from different tribes and sections. It is a step toward unity, and Samuel's part in it, his anointing of the first two kings, is the destiny toward which his life has led him.

With such a beginning, however, such predictions of trouble ahead, the new king's reign can scarcely be a happy one, and Saul who is chosen will be one of the world's great tragic figures.

His story begins with the voice of Samuel tolling out its mournful warning, and ends with that same voice foretelling defeat for Israel and death for Saul the king. Yet, in spite of everything, Saul at first shows great promise, and wins hearts by his many admirable qualities.

CHAPTER SIXTEEN

Toll the Dirge for Saul

> And now across old waters you may hear
> The boom of bells among still trees,
> Like a rolling of huge boulders
> beneath seas.[79]

BELLS have many voices. Some strike clear and sharp like bright winter; the story of Balaam is like this—swift and purposeful. Others boom with warm music, immersing the world in tawny autumn glow of sound like slow honey—such is the harvest tale of Ruth. But ringing longest in memory are heavy bells that toll and clang for death, one stroke for each year of a man's life. Their sound lingers, because awareness of death, especially of tragic death, accelerates the sense of life, sharpens realization of the swift passing of man's days on earth. This heightened sense of urgency is one of the values of tragedy in literature.

Such a tolling sounds through the tragic story of Saul, Israel's first king (1 Sam. 8 to 2 Sam. 1). In it the voice of Samuel the prophet rings out for warning, rings to mark off the steps of Saul's descent to catastrophe. Samuel goes protesting to anoint him king, brings news that he has lost Yahweh's favor, and at the end Samuel returns from the dead to foretell Saul's defeat and death. With Samuel's foreboding the narrative is set in motion, with disasters predicted by his shade the story of Saul ends. It is a tale of slow encroaching night. From the beginning Saul is shadowed, yet he chooses his tragic destiny—step by step he goes into deepening dark. The reader, watching him, feels a tension set up between fate and freedom—that tension which marks all great tragedies. As in them, so here too, the inner, tragic, problematic event is clothed in concrete contemporary reality.

Samuel's words of dread keynote the prologue. Then comes a time of promise when Saul's good qualities appear and he is given the privileges of kingship a step at a time. But God's voice, through Saul's own fault, ceases to speak to him; he begins to sit uneasy on his throne, and so is seized by fear. The next three sections, therefore, center around deeds manifesting fear lest the people turn against him, jealous fear of David his rival, and a nameless fear of final ruin. The last scene is a lament sung by David his successor, and this is followed by a tragic epilogue in which seven of Saul's descendants are killed, and Rizpah, a woman he loved, left to stand guard over their bodies.

The pattern, then, excluding prologue and epilogue, consists of five acts: 1) a time of rising hope; 2) fear of the people which leads to an unlawful sacrifice, a narrow escape from a killing like that of Jephthah the judge, and a defiant delay of a commanded execution; 3) fear of his rival, which starts with a popular song, prompts a shameful persecution, and climaxes in a wholesale and unjustifiable murder; 4) fear of final ruin which brings Saul to forbidden consultation with a witch who brings about the foretelling of his death; 5) David's lament for Saul and Jonathan.

As Saul goes down the movement toward tragedy accelerates. He feels:

> the cold . . . setting in
> on an iron world
> [and hurries] on, sensing
> death close behind
> stalking his own.[80]

An animal or an unreflective man cannot experience the sense of death's pursuit. Saul, though, is sensitively aware of his doom; this makes him cling the more desperately to life. Death by imposing limits intensifies existence.

In the prologue, Israel divided within and threatened by enemies from without, sends a delegation to Samuel asking for a king: "Give us a king to govern us." This request is little to his mind, because Yahweh is Israel's king. To change from theocracy to monarchy is a step weighted with significance. It supplies the serious subject which tragedy must have to go beyond a purely private scope. Samuel answers their plea with a chant of foreboding:

> These will be the ways of the king. . . .
> He will take your sons [for] his chariots . . .
> and some to plow his ground and to reap his harvest. . . .
>
> He will take your daughters to be perfumers
> and cooks and bakers.
>
> He will take the best of your fields and vineyards
> and olive orchards and give them to his servants.

"And in that day you will cry out because of your king, whom you have chosen for yourselves; but the Lord will not answer you in that day." The words bode ill for Saul and for Israel. He will be called to fill a position beyond him; he will be chosen, and so in a sense driven by destiny, yet when confronted with situations of choice he will use his freedom—fighting and falling repeatedly—in efforts to keep his power.

His early promise, his generous response to the call, and his understandable failures, stir the onlooker to pity and fear for a man so great, yet so human in his blunders. But beyond his personal grief, the ruin of this king who never sought the kingship takes on larger implications. When he falls he goes down, not as a single man, a simple citizen, but rather, like a true tragic hero, for his death sweeps all Israel with war's devastation.

> Do you see him whom the Lord has chosen?
> There is none like him among all the people.
> And all the people shouted, "Long live the king."
> (1 SAM. 10:24)

Saul himself comes on stage when, having traveled north and west from his home in Gibeah near Jerusalem, he arrives in "the hill country of Ephraim," at Ramah where Samuel dwells. He is seeking his father's asses which have gone astray. From the first moment he is actual and individual, possessed of kingly qualities that might have led to lasting greatness: handsome, thoughtful of others, diffident about his own worth, prudent, courageous, and magnanimous. These qualities appear in his actions during the three successive steps by which he is brought to kingship.

He is of commanding appearance—"not a man among the people of Israel more handsome than he; from his shoulders upward he was taller than any of the people." His first words show thoughtful concern for his father: "Come, let us go back, lest my father cease to care about the asses and become anxious about us." The man, however, suggests that they first consult Samuel, who lives here in Ramah: "All that he says comes true," and he may have news of the animals.

At this, Saul's thoughtfulness appears again, for he hesitates, knowing it is proper to offer gifts to seers, but their provisions are all used up. The servant, however, produces a coin, and they go on. As they walk, they meet "young maidens coming out to draw water," and an amusing conversation occurs, with the girls giving voluble directions and advice. If the young men will hurry, they may find Samuel "before he goes up to the high place to eat . . . because the people have a sacrifice today on the high place . . . for the people will not eat until he arrives, since he must bless the sacrifice. . . . Now go up, for you will meet him immediately." It sounds as if several are talking at once with little regard for logic, and their chatter furnishes a comic relief which will soon be needed as the story of Saul gathers darkness to itself like some smothering animal pelt thrown over one's head.

Suddenly, as they climb, there is "Samuel coming out toward them on his way up to the high place." This portentous meeting is no accident, for the prophet has been told by the Lord that a man of Benjamin will appear today, and "you shall anoint him to be prince over my people Israel. He shall save my people from the hand of the Philistines; for I have seen the affliction of my people." Samuel's earlier reluctance is in abeyance. It is interesting to note his waverings. In them, as has been said, scholars can trace the hands of editors piecing separate accounts together. Whatever the reason, the text of the Bible pictures Samuel ordinarily harsh and afraid, but at times hopeful and friendly. Now he gives a royal welcome, announcing that the lost asses are safe, and that great blessings wait for Saul.

Hearing his words, the young man shows a winning diffidence: "Am I not a Benjaminite, from the least of the tribes of Israel? And is not my family the humblest of all the families of the tribe of Benjamin? Why then have you spoken to me in this way?" But Samuel answers by leading him to the hilltop and giving him a place of honor at the sacrificial banquet, ordering the best portions of meat to be put before Saul. When the feasting is over, the prophet brings him down into the city, and a bed is "spread for Saul upon the roof" of Samuel's dwelling.

Next morning, Saul and the prophet set out toward Gibeah. Soon Samuel halts, and taking out a phial of oil, pours it on Saul's head, announcing: "You shall reign over the people of the Lord." Such is Saul's vocation—to be a king, but he is not yet to take the throne. Samuel next gives him an important command, and then foretells three events as signs that his call comes from God. When Saul shall come into danger, Samuel says, he must realize that God's help will depend on obedience. No matter the emergency, he must wait seven days, until Samuel comes to show him what he shall do, and "to offer burnt offerings and to sacrifice peace offerings." Upon Saul's later failure to follow these instructions will hinge the beginnings of his tragedy.

Samuel, as he speaks his farewell, then tells of three significant encounters about to take place. These reinforce the truth of the anointing. Exactly as he has said, Saul first meets two men "by Rachel's tomb in the territory of Benjamin," bringing word that the asses are found. Next at "the oak of Tabor" Saul confronts three men on pilgrimage to Bethel:

> one carrying three kids,
> another carrying three loaves of bread,
> and another carrying a skin of wine.

From them he receives two loaves which were probably intended as offerings at the shrine of Bethel. His sharing thus in the Lord's bread signifies that, as king, he is to be Yahweh's representative. Finally Saul meets a band of prophets, and the "spirit of the Lord" comes mightly upon him too, so that he prophesies with them. This means that he will be king with the help of Yahweh's charismatic spirit. After the predictions are thus fulfilled, Saul comes to his home in Gibeah.

Here another of his good qualities becomes evident—a prudence which prompts him to keep his own counsel. His uncle asks where he has been. "To seek the asses," he says, "and when we saw they were not to be found, we went to Samuel." Then the uncle insists, "Tell me what Samuel said to you." But Saul merely repeats that the prophet told him where the asses were to be found. "But about the matter of the kingdom . . . he did not tell him anything."

Perhaps he dreads coming responsibilities; or again, having no proof, he feels it would be rash to announce himself as future king of Israel. Whatever his motives, he can keep the Lord's secret, and however he may feel, with this anointing he has taken the first step toward the throne.

Soon comes the second step of the ascent. Samuel calls an assembly at Mizpah. There he tolls his warning song again, and afterwards arranges that Saul be chosen king by the casting of lots. Speaking in the voice of Yahweh he chants:

> I brought up Israel out of Egypt,
> and I delivered you from the hand . . .
> of all the kingdoms that were oppressing you.
>
> But you have this day rejected your God . . .
> and you have said, "No! but set a king over us."

Then tribe by tribe, clan by clan, man after man the Israelites come forward, and the lot falls on Benjamin; the families of Benjamin come forward and the lot falls on Saul.

But with his usual diffidence he has gone into hiding. Eagerly the people search among the tents, find him, and bring him to stand before Samuel. Then Samuel says before all, "Do you see him whom the Lord has chosen?" And the people cry, "Long live the king!" But some grumble, asking "How can this man save us?" And they bring him no presents. Saul acts as if he has not heard, and even after the acclaim he returns quietly to Gibeah.

Still, for all his thoughtful ways, his prudence and diffidence, he can act with swift courage. One day a messenger comes bearing word that the men of Jabesh-gilead are besieged by the Ammonites, who threaten to put out the right eye of every citizen. Saul, just in from the fields and driving his team of oxen, feels his heart burn with rage. He cuts the oxen into small pieces, and sends the portions by messenger to every part of Israel, saying, "Whoever does not come out after Saul and Samuel so shall it be done to his oxen." In full strength they answer the summons, smite and scatter the Ammonites, and save Jabesh-gilead—a favor which the Gileadites will repay when Saul is dead.

During the victory celebrations some of Saul's adherents call for those who at Mizpah had protested against his election: "Bring the men," they say, "that we may put them to death." But at this Saul shows another of his good qualities, a spirit of forebearance, of magnanimous forgiveness:

> Not a man shall be put to death this day,
> for today the Lord has wrought deliverance in Israel.

Immediately after this comes the last step to full kingship, for Samuel invites them all: "Come, let us go to Gilgal and there renew the kingdom." "And there they made Saul king before the Lord in Gilgal . . . and Saul and all the men of Israel rejoiced greatly."

But Samuel cannot let the day pass without showing his mixed feelings. He reminds Israel again of her rescue from Egypt, and of the saving acts of Yahweh in the days of the judges when he sent Barak and Gideon and Jephthah to rescue them. Yet "when you saw that Nahash the king of the Ammonites came against you, you said to me, 'No, but a king shall reign over us,' when the Lord your God was your king."

> Now behold the king whom you have chosen,
> for whom you have asked;
> behold the Lord has set a king over you.

It is another tolling, a tocsin for warning after the third step that has made Saul king in earnest. Yet Samuel does not leave them hopeless. If they and their king "fear the Lord and serve him and hearken to his voice . . . it will be well." But "if you rebel . . . then the hand of the Lord will be against you and your king."

Soon these warnings prove true, for in the next part of the story Saul appears, openly acknowledged as king, but fearing lest he lose his high place. Because of this fear he takes his first step downward in defiance of Yahweh's will by disobeying Samuel's early command about the offering of sacrifice in time of emergency.

> I repent that I have made Saul king;
> for he has turned back from following me,
> and has not performed my commandments.
> (1 SAM. 15:10)

Saul has come to the kingdom in three stages: he was privately annointed at Ramah, elected by lot at Mizpah, and acclaimed by all the people at Gilgal. Yet he is afraid of the people and shows this fear in three important scenes—a failure, a rescue from the consequences of his own rashness, and another failure. The first happens at a time when the Philistines are threatening the land and the Israelites are "in straits," and hide "in caves and in holes and in rocks and in tombs and in cisterns."

In order to do battle, Saul needs Yahweh's help and blessing, but he has been commanded to wait seven days until Samuel shall come to offer sacrifice. He does wait, but Samuel delays. Men are deserting. Saul grows desperate, calls at the last minute for victims, and usurping the place of the prophet, he himself offers the sacrifice. For fear of losing the support of his men he has sinned against the Lord and his prophet.

No sooner has he finished than Samuel comes in a storm of anger: "What have you done?"

"When I saw that the people were scattering from me, and that you did not come within the days appointed, and that the Philistines had mustered at Michmash, I said, 'Now the Philistines will come down upon me at Gilgal, and I have not entreated the favor of the Lord', so I forced myself, and offered the burnt offering."

"You have done foolishly; you have not kept the commandment of the Lord," and his doom song continues, "The Lord would have established your kingdom over Israel for ever. But now your kingdom shall not continue; the Lord has sought out a man after his own heart; and . . . appointed him to be prince over his people." It is the first loss. Like Shakespeare's tragic Macbeth, he is told beforetime that his dynasty will end, his sons cannot succeed him.

Ironically enough, the eldest of these sons, Jonathan, now proves how brave a king he might have been, and Saul shows once more his fear of the people. With one companion Jonathan storms a Philistine stronghold, working such havoc that among the enemy "there was a panic in the camp" and wild confusion. Quickly Saul follows up the advantage and wins a success made possible by Jonathan's daring. But this day of victory will put Jonathan in jeopardy from his father, and he will be saved only by Saul's fear of the people. For once, the besetting fault will have a good result.

While the army pursues the fleeing Philistines, Saul lays "an oath on the people, saying, 'Cursed be the man who eats food until it is evening and I am avenged on my enemies.' "

In fear of the curse, all remain fasting even when they pass through a glade where honey lies on the ground in golden combs. Jonathan, however, has not heard the orders. He dips his staff into the honeycomb and takes a mouthful from his hand. Then with energies renewed and his eyes brightened, he fights more valiantly than ever.

That evening, offering sacrifice, Saul receives no response from the Lord. He concludes that someone has defied the ban, and repeats his oath, adding with an ironical twist that the transgressor, even "though it be . . . Jonathan my son, he shall surely die." Lots are cast; the signs point to Jonathan.

Courage and pathos contend in his reply: "I tasted a little honey with the tip of the staff that was in my hand; here I am, I will die," or as the older translation puts it, more beautifully, "Only a little money and now I must die." There is an interesting modern poem which combines memories of this scene with the rescue of Isaac laid on the altar by his father, Abraham:

> I did but taste a little of the honey with the
> tip of my rod and my eyes were opened, and behold
> I must die. May God do so and more my father said
> for thou shalt surely die, Jonathan, but the Lord God
> sent leaping from the heart of a bush a saving ram,
> and so I live.[81]

Instead of a ram in the heart of a bush, however, it is the people's protest that leaps out to save the young man, "Shall Jonathan die, who has wrought this great victory in Israel? Far from it! As the Lord lives, there shall not one hair of his head fall to the ground."

Moved by their plea, and undoubtedly by his own love, too, Saul stays his hand and Jonathan lives. Yet, though Saul does not kill his son, he has already lost the kingship for him, and soon, fearing the people again, he will lose his own right to the throne.

Saul's next downward step comes after a battle against Amalek. Samuel has spoken in the name of the Lord of armies:

I will punish what Amalek did to Israel
in opposing them on the way,
when they came up out of Egypt.

Now go and smite Amalek,
and utterly destroy all that they have;
do not spare them . . . man and woman . . .
ox and sheep, camel and ass.

Again Saul disobeys, overcoming the Amalekites, "from Havilah as far as Shur, which is east of Egypt." But he spares "Agag the king of the Amalekites alive," and saves "the best of the sheep and of the oxen . . . and all that was good."

Then "the word of the Lord came to Samuel, saying, 'I repent that I have made Saul king; for he has turned back from following me, and has not performed my commandments.' " All night long Samuel pleads for Saul, but the Lord will not listen, so at morning he hurries to the camp with his unhappy tidings. Saul meets him lightheartedly enough, saying, "Blessed be you to the Lord; I have performed the commandment of the Lord." He has, however, not fulfilled the command, nor can he give a blessing since his sacrifice was made with forbidden fruits.

"What then is this bleating of the sheep in my ears, and the lowing of the oxen which I hear?" says Samuel. "Though you are little in your own eyes, are you not the head of the tribes of Israel? . . . The Lord sent you on a mission. . . . Why, then did you not obey? . . . Why did you swoop on the spoil?"

As he has done before, Saul disclaims responsibility: "I have obeyed . . . I have gone on the mission [and] utterly destroyed the Amalekites. But the people took of the spoil . . . to sacrifice to the Lord."

Angrily Samuel bursts out:

> Has the Lord as great delight in burnt offerings . . .
> as in obeying the voice of the Lord?
> Behold, to obey is better than sacrifice,
> and to hearken than the fat of rams. . . .
>
> Because you have rejected the word of the Lord,
> he has also rejected you from being king.

By his first sin, Saul had lost the succession for his sons, now he loses for himself the right to the throne. He is Yahweh's king no longer.

From this turning point his fortunes will descend swiftly, and at the very end the biblical writer will say that an Amalekite has claimed to be the killer of Saul. This however, may be a stroke of literary irony, showing that Amalek, Saul's occasion of sin, is the instrument of his death, because, as scholars point out, Mount Gilboa, where Saul died, is so far north from Amalekite lands that it is surprising to find any soldiers of Amalek there.

Now Saul, with his usual and winning candor, confesses his motive for disobeying: "I have sinned . . . because I feared the people and obeyed their voice." It is the old weakness. But still he pleads with Samuel to pardon the sin and return with him, that he "may worship the Lord." He hopes that Samuel may yet win him God's mercy, or at least that the prophet's presence will save appearances before the people. He would like to conceal the rift between them.

Unrelenting, Samuel turns away, but Saul catches at his cloak. It tears in his hand, giving the prophet opportunity to point a symbolic meaning—just as the king has torn the garment, so "the Lord has torn the kingdom" from Saul this day, and has "given it to [one] better than you."

Then, surprisingly, Samuel makes a gesture of human mercy and goes with Saul, thus hiding the breach from the people. Still, it is the end of their relationship, and after the sacrifice, Saul kills Agag the Amalekite with his own hands, and goes home; "And Samuel did not see Saul again until the day of his death, but Samuel grieved over Saul. And the Lord repented that he had made Saul king over Israel."

In the next part of the story, the symbol of the torn cloak

which means the forcible tearing away of kingship, will be followed by two scenes in which Saul and his son Jonathan freely choose to dress their destined rival in clothing which symbolizes their power and royalty. It is another aspect of the tension between fate and freedom, destiny and man's own choosing.

> Lying against the throne-room wall,
> Let David play the harp for Saul.
>
> So shall the melancholic brain / Forget . . .
>
> The kingdom's mischief, and the way
> The self disperses, day by day.[82]

Since Saul is no longer Yahweh's chosen king, Samuel is commissioned to anoint another—David of the tribe of Judah. This young man will become a focus for the king's jealous fear, and hating him, Saul will lose, one by one, the things he cherishes: his son's loyalty, the people's support, the fidelity of his daughter, his own integrity, and even the dignity befitting his kingship.

Pursuing his errand, Samuel visits the house of Jesse of Bethlehem—that Jesse whom the book of Ruth listed as the son of Obed, her child. In Jesse's home, Samuel meets seven sons in turn, but the Lord has chosen none of these. Then the youngest is brought in from the fields. "Now he was ruddy, and had beautiful eyes, and was handsome."

"And the Lord said, 'Arise, anoint him; for this is he.' " And Samuel takes the horn of oil and anoints him in the midst of his brothers, and the "Spirit of the Lord came mightily upon David from that day forward." Two things are noteworthy here. The spirit of the Lord which had departed from Saul now rests upon David, and Saul's loss will soon bring David's life into danger. Moreover, the scene of this anointing contrasts vividly with that earlier one of Saul's. The latter, in symbol of the lonely life he was to lead, received his anointing far from home and with only Samuel as witness. David, whose life, as shall be seen in the next chapter, can be chronicled by listing the names of the many people whose fortunes intertwine with his, is anointed in a social situation. He is at home, and his father and brothers witness his election by Yahweh.

Since the spirit no longer rests upon Saul, his personality begins to deteriorate. Evil moods give him no rest. His servants, therefore, offer to seek out "a man who is skilful in playing the lyre; and when the evil spirit . . . is upon" Saul, he will play it, and the king will recover. It is refreshing here to find that Saul's followers show solicitude for him. Though he is never a gregarious man, he is able to inspire affection in others.

By a stroke of irony, the man they hit upon is David the shepherd-musician. The texts that introduce David, as shall be seen in the next chapter, show evidence of composite sources—he appears as shepherd, as musician, and then as accomplished warrior; he has spent some time at Saul's camp, and then the Bible has Saul asking his name. It is another instance, like those often seen before, of the tendency of ancient editors to retain incidents from their sources, even when these do not entirely harmonize.

Saul, welcoming the musician, has no idea that this boy is destined to succeed him, nor that his musical skill will, at the last, be used to compose a dirge for him and Jonathan. So David comes to Saul, and enters "his service. And Saul [loves] him greatly, and he [becomes] his armor-bearer." And the music David plays has power to relieve the king, so that the evil spirit leaves him in peace.

Soon, however, David looms as a rival. He fights a famous battle with a Philistine giant named Goliath. The details belong to David's own story and will be treated later. However, in the preparations for battle the clothing symbol reappears in ominous fashion, for the king makes David wear "his armor." He puts "a helmet of bronze on his head, and [clothes] him with a coat of mail." These garments, belonging to Saul the warrior, signify his prowess; he does not suspect that his gesture foretells his loss of that power.

David, though, is not ready to walk in Saul's clothes. The king is taller and his armor too heavy. Putting it aside, the boy, provided only with a sling and five smooth stones, goes to meet the giant, kills him, and returns with the head as his trophy. When he presents himself before Saul, Jonathan is there, and "the soul of Jonathan [is knit] to the soul of David, and Jonathan [loves] him as his own soul."

So begins one of the world's most famous friendships; it goes so deep that the prince, the heir-apparent, even lends David his robe, armor, sword, and bow. This royal raiment is apparently Jonathan's own, but in reality it is already forfeit to his friend because that friend is the hidden heir-apparent to the throne, the future successor of Saul.

Even though Jonathan remains with his father, and finally dies at his side, still his loyalties are henceforward divided, as Saul sees to his grief. The beloved son will even go so far as to help in furthering the rival's fortunes, and after protecting him from his father's rage, will ask protection from David for his posterity. It is as though Jonathan has a premonition of the future:

> May the Lord be with you, as he has been with my father. . . .
> When the Lord cuts off every one of the enemies of David . . .
> let not the name of Jonathan be cut off from the house of David.

Though he does not know it, the Lord already is with David as he once was with Saul, for the spirit which rested upon Saul, marking him as Yahweh's king, has departed from him and settled upon David, who is even now the king by consecration, though not yet in actuality.

The people, too, whom Saul has worked so hard to hold, now turn to David, leaving the king shaken by helpless anger. His first intimation of their waning loyalty comes one day as he returns from battle, accompanied by the handsome young warrior. Then a chorus of women comes out to greet them singing, with small tact or diplomacy:

> Saul has slain his thousands,
> and David his ten thousands.

As the writer remarks, Saul is "very angry, and this saying [displeases] him." Then he asks himself, "What more can he have but the kingdom?"

Next day Saul begins to suffer jealous frenzies. Several times while David plays to soothe him, he throws a lance, hoping to pin him to the wall. But David slips away safe. Saul has lost the first place in Jonathan's heart, and his preeminence with the people. Soon, by means of his own wily plan to do away with David, he loses the loyalty of his daughter, Michal.

Learning that Michal loves David, Saul makes a resolve: "Let me give her to him, that she may be a snare for him, and that the hand of the Philistines may be against him." And he sends a message, "Thus shall you say to David, 'The king desires no marriage present except a hundred foreskins of the Philistines.'" It seems impossible that David should kill a hundred of the enemy and escape himself. But with his accustomed good fortune, David kills two hundred and marries Michal, who like her brother Jonathan begins to protect David from Saul.

Once when Saul's soldiers pursue him she saves his life, helping him to escape through a window, deceiving the pursuers by placing an image in the bed, with "goat's hair at its head," and claiming that David is too ill to be disturbed. Fooled by the figure in the bed, they return to Saul, who orders them: "Bring him up to me in the bed, that I may kill him," a notion totally unworthy of a king. By this time, of course, David is safely gone, and Saul can do nothing but reproach Michal with sadness: "Why have you deceived me thus, and let my enemy go?"

As all turn from him to his rival, Saul comes to deeper disgrace, forgetting even his personal honor and royal dignity. He pursues David with unremitting envy, and David flees to a priest named Ahimelech, leading him to believe that David has come on a secret errand for the king. Ahimelech gives him bread from the altar, thus repeating the symbol from Saul's early days, when he was given bread intended as pilgrims' offerings. In both cases, sharing the Lord's bread has signified that the young men are chosen by God.

Ahimelech also lets David take the sword of Goliath the Philistine, which has been stored there at the shrine at Nob. Unfortunately, one "of the servants of Saul [is] there that day . . . his name was Doeg the Edomite, the chief of Saul's herdsmen." This man is sometimes fittingly called the Judas of the Old Testament, the treacherous counterpart of Sinon, the traitor at the fall of Troy.

Doeg's betrayal comes one day as Saul is holding court "at Gibeah, under the tamarisk tree on the height, with his spear in his hand, and all his servants . . . standing about him." It is a primitive scene, and recent archeological discoveries by Professor Albright indicate that Saul's court was rough in the extreme—a warrior's place rather than a kingly ruler's. As he sits there surrounded by his men, he speaks with petulance, and then with unreasoning rage: "Hear now, you Benjaminites; will the son of Jesse give every one of you fields and vineyards, will he make you all commanders of thousands . . . that all of you have conspired against me? No one discloses to me when my son makes a league with the son of Jesse, none of you is sorry for me."

Then Doeg the Edomite answers him: "I saw the son of Jesse coming to Nob, to Ahimelech . . . and he inquired of the Lord for him, and gave him provisions, and gave him the sword of Goliath the Philistine." The sword is particularly important, because in these days the Philistines have a monopoly on the working of metals, and "there was no smith to be found throughout all the land of Israel; . . . but every one of the Israelites went down to the Philistines to sharpen his plowshare, his mattock, his axe, or his sickle. . . . So on the day of the battle there was neither sword nor spear found in the hand of any of the people with Saul and Jonathan; but Saul and Jonathan his son had them." The king alone, and Jonathan, carry weapons of metal into battle.

Stirred up now by Doeg, Saul sends for Ahimelech and all his priestly kindred. Ignoring their protests of innocence, he orders his men to kill them. When these refuse, he bids Doeg, "Turn and kill the priests of the Lord; because their hand also is with David." Then Doeg kills "on that day eighty-five persons who wore the linen ephod," the vestment of priesthood. It is Saul's most brutal act; after it he retains little dignity, but dribbles it away in petty persecutions of David.

He pursues his rival over the whole countryside, sending out orders for his men to learn all the secret places where David hides. "I will search him out among all the thousands of Judah." He speaks as if he were hunting a beast, and soon David has a chance to remind him how little such conduct consorts with his noble rank. David's reproach comes during a twice-told incident, whose details differ somewhat. Here the divergence between the two men stands in sharp relief, and the symbolic image of clothing reappears.

David has fled to the "strongholds of Engedi" and Saul seeks him "in front of the Wildgoats' Rocks." Coming to a cave, the king goes in to rest, but David and his men are "sitting in the innermost parts of the cave." Saul is at his mercy now, and

David's followers urge him to make an end of his foe. David, however, looking down upon his sleeping enemy, contents himself with silently cutting off a piece of Saul's clothing. Earlier a torn cloak meant that the Lord would wrest away Saul's kingship; then both the king and his heir freely put their garments upon David; now David takes for himself a clothing token, cut from Saul's royal raiment. He is nearly ready to take Saul's place as king.

When Saul awakes and leaves the cave, David follows, calling aloud: "My lord the king! . . . Why do you listen to the words of men who say, 'Behold, David seeks your hurt? Lo, this day your eyes have seen how the Lord gave you today into my hand; for by the fact that I cut off the skirt of your robe, and did not kill you, you may know . . . there is no . . . treason in my hands." But "I spared you," saying, "I will not put forth my hand against my lord; for he is the Lord's anointed." So he shows himself compassionate, and reverent toward the one God has chosen. But with one of those sudden changes that mark his character, Saul wins sympathy again by noble words, showing that the bitterness of his hate lives in his heart along with a great love for David:

"Is this your voice, my son David? . . . You are more righteous than I; for you have repaid me good, whereas I have repaid you evil." And touched by prophecy, he continues, "And now, behold, I know that you shall surely be king. . . . Swear to me therefore by the Lord that you will not cut off my descendants after me." So David swears to protect Saul's family, and when he comes to the throne he remembers his promise and insures the continuance of Saul's line by adopting Mephibosheth, the son of Jonathan. But he fails to follow the spirit of his oath, when, as shall be seen, he wards off distress from Israel by executing seven men of Saul's posterity.

> Seek out for me a woman who is a medium,
> that I may go to her and inquire of her.
> . . . Behold there is a medium at Endor.
> (1 SAM. 27:7)

Haunted by the brooding presence of Yahweh who has rejected him, Saul tries to win back favor, or at least to get some response from the Lord. For one thing, he has "put the mediums and the wizards out of the land" in an attempt to purify the worship of

Yahweh. Yet in a time of overwhelming danger, when God remains silent in the face of all his entreaties, Saul turns to an enchantress, the famous witch of Endor. Through her, he hears Samuel's last prophecy tolling out doom.

At this time the Philistines have mustered their armies to levy war on Israel's northern borders. Saul goes up Mount Gilboa to look down upon their camp and is dismayed. He prays, but the Lord does not "answer him, either by dreams, or by Urim, or by the prophets"—the three usual ways of discerning the divine will. Urim and thummim were instruments for casting lots; no one today knows just what they looked like; they were carried in a pocket of the priestly apron, the ephod. At any rate, when these means fail, Saul resorts to necromancy, only to hear the shade of the long dead prophet, Samuel, cry out tidings of death.

The scene is smothered in a black anguish like that of the witch scenes in Macbeth, or like the darkness of Hopkins' terrible lines:

> I wake and feel the fall of dark, not day.
> What hours, O what black hours we have spent
> This night! what sight you, heart, saw; ways you went![83]

Like the heavy "fell" or pelt of some nightmare beast, doom presses down on this desolate king, and the fell powers of fate impend in thick darkness. For Saul seeks out a woman who is a medium, and goes to her at dead of night. Here his will is almost thwarted because of his own earlier decree against witches, for when he asks her to "Divine for me by a spirit, and bring up for me whomever I shall name for you," the woman answers him, "Surely you know . . . how [Saul] has cut off the mediums and the wizards from the land. Why then are you laying a snare . . . to bring about my death?"

He swears that "no punishment" shall come upon her, and calls on her to "bring up Samuel." "When the woman [sees] Samuel, she [cries] out with a loud voice," saying to Saul, "Why have you deceived me? You are Saul."

The king says to her, "Have no fear; what do you see?"

"I see a god coming up out of the earth . . . an old man . . . and he is wrapped in a robe." Saul knows that it is Samuel, but his hope is drowned out in the harsh tones that sound doom: "Why have you disturbed me by bringing me up?"

"I am in great distress," says Saul, "for the Philistines are warring against me, and God has turned away from me and answers me no more . . . therefore I have summoned you to tell me what I shall do."

"Why then do you ask me, since the Lord has turned from you and become your enemy? . . . For the Lord has torn the kingdom out of your hand, and given it to your neighbor, David. Because you did not obey the voice of the Lord, and did not carry out his fierce wrath against Amalek, therefore the Lord has done this thing."

> Tomorrow . . . the Lord will give Israel
> into the hands of the Philistines;
> and tomorrow you and your sons shall be with me.

It is Samuel's last warning.

Crushed by despair, Saul falls prostrate, and besides he has "no strength in him, for he [has] eaten nothing all day and all night." It is left for him to receive mercy from this woman who is a witch. She reminds him that she has risked her life by listening to him, "Now therefore, you also hearken to your handmaid; let me set a morsel of bread before you; and eat, that you may have strength when you go on your way."

His men add their own urging, and finally he rises and waits while the woman kills her "fatted calf," and takes flour to bake "unleavened bread." After he has eaten, he sets out to journey the whole night through, traveling in darkness that foreshadows his yet darker journey to death. There is something immeasurably poignant in the courage with which Saul goes along this road that leads to inevitable death.

When the battle is joined on Mount Gilboa, the Philistines surge ahead and Israel must flee. But the enemy overtakes Saul and his sons. They slay Jonathan and Abinadab and Malchishua, the sons of Saul, while he himself is badly wounded. Then he calls upon his armor-bearer, "Draw your sword, and thrust me through with it, lest these uncircumcised come and thrust me through, and make sport of me."

"But his armor-bearer would not; for he feared greatly." "Therefore Saul [takes] his own sword, and [falls] upon it." When the man sees that Saul is dead, then he too falls upon his sword.

Thus Saul died, and his three sons,
and his armor-bearer, and all his men
on the same day together.

Then the Israelites "on the other side of the valley and those beyond the Jordan" all abandon their cities and flee, so that the Philistines occupy the territory, and the country is in a worse state than when Saul began his reign. Saul has gone down, not as a private citizen, alone, but like a true tragic hero, bringing desolation to a whole nation.

Sorrow is heaped upon sorrow when, during the rout that follows upon the disaster, a woman flees with Jonathan's five-year-old son, Mephibosheth. In her haste she falls, and the boy is lamed for life. But even this is not the end.

Next day, coming "to strip the slain," the Philistines find "Saul and his three sons fallen on Mount Gilboa." They "cut off his head," strip him of armor, and send "messengers . . . to carry the good news to their idols and to the people." They also put Saul's "armor in the temple of Ashtaroth; and they [fasten] his body to the wall of Beth-shan." To be disgraced in places of pagan worship—such is the terrible fate of Saul, who with all his faults was yet Yahweh's chosen king.

He still has some friends in the land, however, for the men of Jabesh-gilead, whom Saul had rescued in his first act as king, come to the rescue. These men march "all night," take "the body of Saul and the bodies of his sons from the wall of Beth-shan"; bring them "to Jabesh and burn them there," burying the ashes "under the tamarisk tree in Jabesh," and fasting seven days.

When David hears that Saul and Jonathan are dead, he sings a lament that haunts men's memories to this day and stands among the world's great poems. In theme, design, imagery, it is a masterwork which even in translation has an astonishing power to move the heart. It deserves to be seen as a whole:

Thy glory, O Israel, is slain upon thy high places!
How are the mighty fallen!

Tell it not in Gath,
publish it not in the streets of Ashkelon;
lest the daughters of the Philistines rejoice,
lest the daughters of the uncircumcised exult.

Ye mountains of Gilboa,
let there be no dew or rain upon you,
nor upsurging of the deep!
For there the shield of the mighty was defiled,
the shield of Saul, not anointed with oil.

From the blood of the slain,
from the fat of the mighty,
the bow of Jonathan turned not back,
and the sword of Saul returned not empty.

Saul and Jonathan, beloved and lovely!
In life and in death they were not divided;
they were swifter than eagles,
they were stronger than lions.

Ye daughters of Israel, weep over Saul,
who clothed you daintily in scarlet,
who put ornaments of gold upon your apparel.

How are the mighty fallen
in the midst of the battle!

Jonathan lies slain upon thy high places.
I am distressed for you, my brother Jonathan;
very pleasant have you been to me;
your love to me was wonderful,
passing the love of women.

How are the mighty fallen,
and the weapons of war perished.

Carrying a double theme of sorrow—national and personal—the poem begins with Israel's grief, mentions a song of women, tells the fierce bravery of Saul and Jonathan, speaks of another song of women, and ends with David's personal grief.

The structure is both concentric and progressing: centered in the middle three sections by the theme of bravery symbolized in shield and bow and sword, in eagle and lion; concerned in second and penultimate divisions with songs—warning Israel to keep the disaster secret lest the daughters of the Philistine sing triumph songs, and then inviting Israel's daughters to sing their lament;

framed at beginning and end by images of the mountains of death where sorrow took its rise.

The movement progresses, because it first tells of national grief for the beauty of heroes fallen upon the mountains; it then looks to the enemy who killed them; renews their praises; turns toward home where the women of Israel are reminded of Saul's favors, and ends, not with national, but with personal grief. The images symbolize masculine courage in weapons and fierce beasts, but also softer feminine beauty in such phrases as daughters, dew and rain upon the mountains, scarlet and gold and jewels.

These two poles of masculine strength and feminine loveliness are brought together at the end where the fierce warrior, Jonathan, is "beloved and lovely," and his friendship "wonderful, passing the love of women." Finally, the movement of the poem is carried along by the refrain which gathers meaning as it goes because it is shaped by incremental repetition. At first the poem merely says, "How are the mighty fallen!" Then it adds a phrase: "How are the mighty fallen in the midst of battle!" And finally it tells how even their weapons are ruined: "How are the mighty fallen, and the weapons of war perished!"

But the tragedy of Saul has yet one more step down into darkness. It happens years later, during the reign of David. "Now there [is] a famine in the days of David for three years, year after year." And the Lord says, "There is bloodguilt on Saul and on his house, because he put the Gibeonites to death"—those men whom Joshua had sworn to protect.

Calling for the Gibeonites, David asks what reparation they demand. "Let seven of [Saul's] sons be given to us, so we may hang them . . . at Gibeon on the mountain."

"I will give them," says the king, but he spares "Mephibosheth, the son of Saul's son Jonathan because of the oath . . . which was between them," the oath of friendship made in his youth. He surrenders "the two sons of Rizpah . . . whom she bore to Saul," as well as five sons of Merab, the elder daughter of Saul, who was once long ago promised as wife to the young David, but then given by Saul to another.

And the Gibeonites "hanged them on the mountain [so that] seven of them perished together. They were put to death in the first days of harvest," about the month of April.

Then Rizpah, the daughter of Aiah took sackcloth,
    and spread it for herself on the rock,
from the beginning of harvest
    until rain fell upon them from the heavens;
and she did not allow the birds of the air
    to come upon them by day,
or the beasts of the field by night.

From spring to October she keeps her watch. Among the great tragedies there are few scenes to match this. The nearest, perhaps, is that of the Greek Antigone, who risks and loses her life in order to give ritual burial to her brother after Creon the king has condemned him to lie unburied. Antigone, by scattering ritual dust on his corpse, provides that his spirit may find rest, though she loses her life for her action. The deed is much like that of Rizpah who guards the bodies of her sons, along with those of Merab, saving them from desecration by marauding birds or beasts.

Steadily the narrator has dethroned Saul, showing him step by step left more lonely and deserted. Yahweh has renounced him for his disobedience; Samuel has first left him and then has died. Communications from heaven by dreams, by the casting of lots to determine God's will, by the words of the prophets—all fail him.

He cannot hold the undivided love of his son Jonathan, or Michal his daughter, or Israel his people. He loses his mental balance, his dignity, and his life. All his courageous fighting comes to nothing, for when he dies the Philistines occupy his country. Even when he is dead, his family meets sorrow in the crippling of his grandson Mephibosheth, and the dreadful desolation of Rizpah, left to stand guard over those who have died for belonging to Saul.

No sharper contrast can be imagined than the next story which tells of David. With his winning ways and brilliant good fortune, he gathers all the good gifts Saul might have had. If Saul had not blundered into evil he might have been a great king. But as things stand at the end of his life, this greatness waits for the reign of David.

CHAPTER SEVENTEEN

David: Green Pastures to Royal City

> I discovered inside myself, even in the very midst of winter, an invincible summer.
>
> (CAMUS)

UPON his first appearance, Saul is far from home, trudging desert roads in search of his father's lost animals; David, on the contrary, is found near his father's house, within reach when Samuel comes to anoint him, and caring for sheep in home fields. Saul's meeting with Samuel seems fortuitous; the young man has come on an errand unrelated to the call he is given. Samuel deliberately seeks David out. Saul's first anointing as king occurs on a lonely road between Ramah and Gibeah, and only Samuel is there; David, called in from quiet pasturelands, is anointed while his father and seven brothers look on. Saul may have had brothers, but no mention is made of them or of his mother. David, besides father and brothers, has a mother living, since he later takes pains to provide for her safety. He also has cousins who share his adventures: Joab, Abishai, and Asahel. Saul gives an overwhelming impression of loneliness in spite of Jonathan's affection for him and the loyalty of his followers. David is friendly and gregarious.

Their families after them show a like contrast. Saul mentions his wife only once, and that in a slighting way, when he is angered with Jonathan. Later, Saul's three warrior sons die with him on Gilboa, so that he leaves only Ishbosheth, a weakling, to be put on the throne by Abner. David, however, has many wives, and numerous sons to whom he devotes himself with warm, and even foolish, fondness. His son and successor, Solomon, put on the throne by David himself after a series of palace intrigues, proves himself a strong ruler, though not so great as David, and holds the people together through a long reign.

These outward circumstances symbolize the two men's inmost personalities. Saul is above all solitary—handsome and likable, but alone even in company, never sure of himself or his welcome, suspicious of men's loyalty to him. David is preeminently outgoing, friendly, sure that others will like him, trustful, confident of his own good fortune, his happy destiny. He discovers in himself a disposition like that Camus, the novelist, describes in the lines already quoted. "Even in the midst of winter," he senses "an invincible summer," a buoyant hopefulness and joy in life.

Saul's and David's attitudes toward the Lord show similar tendencies. Saul lives in awe of divinity and fears God's anger; his worship turns to the warrior God whom Joshua knew. David's relationship with Yahweh is one of friendship, many-sided to suit his complex personality, changing in mood with times and seasons, but warm and steadfast—a mutual loyalty. To him the Lord is doom and destiny, hazard, goal, and the greatly beloved one. When David errs, God shows him mercy, and because he knows divine kindness he becomes a merciful man.

Yahweh indeed singles David out for special love, and clearly reaffirms for him the promises of the land, and sons, and a special friendship with the transcendent God himself—promises which Saul never heard, though he too was chosen and specially blessed. David hears all three promises at once:

> I took you from the pasture, from following the sheep,
> that you should be prince over my people Israel,
> and I have been with you wherever you went. . . .
>
> And I will appoint a place for my people Israel,
> and will plant them, that they may dwell in their own
> place. . . .
>
> When your days are fulfilled and you lie down
> with your fathers,
> I will raise up your offspring after you . . .
> and I will establish his kingdom. . . .
>
> I will not take my steadfast love from him,
> as I took it from Saul. . . .
>
> (2 Sam. 7:8 ff.)

The Lord will set Israel's roots so deeply in the promised land that after three thousand years of oppression and exile those roots can still bear life. He will provide that David may live to see his son on the throne. He will offer this king a friendship more familiar than that known by Moses. After such reassurance, David can scarcely doubt Yahweh's love for him. And he never does.

In keeping with his gregarious nature, David leads a life marked by intensely personal relationships with others. Once he is called from the shepherd's slow and lonely world, his fortunes are swept into activity and interwoven with the deeds of others. He hurries from Bethlehem to Ramah, to Nob, to Gath; from the cave of Adullam in the desert, to Mizpah, to the forest of Hereth; then to Keilah, the desert of Ziph, the stronghold of En-gedi, back to Gath, and thence to Ziklag on the borders of Judah.

Through most of his youth he is a wanderer in the tangled heights and valleys of northern Judah. Only when he has driven the Philistines back to the coastal plain and seized Jerusalem, making it a symbol for the union of north and south—only then does he settle into a home again. In the exhilarating highlands he is at home, for Bethlehem, where his father lives, fourteen miles from the Dead Sea, is almost four thousand feet above its sultry blue waters; and Jerusalem, the home of his maturity, can have snow on its high bluff while Jericho stifles in tropical heat. Such climates may in part account for his abundant vitality. And men who are vitally alive always attract others.

David's life might be told by listing the names of those with whom he is involved: Saul and Jonathan; Michal whom he marries; Joab the warrior; Ahimelech the priest; Achish, king of Gath; Abigail the peaceable; Mephibosheth, the crippled son of Jonathan; Bathsheba; and his children, Amnon, Adonijah, Tamar, Absalom, and Solomon. Merely leafing through the chapters of 2 Samuel is enough to show how many people were bound by affection to David. Each stage of his life is marked by new relationships, and at every turn his dominant trait is a serene confidence in his own destiny, in his marvelous good fortune—a confidence engendered by the secure knowledge that he is chosen by God and beloved by men.

His story (1 Sam. 16 through 2 Sam. to 1 Kings 2) is probably the earliest true biography in any language, a literary masterpiece.

Across three thousand years David stands clear and alive, and this in spite of some discrepancies and repetitions, and a certain unevenness of style in the writing. The early chapters, for example, show overlapping introductions in the way they tell of his arrival at Saul's court. These shall be seen later. But such things are minor blemishes; in reality, the narrative is admirable for vivid scenes, keen probing of motivation, and an objectivity which shows David's majestic stature without glossing over his faults.

For with all his gifts, David does fall. He commits adultery and murder, and must listen while Nathan the prophet comes crying words of doom: "The sword shall never depart from your house." But though, at the end, his personal life goes down in sorrow, though he dies surrounded by treachery, the total effect is one of buoyant hope and joy. In spite of everything he is lovable and fortunate; he leaves Israel's fortunes at a peak; and sees, before he dies, the worship of Yahweh central and supreme in the land. Through it all David remains Yahweh's friend and the people's ideal king. Like Jerusalem, his royal city, he too becomes a symbol upon which dreams of greatness converge.

As a young boy, David wins amazing success; as an outlaw he shows blithe disregard for danger; as king he wields power by political acumen and force of personal charm. But as father of a family he tastes defeat, sorrow, treachery, for he cannot manage his own sons; and as an old man he finds himself helpless in the hands of those who love him yet seek their own gain. Such are the five stages of his life: 1) early introductions as shepherd, musician, warrior; 2) days of outlawry touched by the excitement of the chase; 3) kingly triumph by which he unites the people and centers Israel's life upon Jerusalem; 4) a fall and its murderous consequences; 5) the intrigues which put Solomon on the throne, and David's death.

> Let David play the harp for Saul, and sing
> To ease the soul of David, king.[84]

The beginning of David's biography is put together by an editor who wants no facet of the king's personality to be ignored. Though for the most part the account is excellent history, yet at times legends add vividness, such legends as cluster about great men, helping to reveal their inner reality even when not historically true. There are, for example, certain legendary elements in the Goliath tale. As has been said, David is introduced three times, and whether he appears as shepherd, musician, or warrior, each role tells something about the man.

He first appears after Saul has lost his rights as Yahweh's chosen king. Then Samuel the prophet hears the Lord's voice saying: "How long will you grieve over Saul? . . . Fill your horn with oil, and go; I will send you to Jesse the Bethlehemite, for I have provided for myself a king among his sons." Samuel sets out, comes to Bethlehem, and there, in a scene full of suspense, he looks for a king.

Eliab, Jesse's eldest, enters first, and Samuel, admiring "the height of his stature," is about to anoint him, but the Lord stops his gesture. One by one the seven sons appear; each seems to the prophet worthy of kingship, but each time Yahweh intervenes. On none of these does the choice rest. At last, almost as if he has forgotten, Jesse says, "There remains yet the youngest, but behold, he is keeping the sheep." It is to be another instance, so common in the Bible, of the younger son preferred before his elders.

Finally David comes. "Now he was ruddy . . . and handsome," and Samuel, taking his horn of oil, anoints him "in the midst of his brothers." It is a time of shared rejoicing. And "the Spirit of the Lord came mightily upon David"—that spirit which Saul has forfeited. Samuel now goes home to Ramah and the story turns to Saul who has begun to suffer from moods of violence and depression, a direct result, the narrator implies, of Saul's loss of "the Spirit of the Lord." So the scene is set for David's second introduction.

Saul's servants offer to find some skilled musician who will quiet his mind, and he agrees, "Provide for me a man who can play well, and bring him to me." At this a man steps forward, "I have seen a son of Jesse the Bethlehemite, who is skilful in playing, a man of valor, a man of war, prudent in speech, and a man of good presence; and the Lord is with him." So Saul sends messengers to Jesse saying: "Send me David your son, who is with the sheep."

Jesse loads an ass "with bread, and a skin of wine and a kid," and sends them to Saul by David his son. "And David came to Saul, and entered his service. And Saul loved him greatly, and he became his armor-bearer." And whenever Saul's evil moods come upon him, David takes his lyre, and Saul's serenity is restored.

All his life David will remember music: singing three laments which show his gift for friendship, his wily statesmanship, and his love and weakness as a father; composing songs of praise and sorrow that reflect his wonder at the majesty of God, his instinct for worship, and his recognition of his own failings. Still, his prowess as a warrior brings him even more fame than his ability to make music.

One day the Philistines besiege Socoh, in Judah. They stand "on the mountain on the one side, and Israel . . . on the other side, with a valley between them." Each day a gigantic Philistine strides out to taunt the Israelites, calling for one to meet him in single combat, and flourishing his great spear—like a "weaver's beam, and his spear's head weighed six hundred shekels of iron." Then comes the most developed of the stories about David's early days.

> Thinking to cross a blue hollow
> Through the dangers of twilight,
> Feeling that he must run
> And that he will
> Take root forever and stand,
> Does both at once, and neither . . .[85]

Again David, sent by his father, appears in Saul's camp, carrying presents for his brothers in the army. Slight of build, swift of movement, he slips in among the men, and with a boy's curiosity begins to ask questions about this Goliath, the Philistine who defies "the armies of the living God." He learns that "the man who kills him, the king will enrich with great riches, and will give him his daughter, and make his father's house free in Israel." The promises sound like those of popular tales—a princess to wife and a room full of gold!

When Eliab hears the talk, he grows impatient, after the fashion of elder brothers, and accuses David of negligence and boasting: "With whom have you left those few sheep in the wilderness? I know your presumption . . . for you have come down to see the battle." He sounds like the slow Esau, Jacob's brother, or the brothers of Joseph, that spoiled and winning boy.

Soon rumors reach Saul. He sends for the young man and hears his boast: "Let no man's heart fail because of him; your servant will go and fight with this Philistine." His boldness, after the soldiers have been frightened by the giant, is surprising.

"You are not able to go against this Philistine," objects Saul, "for you are but a youth, and he has been a man of war from his youth."

Unabashed, David tells his own feats of strength:

> Your servant used to keep sheep for his father;
> and when there came a lion, or a bear,
>   and took a lamb from the flock,
> I went after him and smote him . . .
>   I caught him by the beard and killed him. . . .
> This uncircumcised Philistine shall be
>   like one of them.

He sounds overconfident, yet his surety has a firm base because his strength rests on trust in God: "The Lord who delivered me from the paw of the lion and . . . bear, will deliver me from the hand of this Philistine."

"Go, and the Lord be with you!" says Saul, and clothes David with his own armor, and girds him with a sword. The young boy tries to walk, but he struggles in vain. He is not used to such clothing. One day he will be ready to wear the armor of Israel's king. But not yet. The story is well told, winning sympathy to this boy who is too slight for armor, too new to war for ease with Saul's sword. And so he goes to battle armed only with "five smooth stones from the brook . . . and his sling . . . in his hand."

As David steps from the ranks of watching men, Goliath shouts defiance, scorning him, for he is "but a youth, ruddy and comely in appearance." "Am I a dog," he shouts, "that you come to me with sticks?"

The taunts are answered by action. David hurls a stone from his sling, and it strikes "the Philistine on his forehead; the stone [sinks] into his forehead, and he [falls] on his face to the ground." The Lord has sent victory without the help of sword or spear.

Now he runs up, takes the Philistine's own sword, cuts off his head, and, carrying the grisly trophy, is led by Abner, Saul's captain, into the king's presence. Both Abner and this sword will play a part in David's future.

During the interview, Jonathan, son of Saul, stands by, and his heart goes out to David, and "the soul of Jonathan [is] knit to the soul of David, and Jonathan [loves] him as his own soul." So the prince makes a covenant of friendship with David, strips "himself of the robe that [is] upon him, and [gives] it to David, and his armor, and even his sword and his bow and his girdle." As John Logan, uniting David the hero with the Greek Odysseus, puts it, in Jonathan's voice:

> Through God my life was knit
> to his who killed the giant king with a stalk he ground
> into the single brazen eye. . . .
> See, I have made myself naked for my brother. I
> have made myself poor.[86]

In the robes of Jonathan the prince, David feels at ease, for in reality he, and not Jonathan, stands next in line to the throne. This first friendship, too, presages the next stage of his life, his time as outlaw in the wilds of desert and mountain. There he will bind many more friends to himself, for David the singer is David the undaunted warrior, whom strong men admire for his courage. He is at home with both sword and lyre.

> I long to dress deeply at last
> In the gold of my waiting brother
> Who shall wake and shine on my limbs.[87]

David's music has brought him to court and won friendship for him; a song not his own will lose him that friendship by stirring Saul's envy. Driven out by that envy, David begins to live in the wilderness, gathering about him a crowd of followers. These days of alienation bind other friends to him: Michal, daughter of Saul; Jonathan, who now proves his love mightily; Ahimelech, who dies for helping David; Abigail, the wife of a surly Calebite; and even the alien kings of Moab and Gath.

At first Saul employs David to lead his fighting forces. His courage and skill in arms make him pleasing to all the people. His popularity grows so great that a victory song names him even greater than Saul. This happens one day when the two men return from battle. Then a chorus of women meets them, "singing and dancing . . . with timbrels . . . and instruments of music," making "merry," because:

> Saul has slain his thousands,
> and David his ten thousands.

Saul, naturally, is "very angry, and this saying [displeases] him," so that he asks "What more can he have but the kingdom?"

In truth he is on his way to the throne: anointed by Samuel, dressed first in Saul's own armor, and then in the crown prince's robes, he has reached such glory that the people are beginning to prefer him to Saul. No wonder the king sees him as a threat. Still, when he falls in love with Saul's young daughter, Michal, Saul is impelled by his own promise of rewarding Goliath's conqueror, and so permits the marriage, but only after imposing his own conditions. To win Michal, David must bring proof that he has killed one hundred Philistines. When he presents evidence for two hundred, there is nothing Saul can do but give him the princess. But though Michal loves David, theirs is a stormy union, as later events indicate.

All along, Saul is tortured by envy. He tries to get David slain in battle, and failing this, he attempts to pin the singer to the wall with a lance. David escapes, but that night Michal learns that he is pursued. She lets him "down through the window," and hides a figure in his bed, putting garments over it, and "goats' hair at its head." Then she tells the pursuers that he lies there sick. So she wins time, and David gets away. Perhaps her subterfuge points to her unconscious feelings; it may be that what she loves is not the real David but an image, for he disappoints her badly later on.

An air of conspiracy now spreads through Saul's camp. Those friendly to David begin to be uneasy about possible spies. For example, David comes back one day, quietly, to speak with Jonathan. As soon as they begin to talk of the king's enmity, Jonathan grows cautious, and invites David, "Come, let us go out into the field." There, safe from eavesdroppers, they swear a covenant of friendship. Jonathan's phrases are beautiful:

> The Lord, the God of Israel, be witness!
> [if] it pleases my father to do you harm,
> the Lord do so to Jonathan, and more also,
> if I do not disclose it to you. . . .
>
> May the Lord be with you,
> as he has been with my father . . .
> and do not cut off your loyalty from my house for ever.

His painful conflict sounds in his phrase "my father." He loves his father and enjoys companionship with him, yet he also loves David and refuses to believe, with Saul, that his friend harbors any evil designs. For his part, David does not let time diminish his friendship. Even when Jonathan is dead, David will search out his crippled son and adopt him. Now, however, they make plans for their next meeting.

On a certain afternoon, David is to come out to this field and "remain beside yonder stone heap," hiding. Then Jonathan will come and "shoot three arrows to the side of it, as though I shot at a mark," and send a boy after the arrows.

> If I say to the lad,
> 'Look, the arrows are on this side of you' . . .
> then you are to come, for . . . it is safe for you. . . .
>
> But if I say to the youth,
> 'Look, the arrows are beyond you,'
> then go; for the Lord has sent you away.

When Jonathan returns to camp and pleads for David, Saul's anger blazes out: "You son of a perverse, rebellious woman, do I not know that you have chosen the son of Jesse to your own shame? . . . For as long as the son of Jesse lives upon the earth, neither you nor your kingdom shall be established." Finding that his father is "determined to put David to death," Jonathan goes out at dawn for their meeting. He shoots his arrows far out, in signal that David's life is in danger, and sends the servant boy home with the weapons.

Then David comes out of hiding and they weep together until

Jonathan sends him away, "Go in peace, forasmuch as we have sworn . . . saying, 'The Lord shall be between me and you, and between my descendants and your descendants, for ever.' " With this they part.

David flees to Ahimelech, the priest at Nob, who is dismayed to find the king's man traveling alone. Here the narrative shows David practicing a deceit which will bring his rescuer to death. Saul's cruelty is making the candid youth crafty. He reassures the anxious priest, claiming that the king has sent him upon a secret errand. Thereupon Ahimelech gives David some of the holy loaves from the altar. Saul, in other circumstances, had received bread intended for worship, in token that he would be Yahweh's king. Now David shares the same sign.

But he needs a weapon: "Have you not here a spear or a sword at hand? For I have brought neither . . . because the king's business required haste."

"The sword of Goliath the Philistine, whom you killed in the valley of Elah, behold, it is here . . . if you will take that, take it, for there is none but that here." He sounds doubtful; perhaps he fears the giant's sword will be too heavy for the youthful David.

But David feels no uneasiness, "There is none like that; give it to me." A short time ago he could not manage Saul's sword, now he can handle Goliath's.

Armed and provided with food, he escapes "to the cave of Adullam," one of the limestone cavities about twelve miles southwest of Bethlehem. From here he sallies out to gather some of his kindred, and "every one who was in distress, [or] in debt, and every one who was discontented," so that he has some four hundred men at his heels.

They make forays upon neighboring peoples, but protect the Israelites, and in turn expect tribute. As so often with David, his actions spring from several motives. He has the complexity of men in real life. He does feel loyalty to his countrymen, and so defends them, but this is not pure altruism. It is a way to make a living. Meanwhile, he is even now, with this army, preparing to win away Saul's kingdom. Wisely, however, he will not take the throne until he is sure of Yahweh's blessing and the people's approval.

Saul soon learns that Ahimelech, his own priest, has aided his enemy, and in fierce anger has him, with eighty-five of his priestly kindred, slain by the sword. David's duplicity has led to terrible consequences. Only one man escapes—Abiathar, who flees to David, bringing with him the ephod, the priestly garment. This, as has been said, was probably a linen apron with a pocket for the Urim and thummim, objects used for divination—a kind of casting of lots by which God's will might be discovered. From this time on, David often consults the Lord in this way. The means may be primitive, and even look superstitious, but David's motive is the noble one of waiting on God's will, of surrender to divine plans. And Yahweh responds with a faithful love for his friend David.

Meanwhile, fearing that Saul may take revenge for his flight upon his family, David makes friends—the Bible does not tell how—with the king of Moab, and asks him, "Pray let my father and my mother stay with you, till I know what God will do for me." David's father and mother, then, are both living and he is anxious to provide for them.

Afterward, relieved, he returns to his guerrilla fighters and resumes his freebooter's life. Saul pursues him, and the story becomes an exciting tale of the chase: the hero runs from an implacable murderer, experiences hairbreadth escapes, proves himself a better man in strength and cunning, and even shows mercy to his foe.

In one scene, told twice in the narrative with different details, David stands over Saul, asleep and helpless, and deliberately spares him. He even cuts off a piece of Saul's cloak in token of his presence there. But for this his heart smites him and he says to his followers, "The Lord forbid that I should do this thing to . . . the Lord's anointed, to put forth my hand against him."

He is motivated by awe at the holiness of the Lord's seal set upon a man, but his gesture is also good policy. He himself will one day be Yahweh's king; he is already sealed by divine anointing; and it will be well if his followers remember and keep such reverence toward himself. The lesson will be repeated in several later incidents. This is again a significant use of the clothing image. His taking a piece of the cloak signifies that David has already usurped Saul's place in part. He is anointed, and he holds the people's favor. But it is only a piece. He is not yet the king.

I passed and saw you
Labouring there, your dark figure
Marring the simple geometry
Of the square fields.[88]

Out of his wilderness adventures comes conflict with the Calebite Nabal, "a churlish and ill-behaved" fellow, who lives in the southern section of Judah. According to custom, David tries to levy tribute; he sends a courteous message: "Peace be to you, and peace be to your house. . . . I hear that you have shearers. . . . Therefore let my young men find favor in your eyes; for we come on a feast day. Pray, give whatever you have at hand to your servants." Outlaw or not, David employs the courtly phrase even to the boorish Nabal.

The reply is rude. "Who is David? . . . There are many servants nowadays, who are breaking away from their masters. Shall I take my bread . . . and give it to men who come from I do not know where?" The words about David's place of origin are an insult to his family as well as to his former position as Saul's right-hand man. Certainly Nabal must have known whence he has come.

At this, David bids his men to gird on their swords, ready to exact vengeance from Nabal, but one man warns the beautiful Abigail, wife to this rich man, "Behold, David [has] sent messengers" but Nabal has "railed at them. . . . Yet the men were very good to us. . . . They were a wall to us both by night and by day, all the while we were . . . keeping the sheep. Now . . . consider what you should do; for evil is determined against our master . . . and he is so ill-natured that one cannot speak to him."

Abigail quickly brings out loaves and wine and raisins, flour and cakes and dried figs. With no word to Nabal she rides out to meet David, who is still enraged. She shows a diplomacy worthy of David's own by appealing to his compassion, his trust in the Lord, and even his vanity—when she refers to a sling, the weapon he once used to slay Goliath in that famous battle. "Upon me alone, my lord, be the guilt. . . . Let not my lord regard this ill-natured fellow, Nabal. . . . Forgive the trespass . . . and the lives of your enemies [the Lord your God] shall sling out as from the hollow of a sling."

When David relents, two of his characteristics come into play—his tendency to show mercy rather than harshness, and his susceptibility to women. Soon after this, Nabal is "holding a feast in his house, like the feast of a king," but "his heart [dies] within him, and he [becomes] as a stone." The stroke ends his life, and then David sends for the wise and courteous Abigail to make her his wife.

Here, too, in a parenthetical sentence, the reader learns that Saul has given his daughter Michal, David's first wife, to another man. It is a way of repudiating any relationship, any claim to inheritance that David might bring as being Saul's son-in-law. Later on, when he is in a position to do it, David will order her return to him. It is strange to see a woman of such decisive character pushed as a pawn from father to husband to father to another husband and back.

Things now grow so desperate that David resolves to take refuge in the country of the Philistines. "Then Saul will despair of seeking me any longer within the borders of Israel, and I shall escape out of his hand." So with a band of six hundred men, he goes to Achish, the king of Gath. Achish welcomes the band of trained and powerful fighters, and David exerts all his amiable personality to assure his welcome. He must have known, in making this move, that he would be expected to fight against his own people, but with his happy optimism he trusts that somehow he can extricate himself. And he is saved by a combination of wise planning and his usual good luck.

With canny foresight he asks Achish to give him the city of Ziklag, far to the south of the Philistine center and on the borders of Judah. He then takes advantage of this position to loot the lands of Achish's allies, winning rich spoils and sending gifts to Judah's leaders, hoping to predispose them in his favor. All the while Achish believes that these forays have been against the Israelites, and he feels that David has alienated his own nation. So complete is his trust in the engaging freebooter, that he says: "I will make you my bodyguard for life."

Luckily for David, however, Achish's chief warriors are not so trusting. The day comes when Philistia musters her forces against Israel for that great battle in which Saul will be killed. David stands fast by his bold fraud, claiming that he is ready to fight alongside the armies of Achish. The situation is ticklish, but his good fortune holds, for the Philistine chieftains protest: "Send the man back," for he may turn traitor during the battle. "Is not this David, of whom they sing to one another in dances, 'Saul has slain his thousands, and David his ten thousands'?"

The words ring of authentic speech; the tones of their grumbling are almost audible. The fame of David's prowess has come even to Philistine ears. Achish is forced to listen, and sends David home. But David covers his secret joy and relief by indignant protests, and Achish actually counters with apology, assuring David that he has never doubted his loyalty to Achish himself.

When David returns, he finds Ziklag in ruins. The Amalekites have taken their chance to revenge his raids upon them. His men, in anger, threaten to stone him, "because all the people [are] bitter in soul, each for his sons and daughters." It is a dark hour, probably the lowest ebb of David's early popularity. But David finds refuge in the Lord, and asks Abiathar to bring out the ephod and instruments for discovering God's will. "Shall I pursue after this band?" "Pursue; for you shall surely overtake and shall surely rescue." So he wins back all they had lost and booty besides, and the men are content.

When the Philistines launch their attack, Saul is defeated and dies with Jonathan on Mount Gilboa. And "when the inhabitants of Jabesh-gilead [hear] what the Philistines [have] done to Saul—[fastening] his body to the wall of Beth-shan—all the valiant men" arise, and walking all night they rescue the bodies and bury them. David's way to the throne is open.

> Gird your sword upon your thigh,
> O mighty one, in your glory and majesty!
> . . . God, your God, has anointed you
> with the oil of gladness . . .
> From ivory palaces stringed instruments
> make you glad. . . .
>
> (Ps. 45:3ff)

Immediately David moves with masterly statesmanship, showing in three instances his genuine reverence for Saul. These acts are also very good policy because Saul is still popular in the north. First, an Amalekite from Saul's army, hoping to win David's favor, comes running with news from the battlefield. He announces that he has killed Saul—though another part of the story says that Saul died by his own hand. David rewards the man with anger, "How is it you were not afraid to put forth your hand to destroy the Lord's anointed?" And he has him killed.

Then by a second wise deed, David sings his haunting lament over Saul and Jonathan, "They were swifter than eagles, they were stronger than lions. . . . How are the mighty fallen." The poetic mastery of this song has already been discussed in Chapter XVI. Though David as friend and musician is most in evidence here, yet David the politician is not absent. Though he is sure of the loyalty of Judah, his own territory, he wants to be king of all the Lord's people, and by his lament he identifies himself with the northern Saul once more. It is another claim to be the logical successor to Saul's kingdom.

Now David inquires of the Lord, and finds he is to move to Hebron, so with "his two wives . . . A-hinoam of Jezre-el, and Abigail the widow of Nabal" and his men, he sets up a dwelling in Hebron. The history of Hebron goes back to Abraham, and until the winning of Jerusalem, it is a natural center for Judah. Here the men of the south seek him out and name him king. He has part of his ambition, but he is not king of a united country yet.

Next comes his third wise move, when he sends a message to Jabesh-gilead, to the men that had buried Saul:

> May you be blessed by the Lord,
> because you showed this loyalty to Saul your lord. . . .
> And I will do good to you because you have done this thing.
>
> Now therefore let your hands be strong, and be valiant;
> for Saul your lord is dead,
> and the house of Judah has anointed me king over them.

They are gracious words, and he ends with an implied question: Judah has a ruler, but what about you, now that Saul is dead?

These northern tribes, which have gradually come to be called Israel in contrast to Judah in the south, might also have fallen quickly to David. But Saul's strong captain, Abner, intervenes by setting up Ishbosheth, Saul's son and a weakling, as king at Mahanaim, east of Jordan. Then begins a seven-year struggle between Saul's house and David's, but the power of David grows, partly because of his superb statesmanship, again through the devotion he wins from others, but most of all because Yahweh's blessing rests on him. He draws the love of God and man, and on the whole he deserves it.

His rise is furthered by two early killings which rid him of possible rivals. By quick thinking he averts from himself all blame for these deaths. The first to die is Abner, because of a blood feud with Joab, the fanatically loyal captain of David's forces. The feud had begun after a fierce battle at Gibeon, when Abner, in flight, was followed by Asahel, brother of Joab, "swift of foot as a wild gazelle." He would not stop even when Abner cried a warning, "Turn aside from following me; why should I smite you to the ground? How then could I lift up my face to your brother Joab?" Heedless, the youth runs on, until Abner smites "him in the belly with the butt of his spear," and Asahel dies there on the path. Then a bitter will to vengeance is born in Joab's heart.

His chance comes when Abner turns from Ishbosheth, his puppet king. The old soldier has taken to wife a former concubine of Saul's named Rizpah; foolishly Ishbosheth taunts him about this—made uneasy, perhaps, because the wives of a dead king usually went to his successor. By the marriage, therefore, Abner may be showing a desire to reign in Saul's place.

Furiously Abner replies, "Am I a dog's head of Judah? This day I keep showing loyalty to the house of Saul your father . . . and yet you charge me today with a fault concerning a woman. God do so to Abner . . . if I do not . . . set up the throne of David over Israel and over Judah, from Dan to Beer-sheba." But Ishbosheth cannot "answer Abner another word, because he [fears] him."

Now Abner sends a message to David, offering "to bring over all Israel" to him. David answers courteously, but stipulates that Abner cannot be heard unless he brings Michal, Saul's daughter, with him. So she is taken "from her husband Pal-ti-el the son of Laish. But her husband [follows], weeping after her all the way to Bahurim." She, too, must have been one who could win love. Nothing, however, is said of her own feelings, but the reunion cannot have been happy, since in a little while she is seen ridiculing David in public. In insisting on her return, David is possibly motivated by his old love, but this is also a stroke of policy aimed to solidify his position as Saul's son-in-law.

Abner comes. The conference is amicable, and he leaves to rally Israel to David's side. He has not gone far, though, when Joab, that fierce warrior cousin of David's, returns from battle, and hearing that Abner has visited the king, and they have parted friends, he shouts:

> What have you done?
> Behold, Abner came to you. . . .
> You know that [he] came to deceive you,
> and to know your going out and your coming in.

Therefore Joab sends messengers after Abner, and they bring him back without David's knowledge. And Joab takes "him aside into the midst of the gate to speak with him privately, and there he smote him in the belly, so that he died, for the blood of Asahel his brother." His motive of revenge is probably mixed with fear that Abner will supplant him as captain of David's army, yet all the while he claims the deed is done to protect David.

When David hears of it, he says, "I and my kingdom are forever guiltless . . . for the blood of Abner the son of Ner. May it fall upon the head of Joab." Yet he lets Joab off with light punishment. It is the first instance of that weakness with those close to him, which will bring David so much grief with his sons. Here he speaks truly. He has had no part in the death. Yet he has profited by Joab's act, for it has removed a threat to his throne.

David, therefore, bids Joab to put on sackcloth, and go mourning at Abner's funeral, while he himself, weeping, sings a lament at the tomb. It is believed that what the Bible preserves of the song is a fragment of the original:

> Should Abner die as a fool dies?
> Your hands were not bound,
> your feet were not fettered;
> as one falls before the wicked
> you have fallen.

David's grief for the death of a good man is sincere: "A prince and a great man has fallen this day in Israel." At the same time he denies complicity, "I am this day weak, though anointed king; these men the sons of Zeruiah," Joab and his brothers, "are too hard for me." And "everything that the king [does pleases] the people," and all Israel understands that it has "not been the king's will to slay Abner the son of Ner." No man afterward blames David for the slaying. As so often he follows his heart, and it leads him to wisdom, even worldly wisdom.

Soon Ishbosheth, too, is taken out of his path without his connivance. The rival king rests one summer day, and "the doorkeeper of the house" has grown "drowsy" over the task of "cleaning wheat." Then two Benjaminite malcontents slip in and kill him, cutting off his head and journeying with it all night across the desert to David. They expect a reward, but just as it was with the Amalekite who claimed he had killed Saul, so it is now. David orders their death for having killed an anointed king. But they take "the head of Ishbosheth" and bury it "in the tomb of Abner at Hebron."

> Those who trust in the Lord
> are like Mount Zion, which cannot be moved. . . .
> As the mountains are round about Jerusalem,
> so the Lord is round about his people. . . .
> (Ps. 125:1–2)

Now the northern tribes rally to David at Hebron saying,

> Behold, we are your bone and flesh.
> In times past, when Saul was king over us,
> it was you that led out and brought in Israel,
> and the Lord said to you,
> "You shall be shepherd of my people Israel."

The narrator is careful to show that both the people and the Lord want David to rule. By this action, all tribes are united—David is king over Israel and over Judah.

One of his first actions after his accession—an important one—is the choice of a new capital. He selects Jerusalem, an ancient Canaanite stronghold, built on a hill difficult of access on three sides and easily defended on the north. Its position, which makes it attractive to David, also makes it hard to win. Men called

Jebusites live there, and when he lays siege, they peer over the walls to shout jibes at David's forces.

He promises that the first man to make his way in shall be captain of all his armies. This is all that Joab needs to hear. Now the Jebusites had built an almost vertical "water shaft" into the limestone hill to obtain water from the spring. "The account of the capture of the town . . . seems to imply that Joab crept up the shaft and took the Jebusites entirely by surprise" (Grollenberg). The aggressive Joab is the hero of the exploit.

The significance of David's victory goes beyond the mere establishment of a new capital. Especially, it brings three kinds of unity—to the nation, to the geographical state, and to church and state. Not only is it the first capital of the whole Israel, but it draws the tribes together in a way that Saul's rule could never do. For Jerusalem has no traditional associations with either north or south to stir their rivalry; it is more central than Hebron of Judah, or Shechem which has been a northern stronghold. This Jerusalem "was a very ancient city. Its name has been found on one of the potsherds which an Egyptian of about 2000 B.C. covered with the names of enemy cities."[89]

Further, there is no more mention during David's time of those pockets of Canaanite resistance which gave the judges so much trouble. They seem to have been absorbed into the new state by conquest or by their own choice, so that divisive element is eliminated. Unity, then, of the people, and of the territory—these are gained. But David, enthroned at Jerusalem, goes further and unifies church and state.

This is most important, for the people's relationship with the Lord, their haunting desire for the fulfillment of his covenant promises, is at the heart of their national life. Now by a single stroke of genius, David links Israel's sacred traditions with his new kingdom.

He first makes the city strong and beautiful, receiving help especially from Hiram, king of Tyre, who furnishes "cedar trees, also carpenters and masons who built David a house." It is a recognition of the new nation as a political power. When all is ready, he moves, to make this not only the city of David, but the city of Yahweh.

I was glad when they said to me,
"Let us go up to the house of the Lord!"
Our feet have been standing
within your gates, O Jerusalem!
(Ps. 121:2)

Victory gives opportunity for David's wisest move, and he sets out "to bring . . . the ark of God, which is called by the name of the Lord of hosts who sits enthroned on the cherubim." It is the old symbol of Israel's faith, the visible sign of the third great promise, of Yahweh's intimate presence with his people.

During the triumphant procession, with its music of "songs and lyres and harps and tambourines and castanets and cymbals," two incidents shadow David's rejoicing. The first happens when a man named Uzzah impulsively stretches his hand to steady the ark, and is struck dead. The narrative suggests either that his act was irreverent, or that even to approach holiness with all respect can be dangerous. David, frightened at the incident, leaves the ark with Obed-edom the Gittite. But Obed-edom prospers, and after three months the procession is resumed. The king then goes dancing "before the Lord with all his might," and "girded with a linen ephod." So he brings the ark to Jerusalem.

Then another shadow falls when Michal, the daughter of Saul, sees David dancing in the Lord's presence, and despises him in her heart. But to her reproaches, David only replies:

It was before the Lord,
who chose me above your father . . .
to appoint me prince over Israel . . .
and I will make merry before the Lord,
[therefore] I shall be held in honor.

And Michal, the storyteller remarks, interpreting his hindsight as cause and effect, "had no child to the day of her death." Perhaps, too, from that day David had nothing more to do with her.

Until now the ark has been housed in a tent, but since desert wanderings are ended, David looks at his own palace and dreams of further glory for God and Jerusalem: "See now," he says to his prophet Nathan, "I dwell in a house of cedar, but the ark of God dwells in a tent." Many details of his plans for building a temple to honor the Lord are given in the books of Chronicles. Some of these have been added by later editors. But David is not to build the temple. This will be left for Solomon, his son. Solomon will carry on David's wisdom and ambitions, but also those weaknesses of his father which come to view once David is settled on his throne—weaknesses especially toward his own family. Still, the Lord is pleased with his desire to build a house of worship, and renews his three promises.

The final magnificent chapters of David's story are concerned with his human weakness and his winning kindness. For the supreme statesman, the man gifted for friendship, proves unequal to the task of ordering his household, unable to hold the loyalty of his sons. Still, he meets sorrow with noble courage, and with mercy for others, even while he knows that his black distress comes as a result of his own sins.

From hill fastnesses of his outlaw days and open fields of warfare, David's story now moves to a life at home. All his days are a tissue of relationships, but here he is more than ever close to others, and at the same time alienated from them. This section throngs with people presented in psychological reality. But here three may be singled out—three who symbolize David's past affections, his present love and sin, and the future of his kingdom. They are Mephibosheth, Bathsheba, and Absalom.

> Poor twist and tangle of my friend,
> Receive my hand. . . .
> Come, I will not offend thee, though
> The clangors hunt thy heart again.
> Sing to me of Jonathan.[90]

With a quieter life, David's thoughts turn to the past, and he wonders, "Is there still any one left of the house of Saul that I may show him kindness for Jonathan's sake?" Both friendship and mercy are here; kings did not ordinarily seek to insure the continuance of their predecessors' families. He finds Mephibosheth, the crippled grandson of Saul by Jonathan. "He was five years old when the news about Saul and Jonathan," about their deaths on Mount Gilboa, was brought to Jezreel. "And his nurse took him up, and fled; and as she fled in her haste, he fell, and became lame. . . . So Mephibosheth dwelt in Jerusalem; for he ate always at the king's table. Now he was lame in both his feet."

Later, in David's days of sorrow, Mephibosheth will prove unfaithful, yet still David will forgive him for the sake of Jonathan. James Wright, in his poem "David," quoted at the beginning of this section, pictures the scene in which the king seeks the young man out:

After thy father's form
Returned to earth to keep him warm,
And sheep despaired of summer,
I came to thee, Mephibosheth. . . .

Broken myself, and full of blame,
Mephibosheth, I called thy name. . . .
Hoping to hold thee as my son,
Thou crippled child of Jonathan.[91]

David can love greatly, but a heart like his carries its own hazards. Hitherto he has gone out to fight with his men, but now, when spring returns, "the time when kings go forth to battle," David sends Joab to besiege Rabbah, while he himself remains at Jerusalem, and his real troubles begin.

That enravished voice shall drive
Uriah from honey in the hive.[92]

A life of luxury is not good for this hardy soldier, and one day in idleness he is "walking upon the roof of the king's house." From here he sees a woman of rare beauty, Bathsheba, wife of Uriah the Hittite, one of his soldiers. Whether she deliberately set herself to catch his eye the story does not tell. He sends for her. She comes unprotesting, and when he had his will, she returns home.

Soon, however, a message comes—she is with child. David sends for Uriah who is away, fighting David's wars at the side of Joab. When Uriah comes, David, hoping that the child may appear to be the husband's, tries to persuade him to go home to Bathsheba. But the plan fails because of the soldierly goodness of Uriah. He says that "the ark and Israel and Judah dwell in booths; and my lord Joab [is] camping in the open field. . . . Shall I then go to my house to eat and to drink, and to lie with my wife? . . . As your soul lives, I will not do this thing." So he sleeps that night at the palace gates. Nothing David can do will change him, and his obduracy in goodness rouses an obduracy in David which brings him to the lowest point of his career.

He bids Uriah return to the field carrying a sealed letter to Joab. The letter, by a cruel irony, carries Uriah's own death sentence. Joab is to find a place for him "in the forefront of the hardest fighting, and then draw back from him, that he may be struck down and die." So a brave man goes to death, and Joab sends a laconic message assuring David: "Your servant Uriah the Hittite is dead." It may be that this is the reason Joab later has no use for Bathsheba's son Solomon; he may also resent her life-long hold over David. Certainly, after this, his insolence to the king grows more marked. "But the thing David had done displeased the Lord." This statement, too, shows the high moral standards of the Israelites. Among other nations at this time it was not thought a moral wrong for a king to appropriate one of his subjects' wives.

Nathan the prophet now hastens to court and tells David a parable about a rich man with many flocks, who perversely feasts his guests with the one lamb owned by his poor neighbor—"it used to eat of his morsel, and drink from his cup . . . and it was like a daughter to him." Then David's anger is "greatly kindled against the man," and the king cries out that such a one "deserves to die . . . because he had no pity."

Courageously, then, Nathan makes his point: "You are the man!" His boldness shows that Isarel's king is not an absolute ruler, but one who listens to the voice of the Lord brought to him through the prophets. Nathan goes on, "Thus says the Lord, the God of Israel:

> I anointed you king over Israel,
> and I delivered you out of the hand of Saul . . .
> I gave you the house of Israel and of Judah. . . .
> Why have you [done] what is evil in [my] sight?

You have slain Uriah the Hittite "with the sword of the Ammonites. Now therefore the sword shall never depart from your house." It is a tremendously dramatic scene, and David responds with simple honesty: "I have sinned against the Lord."

God accepts his repentance, but the events set in motion by the sin move inexorably forward. Bathsheba's child dies, and David's sorrow is great. And after this, much of his life becomes a vipers' tangle of evil and treachery shown him by those he has loved best.

And Absalom shall strangle in
the harpstrings eloquent and thin.[93]

David's eldest son, and heir to his throne, fails him first. This young man, Amnon, conceives a violent passion for his half-sister Tamar. He pretends to be ill, and persuades David to send Tamar to make him some cakes. When she comes to serve his food, however, he ravishes her, forcing her to his will. But afterwards he hates "her with very great hatred; so that the hatred with which he [hates] her [is] greater than the love with which he [has] loved her."

He drives her from his house, bolting "the door after her." And Tamar puts "ashes on her head, and [rends] the long robe which she [wears]; and she [lays] her hand on her head," and goes away, "crying aloud" as she goes. Her clothes, her posture, her tears all combine to make a classic picture of grief.

David feels great sorrow over the disgraceful event, but he does not reprove Amnon his son because this is his firstborn, and he loves him. Absalom, however, who is full brother to Tamar—a handsome man and inordinately proud of his long hair, a sign of virility—broods in bitter silence for two years. Then he seizes a chance for revenge during a festival that celebrates the shearing of his sheep.

Beforehand he instructs his men, "Mark when Amnon's heart is merry with wine, and when I say to you, 'Strike Amnon,' then kill him." Dante, in his *Divine Comedy*, would have put both young men among the betrayers of kindred in Caina of deepest hell—a place named for Cain, son of Adam, who murdered his brother Abel.

When the murder is done, then "all the king's sons" arise, mount their mules, and flee in terrified disorder. Rumors reach David before their homecoming, and a scene of pathos and suspense ensues. Believing that all his sons are slain, the old king tears his garments and casts himself upon the ground. Then Jonadab, a nephew who had helped arrange the seduction, and could have foreknown the revenge, assures him that "Amnon alone is dead, for by the command of Absalom this has been determined from the day he forced his sister Tamar." At this, a "young man who kept the watch" lifts up his eyes and calls out, "Behold, the king's sons have come," for he sees them descending the mountain path. All are safe but Amnon.

Now Absalom, in fear of his father, flees the country, remaining away for three years, while David goes on mourning for his son. But growing restless at last, Absalom persuades the canny Joab, who likes men of action, to plead for him. Joab calls on a wise woman of Tekoa to go to the king with a parable that is a masterpiece of circumlocution and evasive phrases. She says that her own remaining son is about to die for having killed his brother. But this will leave her desolate. Cannot the king save him? When David promises to protect him, she reveals that she is really pleading for the return of David's own son Absalom. Her mode of speech should be contrasted with the clear and candid parable spoken by Nathan the prophet about the rich man who took his poor neighbor's only lamb.

Joab's worldly-wise ruse is successful, just as Nathan's parable was successful, in bringing the king to repentance. David allows Absalom to come home. But soon the prince grows restless again, because the king has grown old without appointing a successor, and he frames a speech full of his own kind of guile. Absalom provides for "himself a chariot and horses, and fifty men to run before him." And he begins "to rise early and stand beside the way of the gate; and when any man [has] a suit to come before the king for judgment," Absalom says to him, "See, your claims are good and right; but there is no man deputed by the king to hear you. . . . Oh that I were judge in the land . . . I would give justice." With such words he alienates "the hearts of the men of Israel" from David.

Soon a messenger comes to David to tell him that the men of Israel have gone after Absalom, and among them is Ahithophel, David's trusted counselor. Then Absalom gives orders which many in the land obey: "As soon as you hear the sound of the trumpet, then say, 'Absalom is king at Hebron!' "

The rebels move on Jerusalem, and David flees just in time. Upon entering the city, Absalom's first act is to take to himself

David's concubines left behind in the palace. In this way he signalizes his intent to usurp David's kingly place.

Then the biblical writer paints another unforgettable picture of grief. It is the old king, in flight from his son, crossing the Kidron valley, climbing the Mount of Olives "weeping as he [goes], barefoot and with his head covered; and all the people . . . weeping" as they follow.

Still, he is not without majesty, nor deprived of resources. He shows both hope, and surrender to Yahweh's will when his followers bring the ark of the covenant before him. Halted by the side of the road, he bids them:

> Carry the ark of God back into the city.
> If I find favor in the eyes of the Lord,
> he will bring me back and let me see . . . his habitation;
> But if he says, "I have no pleasure in you,"
> behold here I am,
> let him do to me what seems good to him.

Among his friends, too, is Hushai the Archite, a man of wisdom. He wishes to follow David into exile, but the king sends him back to the city to pose as counselor to Absalom and to foil the crafty plans of Ahitophel.

In the city, Ahitophel advises Absalom to attack David at once while the king's forces are in disorderly flight. But Hushai, secretly on David's side, argues that the best policy lies in delay. Hushai wins out, thus giving David time to organize resistance. As for Ahitophel, when he finds his good advice unheeded, that traitor saddles his ass and goes home. There he sets "his house in order," and then hangs himself. And he is "buried in the tomb of his father."

David's journey and short exile are full of human incidents. One even adds humor to the grim situation when it shows two young men carrying a message from Hushai to David, and hard beset by Absalom's pursuivants. They come "to the house of a man at Bahurim, who [has] a well in his courtyard; and they [go] down into it." The well is not brimful of water. Nor is their hiding place discovered, for a "woman [spreads] a covering over the well's mouth, and [scatters] grain upon it," so that the pursuers cannot find the fugitives, and return home baffled.

Such touches of realism have led a number of scholars to believe that much of this so-called court history of David was told by eyewitnesses—perhaps even one of these young men. Who else, they ask, could know how they hid in the well, or how a woman spread a cloth over it to hide them?

Now David gives strict orders that all are to "deal gently for my sake with the young man Absalom," and then immediately launches an all-out attack. When Absalom's forces are routed, he himself flees, "riding upon his mule."

> And the mule [goes] under the thick branches
> of a great oak,
> and his head caught fast in the oak,
> and he was left hanging between heaven and earth.

This narrator, a master of clear visual pictures, has left another memorable scene which is treasured in the world's literature.

After Absalom has been hanging there for some time, Joab, who was formerly his friend, comes with "three darts in his hand, and [thrusts] them into the heart of Absalom, while he [is] still alive in the oak." Joab has again defied David. Then the people take "Absalom, and [throw] him into a great pit in the forest, and [raise] over him a very great heap of stones."

In the meantime, David is waiting for news. He hears a watchman on the roof cry out that a runner is coming all alone. And the king says, "If he is alone, there are tidings in his mouth." Then another messenger appears and David, unaware of the kind of news he brings, recognizes him as Ahimaaz the son of Zadok, and speaks out his hope, "He is a good man, and comes with good tidings."

To the messengers, the king's first question phrases his greatest fear, "Is it well with the young man Absalom?" But instead of answering the question, they tell first of the victory, referring only obliquely to Absalom:

> Blessed be the Lord your God,
> who has delivered up the men
> who raised their hand against my lord the king.

David asks again, "Is it well with the young man Absalom?" Then he receives his answer, "May the enemies of my lord the king, and all who rise up against you for evil, be like that young man."

Then the king "is deeply moved, and [goes] up to the chamber over the gate" to weep. Here he composes the third and most desolate of his lifetime's laments:

> O my son Absalom, my son, my son Absalom!
> Would I had died instead of you, O Absalom,
> my son, my son!

From the wonderfully poetic lament over Saul and Jonathan, to the sophisticated elegy for Abner which is a mixture of grief and politics, to the sorrowful simplicity of these bare lines, David has come a long road. In the first, his anguish was tempered by hope and ambition—the future was open. In the second, he sees the last obstacles to his reign removed, for without Abner, David's northern rival has no hope of holding the throne. In this last lament, the old king grieves for all that might have been and now will never be.

After the victory he returns to Jerusalem along a road he strews with deeds of mercy—forgiving Shimei, a Benjaminite who had cursed him on his flight; accepting Mephibosheth's weak excuses when he tells why he failed to fly from Jerusalem with David; promising favors to the faithful Barzillai, so old he can no longer "discern what is pleasant and what is not." "Can your servant," he says, "taste what he eats or what he drinks? Can I still listen to the voice of singing men and singing women?"

Once home, David must face three more crises: a minor rebellion, the misfortunes consequent upon a treaty broken, and a Philistine attack. In the first, comes another of those wise women who keep appearing in the Bible. It happens that a certain Sheba, the son of Bichri, a Benjaminite, blows a trumpet for war, shouting:

> We have no portion in David,
> and we have no inheritance in the son of Jesse;
> every man to his tents, O Israel!

Then David, probably because of Joab's murder of Absalom, slights his captain by sending another man, Amasa, to put down the rebellion.

Joab, however, kills Amasa, as he has killed Abner and Absalom, and then goes on to defend the king in his own way. He pursues Sheba to the town of Beth-maacah, where the rebel takes refuge.

"Then a wise woman [calls] from the city, 'Hear! Hear! Tell Joab, Come here, that I may speak to you.'" When he comes, she tells him, "I am one of those who are peaceable and faithful in Israel; you seek to destroy a city which is a mother in Israel; why will you swallow up the heritage of the Lord?"

Joab answers that he does not seek to "swallow up or destroy." But a "man of the hill country . . . called Sheba . . . has lifted up his hand against King David; give up him alone, and I will withdraw from the city."

Then the woman goes "to all the people in her wisdom. And they cut off the head of Sheba the son of Bichri, and [throw] it out to Joab." So the insurrection ends.

In the second crisis, a famine descends upon the land, and David is told that this is a punishment for a treaty broken. It had happened during the time of Saul, that the ancient treaty made by Joshua with the Gibeonites was disregarded, for Saul put some of them to death. Now when they are asked what reparation is due, they demand the lives of seven of Saul's descendants: "Let seven of his sons be given to us, so that we may hang them up . . . at Gibeon on the mountain of the Lord."

David gives them the young men, sparing only Mephibosheth, the son of Jonathan. Then it is that Rizpah, the mother of two of them, stands guard over their bodies from April to October, protecting them from vultures and prowling animals.

In the third incident of crisis, a battle against the Philistines, which is told here, but may have happened earlier in David's career, there appears another proof of that staunch loyalty he can still inspire. He is in the field, and narrowly escapes an enemy spear. Then his men swear to him, "You shall no more go out with us to battle, lest you quench the lamp of Israel."

Here, too, the writer, perhaps moved by the theme of loyalty, adds another incident which also probably belongs earlier. He tells how David, once encamped near Bethlehem and at war with the Philistines, exclaims aloud, "O that some one would give me water to drink from the well of Bethlehem which is by the gate!"

Thereupon three soldiers break through the enemy lines and bring him water. His response shows how it is that he calls forth such devotion:

Far be it from me, O Lord, that I should do this.
Shall I drink the blood of the men who went at
the risk of their lives?

And he pours it out as an offering to the Lord.

Toward the end of David's biography, the writer returns to the early theme of David the musician, quoting at length a beautiful song of thanksgiving and a last psalm attributed to David. Both show his lifelong belief in his own good fortune, his surety in Yahweh's love:

The Lord is my rock, and my fortress, and my deliverer. . . .
He drew me out of many waters. . . .
He made my feet like hinds' feet, and set me secure. . . .

When one rules justly over men, ruling in the fear of God,
he dawns on them like the morning light,
like the cloud shining forth on a cloudless morning,
like rain that makes grass to sprout from the earth.

Still, even the immortal David grows old and chilled with age, and "although they [cover] him with clothes, he [can] not get warm." So his attendants bring "a beautiful maiden . . . Abishag the Shunamite," and she becomes "the king's nurse and [ministers] to him . . . that the king may be warm."

Days go on and yet he delays appointing a new king, until his son Adonijah, like to Absalom, "a very handsome man," begins to boast that he will be king. He draws after him both Joab and Abiathar the priest, friends of David since his earliest youth. At this, Nathan the prophet hurries to Bathsheba, who has never lost her influence over David.

Gaining access to the king's own room, where he sits "very old, and Abishag the Shunamite . . . ministering" to him, Bathsheba pleads for her son Solomon:

Did you not, my lord the king, swear to [me], saying,
"Solomon your son shall reign after me,
and he shall sit upon my throne"?
Why then is Adonijah king?

Now the "eyes of all Israel are upon you," she goes on, "to tell them who shall sit upon the throne."

Acting, then, with some of his old decision, David orders a

triumphal procession to escort his son Solomon, mounted upon the king's own mule, to Gihon. There "let Zadok the priest and Nathan the prophet . . . anoint him king over Israel; then blow the trumpet and say, 'Long live king Solomon!' " It is done, and at the celebration there is "playing on pipes, and rejoicing with great joy, so that the earth was split by their noise." The incipient revolt has failed, and Solomon reigns.

"When David's time to die [draws] near," he renews in his last speech to Solomon the old theme, the early promise of sons to hold the land—a promise first given to Abraham:

> I am about to go the way of all the earth. . . .
> Keep the charge of the Lord your God,
> walking in his ways. . . .
> that the Lord may establish his word . . .
> so there shall not fail you a man on the throne of Israel.

Here David's heart speaks, showing especially his love for the Lord and his hope that Solomon, too, will be Yahweh's friend.

Then David, the man of affairs, the foresighted politician comes to the stage for one last time. He sees that Shimei the Benjaminite, who was forgiven for cursing the king on the road to Olivet, may become a center for rebellion, and that Joab, who bears no loyalty to Solomon, may prove more than the young king can manage. He therefore advises Solomon to execute both. It seems a sad ending for the merciful David, a cruel ending for Joab, that defiant but fanatically loyal friend. "Then David slept with his fathers, and was buried in the city of David. And the time that David reigned over Israel was forty years."

David has received a loose federation of tribes from Saul and has built it into a stable nation. He has won Jerusalem and centered the people's life and worship there. Solomon will glorify the city and build a temple to bring honor and dignity to Yahweh's worship. But he will plant a wedge between north and south by forcing especially those of the north to labor at his public works. His son, Rehoboam, in turn, will drive that wedge in and split David's kingdom apart.

David has been a man of wisdom and political acumen, but even more a man of mercy, a man of heart. Solomon will be noted for his wisdom; his skill in governing will make Israel a world power, but he will lack David's personal warmth. With Solomon's reign David's dreams for Israel are realized because the Lord's promises of land and sons seem to have reached lasting fulfillment, and because Yahweh now dwells in a special manner with his people in his own city and temple.

But because Solomon, like David, is weak toward his family, he will allow his foreign wives to corrupt the pure worship of God, and plant seeds of that future apostasy which the great prophets will fight. The dream of a city with golden streets and gates of pearl almost comes true in the days of Solomon's magnificence. But even his Jerusalem is not the apocalyptic city. That waits in the future, waits to beckon Israel on through dark days yet to come.

Afterword

Adam's Haunted Sons, like the Bible itself, has begun in a garden and ended in a city—the same garden of Eden but different cities. The garden is a free gift given to a human couple who live there in primeval innocence. They did not plan or plant it. David's Jerusalem, like the apocalyptic city, is a hard-earned haven, a home shaped by human deeds and decisions.

This book ends with David's city, but the people's adventures are not ended, nor is this a lasting city. Still, their possession of it is a climax, a fulfillment in part of the Lord's promise to give them a land. They stop here for rest, but they will go on into other exiles, across other strange deserts, searching for another city, a symbolic one which contains all the joy of man's desiring.

Each goal reached has left them with ambivalent feelings, each of Yahweh's promises is built on ambiguity. The land is theirs, but this is not the ultimate land. The home of their longing is in some unimaginable life of friendship and family living with the transcendent God. The first promise merges with the third. They are Yahweh's people; they know it even when the knowledge is hard to live with.

Through longing and joy and apparent disaster they hunger for life—to live fully now, to keep on living hereafter. This accounts in part for their eagerness to see the second promise fulfilled—the pledge of sons to hold land and future. But this one, too, is ambiguous. Their longings are answered, not as they plan, but in Yahweh's own fashion. He keeps their days in his hands.

He gives sons, but seldom is any man's heir the one he would have expected. Adam's eldest is Cain the murderer; Adam's real heirs come later. Abraham's second son, Isaac, carries on the family, and lives to transmit, unwittingly, the inheritance to Jacob, his second son. Jacob in turn deliberately blesses Ephraim, Joseph's younger son, before his brother.

Moses' sons do not carry on his work; Joshua seems to have none; Gideon refuses a throne for his children. With Ruth, the most peaceful book among the narratives of the Old Testament, the expected does—surprisingly—happen: her first son Obed is father to Jesse who is father to David. Samuel's sons are wicked, but he may be seen as father of the kingship. Here, again, the paradoxical pattern holds. His first-chosen king, Saul, fails, and the younger David wins the throne. Yahweh keeps his promises, but in his own way.

Besides the three promises, the Bible is further unified—as is *Adam's Haunted Sons*—by five salvation events, five turns of fortune, five revelations of Yahweh's care for these, his chosen people. One of them comes to Abraham, three are worked out mainly in the life of Moses, and the last belongs to David.

To Abraham the promises are given. Through Moses the people march into freedom, with him they meet the Lord on a mountain of fire where he gives them a law and they give him their whole future, and under Moses' leadership they come at last to the hoped-for land. After long attempts at full conquest, that land becomes finally their settled home under David.

One other great biblical theme has moulded the lives of the people treated in *Adam's Haunted Sons* the great reality of the call. Besides the call of the whole people, each man hears a call which gives direction to his life. His response is the force which makes his personality, the measure of his fulfillment. In this sense the men of the Bible are dynamic characters. They move and change. At the end of each story, its main character is forever different from the man he was at the beginning. Moreover, his response to his individual call often changes the world around him.

Certainly the people who came from Ur of the Chaldees were different after their lives were touched by Abraham's faith, which was his answer to God's choice of him. Even their mode of life changed when the call brought them out of a prosperous city to the desert wanderings of a nomadic people. The city can never be built except by those who sojourn in the desert, nor new life spring up from any place except the dark waters of pain. Again, Moses, the first single individual to have influenced the whole world after him, might have remained and been lost in Egypt's court, had it not been for God's choice of him, for that call which he at first resisted.

And so with all the rest. When the Lord intervenes in history, things begin to move forward, in individual lives, in the destiny of this wonderful, vital, stuborn people, and through them in the whole world.

Oliver Wendell Holmes once said that "man's mind, stretched to a new idea, never goes back to its original dimensions." The people of scripture have not only their minds but their whole existence stretched by a new vision. They can never go back to their original dimensions of routine, of rise and fall without goal, but forever lean forward in their urgency to seek the future.

For all who read it, too, the Bible holds a life-enhancing quality. It has the power to return one to the daily world with a deeper sense of the meanings that lie hidden under its hours. Long immersion in the scriptural world of deep meaning and vibrant life tends to send the human being out beset by urgency. The Bible people are haunted by call and covenant and promises, by a God who will not leave them alone, by the empty spaces in themselves which wait for a fulfillment they have only glimpsed in fleeting light and shadow. All Adam's sons are haunted by hope.

Notes

1. *The Holy Bible,* Revised Standard Version. New York: The World Publishing Co., Meridian Books, 1964. Copyright Division of Christian Education of the National Council of Churches of Christ in the U.S.A. Used with permission.
2. *The Apocrypha,* Revised Standard Version. New York: Thomas Nelson and Sons, 1957. Copyright as above.

* * * * *

1. G. Ernest Wright and Reginald H. Fuller, *The Book of the Acts of God.* New York, Doubleday & Company (Anchor Books), 1960, pp. 8–9.
2. C. S. Lewis, *The Weight of Glory.* New York, The Macmillan Company, 1949, pp. 1–15, *passim.*
3. Edwin Muir, "The Days," *One Foot in Eden.* New York, Grove Press, 1956, p. 17. Copyright Faber and Faber, London, used with permission.
4. T. S. Eliot, "The Dry Salvages," *Complete Poems and Plays.* New York, Harcourt, Brace and Company, p. 130.
5. Donald Justice, "Ladies by Their Windows," *The Summer Anniversaries.* Middletown, Conn., Wesleyan University Press, 1960, p. 11.
6. Barbara Howes, "The Triumph of Time," *Light and Dark.* Middletown, Conn., Wesleyan University Press, 1959, p. 29.
7. Alex Comfort, "The Atoll in the Mind," *The Song of Lazarus.* New York, The Viking Press, 1945.
8. Alexander Eliot, *Sight and Insight.* New York, E. P. Dutton & Co., 1960, p. 75.
9. Dylan Thomas, "Fern Hill," *Collected Poems of Dylan Thomas.* New York, New Directions, 1946, p. 178.
10. John Montague, "Soliloquy on A Southern Strand," *Poisoned Lands.* Chester Springs, Pa., Dufour Editions, 1963, p. 26.
11. Richard Wilbur, "The Problem of Creative Thinking in Poetry," *The Nature of Creative Thinking.* New York, New York University Press, 1952, p. 58.
12. Edwin Muir, "The Days," *One Foot in Eden,* p. 18.
13. T. S. Eliot, "The Dry Salvages," *Complete Poems and Plays,* p. 132.

14. *Ibid.*
15. *Ibid.*, "Choruses from 'The Rock,' " p. 113.
16. Arthur Charles Fox-Davies, *A Complete Guide to Heraldry*. London, T. C. and E. C. Jack, Ltd., 1925, pp. 211, 185.
17. Ned O'Gorman, "L'Annunciazione: From Bellini," *The Night of the Hammer*. New York, Harcourt, Brace and Company, 1959, p. 32. Jonathan Cape, Ltd., 1965, p. 25.
18. William George Heidt, O.S.B., *The Book of The Apocalypse*. Collegeville, Minn., The Liturgical Press, 1962, commentary on 12:3.
19. Sigrid Undset, *The Master of Hestviken*. New York, Alfred A. Knopf, 1934, p. 985.
20. C. S. Lewis, *The Weight of Glory*, pp. 1–15, *passim.*
21. T. S. Eliot, "Little Gidding," *Complete Poems and Plays*, p. 145.
22. Ignatius Hunt, O.S.B., "Commentary," *The Book of Genesis*. New York, The Paulist Press, 1960, p. 15.
23. *Ibid.*
24. Ned O'Gorman, "The Rose and the Body of the Rose," *The Night of the Hammer*, p. 24.
25. John Moffit, "The Apple," *The Living Seed*. New York, Harcourt, Brace and Company, 1962.
26. Conrad Aiken, "Seven Twilights: I, II," *Collected Poems*. New York, Oxford University Press, 1955, p. 364.
27. Donald Justice, "Sonnet," *The Summer Anniversaries*, p. 33.
28. Edwin Muir, "The Days," *One Foot in Eden*, p. 18.
29. Elder Olson, "The Cry," *Collected Poems*. Chicago, University of Chicago Press, 1963.
30. T. S. Eliot, "The Dry Salvages," *Complete Poems and Plays*, p. 135.
31. Hayden Carruth, "Depression," *The Crow and the Heart*. New York, The Macmillan Company, 1962, p. 30.
32. John Holmes, "Noah and His Ark," *The Double Root*. New York, Twayne Publishers, 1950, p. 54.
33. Dylan Thomas, "Author's Prologue," *Collected Poems of Dylan Thomas*, p. xv.
34. Elizabeth Bishop, "The Prodigal," *Poems*. Boston, Houghton Mifflin Company, 1955, p. 77.
35. Samuel Hazo, "The Carnival Ark," *The Quiet Wars*. New York, Sheed and Ward, 1962, p. 71.
36. Richard Wilbur, "Still, Citizen Sparrow," *Ceremony and Other Poems*. New York, Harcourt, Brace and Company, 1950, p. 38.
37. *Ibid.*, p. 38.
38. William Plomer, "Another Country," *Visiting the Caves*. London, Jonathan Cape, Ltd., 1965, p. 25.
39. Rob Lyle, "Eighth Elegy," *Poems from Limbo*. Chester Springs, Pa., Dufour Editions, 1961, p. 59.
40. Arnold Kenseth, "Birds at the Feeding Station," *The Holy Merriment*. Chapel Hill, University of North Carolina Press, 1963, p. 17.

41. Daniel Berrigan, "Pentecost," *Time Without Number*. New York, The Macmillan Company, 1957, p. 5.
42. Mircea Eliade, *Cosmos and History*. New York, Harper and Bros., 1959, pp. 139 ff.
43. Søren Kierkegaard, *Fear and Trembling*. Garden City, N.Y., Doubleday & Company, 1955.
44. Erich Auerbach, *Mimesis: The Representation of Reality in Western Literature*. New York, Doubleday & Company, 1957.
45. Conrad Aiken, "Seven Twilights: I, II," *Collected Poems*, p. 364.
46. Edwin Muir, "Abraham," *One Foot in Eden*, p. 33.
47. George Garrett, "Abraham's Knife," *Abraham's Knife and Other Poems*. Chapel Hill, University of North Carolina Press, 1961, p. 53.
48. Rainer Maria Rilke, "The Second Elegy," *The Duino Elegies*, trans. Harry Behn. Mount Vernon, N.Y., Peter Pauper Press, 1957.
49. G. Ernest Wright and Reginald H. Fuller, *The Book of the Acts of God*, p. 71.
50. E. A. Speiser, "Introduction," in *The Anchor Bible: Genesis*. Garden City, N.Y., Doubleday & Company, 1964, p. 319.
51. Gerard Manley Hopkins, "The Wreck of the Deutschland," *Poems*, ed. W. H. Gardner. New York, Oxford University Press, 1948, p. 55.
52. S. H. Hooke, "Genesis," *Peake's Commentary on the Bible*, ed. Matthew Black and H. H. Rowley. London, Thomas Nelson & Sons, Ltd., 1962, ⁂ 166e.
53. Gerard Manley Hopkins, "Carrion Comfort," *Poems*, p. 106.
54. Allen Kanfer, "Jacob," *Yale Review*, Winter 1953, p. 198.
55. S. H. Hooke, "Genesis," *Peake's Commentary on the Bible*, ⁂ 164a.
56. Brooke Peters Church, *The Golden Years*. New York, Rinehart and Company, 1947, pp. 73–74.
57. *Ibid.*
58. I. R. Orton, "The Cry," *Collected Poems*. Chicago, University of Chicago Press, 1963, p. 71.
59. S. H. Hooke, "Genesis," *Peake's Commentary on the Bible*, ⁂ 88.
60. Christopher Fry, *The Boy with a Cart*. New York, Oxford University Press, 1951, p. 16.
61. Arnold Kenseth, "Notes for a Marriage Vow," *The Holy Merriment*, p. 30.
62. Howard Nemerov, "The Finding of the Ark," *Mirrors and Windows: Poems*. Chicago, The University of Chicago Press, 1958, p. 38.
63. *Ibid.*
64. Fleming James, *Personalities of the Old Testament*. New York, Charles Scribner's Sons, 1939, p. 13.
65. Mary Ellen Chase, *The Bible and the Common Reader*. New York, The Macmillan Company, 1962, p. 126.
66. F. T. Prince, *Poems*. London, Faber and Faber, Ltd., 1937, p. 50.
67. Fleming James, *Personalities of the Old Testament*, p. 144.

68. George S. Glanzman, S.J., *The Book of Deuteronomy*. New York, The Paulist Press, 1960, introduction, p. 20.
69. G. Henton Davies, "Deuteronomy," *Peake's Commentary on the Bible*, ⁂ 244a.
70. T. R. Henn, "The Bible as Literature," *ibid.*, ⁂ 16b.
71. Norman K. Gottwald, *A Light to the Nations*. New York, Harper & Row, Publishers, 1959, p. 156.
72. William F. Albright, as quoted in *Introduction to The Book of Josue*, ed. Joseph J. De Vault, S.J. New York, The Paulist Press, 1960, p. 17.
73. Homer, *The Iliad*, trans. Richard Lattimore. Chicago, The University of Chicago Press, 1961, 17: 424–425.
74. Joseph J. De Vault, *Introduction to The Book of Josue*, p. 20.
75. Gerard Manley Hopkins, "The Wreck of the Deutschland," *Poems*, p. 55.
76. Rainer Maria Rilke, "The Second Elegy," *The Duino Elegies*.
77. James Hastings, "Nazirite," *The Dictionary of the Bible*. New York, Charles Scribner's Sons, 1963.
78. John Hollander, "Orpah Returns to Her People," *A Crakling of Thorns*. New Haven, Yale University Press, 1958, p. 6.
79. Conrad Aiken, "The Divine Pilgrim," *Collected Poems*, p. 88.
80. Raymond Souster, "Winter Valley," *Poetry* (Chicago), September 1963, p. 302.
81. John Logan, "Monologues of a Son of Saul," *Spring of the Thief*. New York, Alfred A. Knopf, 1963, pp. 3–5.
82. Adrienne Rich, "The Boyhood of David," *Poetry* (Chicago), August 1957, p. 302.
83. Gerard Manley Hopkins, "I Wake and Feel," *Poems*, p. 109.
84. Adrienne Rich, "The Boyhood of David," *Poetry* (Chicago), August 1957, p. 302.
85. James Dickey, "For the Mighty Ascent of the Hunter Orion over a Forest Clearing," *Drowning with Others*. Middletown, Conn., Wesleyan University Press, 1963, p. 28.
86. John Logan, "Monologues of a Son of Saul," *Spring of the Thief*. New York: Alfred A. Knopf, 1963, p. 3.
87. James Dickey, "Armor," *Drowning with Others*, pp. 45–46.
88. R. S. Thomas, "Iago Prytherch," *Poetry for Supper*. Chester Springs, Pa., Dufour Editions, 1958, p. 36.
89. L. H. Grollenberg, *Atlas of the Bible*, trans. and ed. Joyce M. H. Reid and H. H. Rowley. London, Thomas Nelson & Sons, Ltd., 1965, p. 68.
90. James Wright, "David," *Yale Review*, Winter 1957, p. 222.
91. *Ibid.*
92. Adrienne Rich, "The Boyhood of David," *Poetry* (Chicago), August 1957, p. 302.
93. *Ibid.*

INDEX

INDEX